LEMON SHERBET AND DOLLY BLUE

Lemon Sherbet

and

Dolly Blue

The Story of an Accidental Family

LYNN KNIGHT

Atlantic Books
LONDON

First published in hardback in Great Britain in 2011
by Atlantic Books, an imprint of Atlantic Books Ltd.

1 3 5 7 9 8 6 4 2

A CIP catalogue record for this book is available
from the British Library.

ISBN 978 184887 416 9

Printed in Great Britain by the MPG Books Group

Atlantic Books
An Imprint of Atlantic Books Ltd
Ormond House
26–27 Boswell Street
London
WC1N 3JZ

www.atlantic-books.co.uk

For my brother
who shares this history with me

Contents

PART THREE

Cast of Characters

Kitty Martin /Ball – daughter

Margaret Martin /Ball – daughter

Annie Martin /Ball – youngest daughter, who becomes *(Doris) Eva Nash* on adoption

Jessie Mee – Cora's birth mother

Mrs Sedgwick – her employer

Frances M. Wood (née Mee) – Jessie's married sister

Jessie's baby – my mum – becomes *Cora Thompson* on adoption

FAMILY CONNECTIONS AND SUNDAY VISITORS

Annie Wardle (née Ward) – Betsy's oldest sister, a former ladies' maid

George Walter Hardcastle – friend of family; sweet on Annie

Annie Wardle's son Jack – killed, First World War

Annie Wardle's son Charlie – invalided out, First World War

Edie Wardle – Charlie's wife

Liza – Betsy's youngest and favourite sister

SOME FRIENDS AND NEIGHBOURS AT WHEELDON MILL

Florrie Stokes – neighbour and mother of Annie's friend Ethel

Ethel Stokes – Florrie's daughter, Annie's lifelong friend and childhood defender

Rolly Cook – Ethel's second husband (also the name of Ethel's son)

Nora Parks – collier's wife

Edna Parks – one of Nora's daughters, marries Clem Stokes

Kathleen Driver – soaps the stairs

Clara Tissington – neighbour (lives higher up the hill)

Zoe Graham – publican's daughter, Annie's childhood friend

Carrie Rice – Eva's lifelong friend

Mildred Taylor – collier's wife, has pony-driver sons

Jimmy Frith – neighbour; shell-shocked, First World War

Maud Cartwright – back-door visitor to corner shop

Pearl Cartwright – Maud's daughter; Saturday visitor to corner shop

Clem Stokes – one of Ethel's brothers; injured First World War, marries Edna Parks

Georgie, Katie and Punka Stokes – some of Clem and Edna's children

Charles/Charlie Parks – Edna Stokes' brother and lodger

(SOME OF) WILLIE'S FAMILY

Jim Thompson – Willie's brother and employer; Mayor of Chesterfield 1939–40

Edith Thompson – his wife

Bernard and Ida Thompson – Willie's brother and wife; Ida works in Derbyshire's outfitter's, Whittington Moor

NEIGHBOURS RACECOURSE ROAD

Mrs Blake – trusted next-door neighbour

Grace and Tommy Blake – two of Mrs Blake's children; Cora's playmates

See Chapter 23 for a discussion of the variants in the spelling of my great-grandfather's name

MOST NAMES HAVE BEEN CHANGED

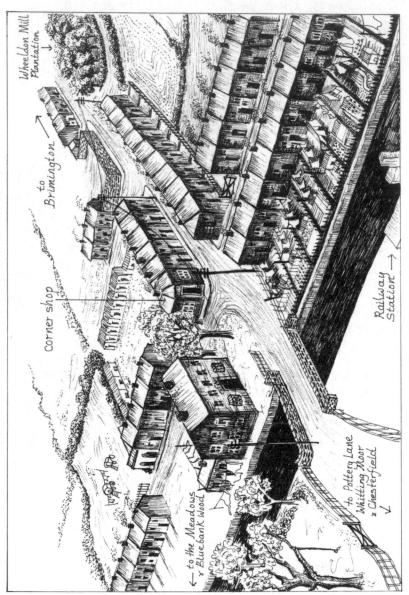

Wheeldon Mill

List of Illustrations

LEMON SHERBET AND DOLLY BLUE

'I'm adopted, because mummy and daddy have no children. I think that's better fun, don't you?'

'Yes,' replied Herbert, after consideration; 'anybody could be born.'

From 'The Tommy Crans', Elizabeth Bowen

Prologue

There is no childhood photograph of my great-grandfather. His parents gave him away when they left for America. They did not even tell Dick when his birthday was, and so were hardly likely to pose for a family group (and I doubt they had the sixpence to spare). There is a photograph of my great-aunt, Eva, however, and she's standing in the garden shortly after she was brought home to the corner shop. And there are several pictures of my mum, a babe in arms, soon after she joined the family. All the women wanted to be photographed with Cora.

It is said that you can't choose your relatives, but some of my family did. Dick, Eva and Cora were all adopted, and adopted in three distinct ways. I know of no other family like this one. Perhaps it was their precarious beginnings and their sense of how slippery facts can be that made them enthusiastic storytellers. I grew up hearing their stories and have been longing to pass them on, but I've also wanted to uncover some of the mysteries and silences behind them. In exploring a family stitched together by adoption, there is much I have needed to discover for myself. I've also been longing to recreate a place which was a rich part of my family's life and the tales told to me during childhood. I never knew my great-grandma's corner shop, but I've heard its stories so many times I feel I know the ching of its bell.

My great-grandparents died before I was born, but I spent a lot of time with my grandma and great-aunt, Annie and Eva. I had my own shop too, courtesy of a game we played in their pantry. Buttons were my ready currency (and, on other days, the buttons themselves entertained me: Annie saying, 'Oh, those jet buttons were Mam's. I remember…' and heading into another story). Annie and Eva bought imaginary chocolate and ice cream, as well as soap powder and pegs, and quarters of cough drops (red buttons) and, Eva's particular favourites, Pontefract cakes (large, black). To lend authenticity to our game, Eva approached the pantry with her shopping bag, but she had not forgotten her days on the other side of the counter and showed me how to twist newspaper into the narrow cones in which I sold the imitation sweets.

The real corner shop stood in a tu'penny-ha'penny district, hardly a district as such, on the edge of Chesterfield, Derbyshire, the county where, in the words of native-born Violet Markham, 'north meets south and the Pennines swoop down to gather up the flat and placid midlands into a stern embrace of rock and moor'. Administratively, Chesterfield is defined as the East Midlands, but it is North Derbyshire, twelve miles south of Sheffield ('the true North-country', according to J.B. Priestley) and its characteristics (and humour) have always seemed northern to me. Today, the town is famed for the Crooked Spire on its parish church, St Mary and All Saints. Some say the devil sat on it; others that, on observing the rare sight of a virgin marrying within, the spire leaned down to take a closer look and could not straighten up again.

You could see the tip of the Crooked Spire when you stood outside my great-grandma's shop. Those first photographs of my mum were taken on the shop's doorstep, which overlooked the pub and had a clear view of the branch-line railway station below. Shank's pony was the more usual transport for those in the immediate vicinity, but Betsy's shop was a good place to pause and see who might arrive on the next train. It functioned as a kind of drop-in centre too: people came to talk as well as shop.

The shop's main window, reserved for sweets, held the large glass-stoppered jars of dolly-mixtures, humbugs and a dazzle of Quality Street in coloured foils, but individual chocolate bars were kept behind the counter, beyond the reach of thieving hands. In the sunny window to the side, where advertisements curled and faded, a cardboard Vim declared that modern women had been released from household drudgery, though everyone round about took that for the nonsense it was.

By the time I knew my great-aunt Eva, she was the spirited adventurer. Being with her was sometimes like being with an older child, a wholly reliable protector, but someone who knew about fun. My grandma, Annie, was more reserved, but hers was the lap I snuggled into, her big doughy arms wrapped about me while we read the same books she'd read to my mum. My grandma read to me each Sunday, the two of us sinking into her leatherette chair, the Jacobean-print curtains behind us screening us from the afternoon sun.

They were great keepers of things, Annie and Eva (keepers of secrets too, I've since discovered): clothes and jewellery, beaded purses, handbags – my visits in later years were like feasting in a vintage shop. They also kept family documents and papers;

newspaper cuttings in biscuit tins; handwritten recipes; notebooks. That vital documents were saved should not surprise me, but in a family shaped in such an unusual way, it feels remarkable that they were. All kinds of material survives, whether by happenstance or intention; the cuttings in my grandma's commonplace book, for example, helped me understand more about the young woman she was in the years before I was born.

My mum picked up the habit of keeping record: notebooks, childhood poems, drawings; the minutiae of her young life. She also learned the habit of telling stories – her tales of her grandparents and the corner shop expanded those told me by Annie and Eva. She had her own fund of stories too, some involving the dance dresses of her youth – pink sateen with ric-tac braid, or yellow with a sequined heart in emerald green – which became the dressing-up clothes of my childhood.

One of my favourite excursions when I was young was lunch with my mum at Woodhead's Café, all dark wood panels, chrome and pistachio green, its decor barely changed since the 1930s. Here, provincial ladies lunched on creamed carrots and shepherd's pie, as provincial ladies had lunched for many years, the sound of an EPNS teaspoon scraping the last of a strawberry ice the only disruption to their quiet afternoon. In London the 1960s were happening, but London was a million miles away.

By the time I was a teenager, we'd shrugged off Woodhead's and the High Street and headed, instead, for Sheffield and its shops, scudding along leafy lanes in Mum's powder-blue Mini, talking ten-to-the-dozen all the while. We've talked (and laughed) a lot in recent years, sitting at her dining table, sifting through old photographs and papers, reluctant to interrupt our conversation to get up and peel potatoes at the sink.

My mum's dance dresses are long gone, but I live surrounded by everyday objects that tell their own stories. There is something of the past in every room: the squat Gray, Dunn & Co's Biscuits tin, a reminder of the corner shop; the wooden box with a sketchy cottage scene on its lid that my great-grandfather bought years ago; the huge chest of drawers that was Betsy's and then Annie's before it came to me, and it was my turn to tug on its large glass handles or prise open its secret drawer. ('When I die,' Annie told me, more than once, 'don't forget to look in the secret drawer.')

In my attempts to uncover further stories about my family, I've been discovering distant histories, but also exploring those closer to home. When I started writing this book, I knew little of my mum's birth mother, and had no idea if I – and, far more importantly, she – would ever know more. Writing about people you love is a tremendous responsibility; stranger, still, is the act of taking someone's childhood and playing it back to them, as I'm doing here, with my mum's.

My grandma made the dress in which Cora was photographed shortly after her adoption. Annie also made a 'weighty' for her pram, just as she and Betsy, my great-grandma, made weighties for their own beds: eiderdowns named for their comforting heft and bulk; layer upon layer of fabric. Each layer told a different story – the cotton print Eva wore to stride across the gala field with her sweet tray; a strip of silk from Annie's favourite sash; the yards left over from serviceable flannel petticoats and Dick's work shirts; the crimson brocade Betsy favoured for best curtains. To sleep beneath a weighty was to be embraced by the past and the security of knowing you were home.

Some of my family stories, like those layers, are as light and colourful as silk or sprigged cotton; others, darker and heavier.

Some belong to the people without whom the family could not exist, who, though invisible, are present all the time as shadows behind their narratives – the stories of those who gave up their children for adoption. If I could, I'd invent a different beginning for at least one of the adopted children. But that part of the story comes later. The best place to start is when my great-grandfather was brought to the town.

Part One

I

I Deliver My Son

20 July 1865 was one of those fine mornings that promise heat
by lunchtime. Even before the sun reached anywhere near its full
height in the sky, the day shimmered with a sense of possibility.
It was not just rising temperatures that marked out this date.
From an early hour, the road from Chesterfield was crammed with
flys and barouches, gentlemen on horseback and pedestrians in
holiday mood. The *Derbyshire Courier* was there to record them:
'Everything was hurry, bustle and excitement.' This was the start
of the Chesterfield Races.

Spectators streamed past the town's lace and cotton mills, its
gingham and check manufacturer, grubbier workshops, earthen-
ware potteries, tanneries and foundries. By midday, shopkeepers
were putting up their shutters and escorting wives and daughters
to the course, and the town's straw-hat makers turning out to
count the numbers showing off new bonnets. Race Days were not
merely sporting occasions, but opportunities to promenade and
be seen, and to enjoy the general carnival atmosphere descending
on the town. The Theatre Royal provided a special programme

Bonny Scotland   Blunderbuss & Shylock   Sour Beer & Turncoat   Lackey & Young Tom

CHESTERFIELD RACES

Nov. 1863.

STEWARDS.

His Grease the Duck of Derbyshire.
The Right dis-Honourable Lord Gorge Carving Plate.

THE

Council Sweepstakes

Of 50 Sovs.

Capt. B——'s b h Bonny Scotland, out of Auld Lang Syne	Tartan Plaid.
Admiral B——k's Blunderbuss, by Floor'em, out of Paint Pot ..	Red, White and Blue.
Mr. G——n's Shylock, out of Bonny Bess by Sugar Sand dam, lt. wt.	Princes Mixture.
Mr. B——g's Sour Beer by Devils Mixture, out of Doctor's Shop ..	Red
Mr. W——l's Turncoat, by Young Conspirator, out of West-end Pandemonium	Dirty.
Mr. W——d's Lackey, out of Duke's Court, by Conspirator dam Polly Owen	Transparent.
Mr. T. W——d's Young Tom, by Old Tom, out of Glasshouse by Photographer	Green.

WEST END

Pony Races,

Mr. Bissey B's Berkshire Cob, by Builder out of Bankruptcy dam Consequence	Yellow.
Mr Joseph the Good's Deception, out of Laundress by Washerwoman	Puce.
Mr. Hare's Axem Round, out of Good Oth Town, by old Coach Boy	Blue
Mr. Dawb's Stick in the Mud, by Wingfield Tyrant, out of Ralph Lowe's Fancy	Drab.

LATEST BETTING.

Friday Night 12 *o'clock.*

6 to 4 on Bonny Scotland, Even betting on Blunderbus, 3 to 2 agst Sour Beer, 5 to 4 agst Turncoat, Lackey scratched,   Young Tom disqualified.   Any odds agst Shoe's lot.

Judge, Right Honourable F. B. Farmer.
Clerk of the Course, Mr. John Patteson,

throughout the week, while the Assembly Room boasted perform-
ances by Messrs Leclercq and A. Wood's Dramatic, Burlesque and
Ballet Company.

For two days each year, Chesterfield Racecourse rang with
thudding hooves and expectation. One of the oldest fixtures in the
sporting calendar (and more usually taking place in the autumn),
the Chesterfield Races were established by the end of the seven-
teenth century, and regularly reported from 1727. During their
heyday, the Races enjoyed as considerable a following as those at
Doncaster, or the Derby, on which the town's remodelled Grandstand was based.

The course extended for two miles on the outskirts of Chesterfield and crossed the Sheffield–Chesterfield Road in four places.
One of its more remarkable features was its situation: the track
circled land on Whittington Moor. What was originally a strip of
pasture, with all aspects visible to the eye, came to be interrupted
by washing lines and chimneys as more and more houses were
built. Until the races were disbanded in the 1920s, their occu-
pants had ringside seats. Fortunately, the race-goers of the 1860s
still had an unhindered view of starting flag and finishing post.

The course was a babble of noise and commotion: official vend-
ors waving race cards, bookmakers calling the odds on Countess,
Picaroon, Locket Lucy, Maid of Usk. Who'll stake their money on
Pretty Queen in the Nursery Handicap or King Tom in the
Chatsworth Stake? Publicans heaved casks of ale into booths
specially auctioned for the event. The Britannia Inn had secured
the best spot, the Grandstand booth in Cundy's Lot, at a cost of
£3 5s, and expected to make its money back from the gentry.
Elsewhere, dotted about the course, smaller booths vied with one
another for the attentions of the lowlier crowd and their winnings.

We found Derbyshire not indeed so extensive a county, but as more romantic it's more pleasing than Yorkshire, and though at the same time remarkable for producing many commodities in great plenty. The finest lead in England, iron, etc, 'tis full of quarries of free stone, greatstone, brimstone, black and grey marble, crystal, alabaster, and sometimes there is found antimony. The vales produce great quantities of corn, and the mountainous parts coal pits; but what adds beauty to this county is the parks and forests, and inequality of hills and dales that so diversify the landscape... About a week after our large party arrived...there came two other ladies and four gentlemen to the races, which were to begin on the next day... On the Wednesday, having dined early, we set off in different carriages, and seven gentlemen on horseback for the course, about three, came back to tea about eight...about ten we went to the Assembly Room, where the Duke of Devonshire always presided as master of the ceremonies, and after the ball gave an elegant cold supper...We got home about five. The next evening were at the concert...and on the third day again went to the course...That evening's ball was equally brilliant as the first night, and both gave us as strangers a high idea of these annual assemblies at Chesterfield, which town in itself has but a poor appearance.

– Description of Chesterfield Race Week, by diarist, Mrs Lybbe Powys, 1757

The Grouse Inn, the Spinning Wheel, the Red Lion, the Griffin – landlords the length and breadth of Chesterfield turned out in best bibs and tuckers to supply champagne, fine spirits, ale and porter. Some enthusiasts were so ardent in their support of the local hostelries they missed the actual races. Revellers seeking more substantial fare could frequent the gaily painted stalls circling the perimeter, selling piles of gingerbread, sandwiches and dubious cuts of meat. Darting among the snobs and swells that afternoon were the light-fingered Johnnies who could snaffle a pocket watch without so much as blinking, and the 'spots' for the numerous card sharps setting up trackside scams. There were many ways to lose your shirt on Race Days.

The local aristocracy had well-worn seats in the stand, but Race days also attracted well-heeled outsiders, and had done so since the mid-eighteenth century when Derbyshire joined the tourist itinerary. Ladies and gentlemen touring the Peak liked to take in the Chesterfield Races. A morning surveying Chatsworth House, Haddon Hall or Hardwick; the dour Romance of Curbar Edge, or the Blue John Mines at Castleton (the latter providing the especial titillation of the mine known as the Devil's Arse), could be followed by an afternoon's idling at the racetrack, and an evening's cold collation at the Angel Inn, courtesy of his Grace the Duke of Devonshire, long-standing friend of the turf. (His annual purse for the Chatsworth Stake was fifty sovereigns.)

Racing was one of the few sports which enabled the social classes to mix. Chesterfield Race Days produced scenes every bit as vivid as William Frith's famous painting of *The Derby Day*. Mechanics and day-tripping clerks rubbed shoulders with school teachers, domestic servants and gypsies selling lavender and pegs. Colliers, chancing a day's pay, stood feet away from ladies trying not to crush their crinolines, and school children granted a holiday. This was a chance for the gentry to view the hoi polloi and for the hoi polloi to thank their own good fortune when regarding the numerous beggars working the course and the poor unfortunates on show – entrance, one halfpenny – in assorted curiosity booths.

Special trains from Sheffield, Nottingham and Derby disgorged passengers, who, in these still relatively early days of locomotion, were thankful to reach their destination unscathed. In the years before the railways, poorer race-goers had walked enormous distances from one race to the next; the advent of excursion trains changed all that and delivered larger numbers to the course.

By day, the rowdiness was good-natured; come nightfall, it could thicken into something less benign. Few wanted to find themselves at the shadowy margins of the racetrack as daylight drained away. The brawling and carousing that accompanied this annual shindig led to frequent debates about vice and immorality, but although the occasion was a focal point for gambling and the fleecing of fools, and doubtless attracted 'nymphs of the pave', loutish behaviour was not confined to Race Days. Even a cursory glance at the *Derbyshire Courier* reveals accounts of drunkenness on the part of both sexes, and in boys as young as eleven, as well as fist fights and stabbings.

Wandering among the crowds that day were Thomas and Sarah Walker, and their three-year-old son, Richard Dorance. The Walkers were fairground people, Romanies possibly, for whom Chesterfield was just another stopping point on the road. Race Days attracted a rich mix of entertainers: practitioners of 'the noble art' drummed up custom for the ring, 'photographic studios' promised exact likenesses for sixpence. Tumblers performed feats of strength and agility; conjurers bamboozled the crowd, balladeers serenaded it. There were rifle galleries, peep shows, Aunt Sallies and coconut shies, as well as stalls selling cheap toys and gaudy trinkets. I don't know how the Walkers plied their trade – whether he was Thomasino with his Raven-Haired Assistant, or she, Gypsy Sarah, weaving fantastical tales of good fortune while gold bangles played up and down her arms, but, for showmen reliant on the fairground calendar, the hectic camaraderie of Race Days provided an essential way to turn a shilling.

Entertainers travelled between the country's racecourses and the larger town fairs, taking in village feasts and wakes along the way. The nearby villages of Dunston, Newbold and Hasland scheduled their feasts for Chesterfield Race Sunday; there were also opportunities to entertain the town's theatre queues or to perform at the edge of the bustling market square. (In the years when the Chesterfield Races took place in the autumn, the Walkers could also tag on to the town's annual Feast, and link up with Nottingham's famous Goose Fair.)

Many showmen drifted into the roving life because of harsh circumstances elsewhere: the past left behind and good riddance. Successful fairground entrepreneurs were few, however; for the majority, theirs was a precarious existence. The poorest showmen travelled miles on foot, carrying their belongings and staying in the kind of the hostelry where the cutlery was chained to the table. The open road could rapidly lose its romance.

Whether good takings prompted the Walkers to change their lives that year, or hunger and a pittance drove them to it, they decided to leave England and make a fresh start in America. Entertainers regularly crossed to mainland Europe, lured by advertisements like this one: 'Wanted, for Bell and Myer's Circus,

France, a Stud-Groom and 2 Under Grooms. Liberal Salaries to competent men; also Equestrians and Gymnasts, for future Engagements. No Stamp. Silence a negative.' By the 1860s, America was also beginning to attract entertainers. All that was needed, according to one confident theatrical report, was 'a day's notice, a wide-mouthed bag and your ticket'. The new country had circuses and fairs aplenty, and anyone good with their hands could find work in that vast, expanding economy. Steam ships had reduced some of the terrors as well as the length of transatlantic crossings, although travelling in the confined and claustrophobic spaces of steerage was still a fairly desperate enterprise. Whatever their intentions, and however unsure their scheme, one thing was certain: Thomas and Sarah Walker planned to travel without their son.

At three years old, Richard was perhaps judged to be both too young and too old for the journey – too big, too lively, too inquisitive, too hungry – too much of everything to be anything but an encumbrance en route, though this was not a decision most emigrant parents reached. If Thomas and Sarah had already removed themselves from square walls and solid ground, however, they may have found it easier to remove themselves once again, and on this occasion, relinquish their child.

Thomas Walker was illiterate, but someone had taught Sarah her letters, plus a vague understanding of the law. Her writing has a hammy style, with extra 'hs's, in which I hear the call of the impresario summoning his audience. If Sarah was the woman who haunts nineteenth-century stories and songs, and who cast off the corsetry of Victorian propriety to run away with the raggle-taggle gypsies, I doubt she was leaving a comfortable home. But casting off was evidently something Sarah was good at. Fairground life was about moving forward always, even if following an annual circuit: the next town, the next audience – who will surely be more appreciative than the last: keep looking forward, not back. And what could be more forward-looking or a more complete way of severing the past than a passage to America?

There were many people like the Walkers: ordinary, undistinguished emigrants who crossed the Atlantic in the hope of making something new of themselves. ('Go West,' the *New York Times* advised immigrant hopefuls.) In 1865, 264 ships left Liverpool for America and transported nearly 5,000 cabin and around 90,000 steerage passengers between them. Several hundred steerage passengers each voyage; typically, one third single male adventurers, the remainder married couples with children: whole families uprooting themselves and what little or nothing they had, crammed into airless spaces and headed for America and the promise of a better life, undeterred by news of its civil strife. (Even the *Derbyshire Courier* carried reports of the Civil War.) The Walkers took up that promise.

The landscape of the fairground was changing. Three London fairs, most famously, Bartholomew's Fair, had come to an end in the past ten years. With increasing urbanisation, fairs were no longer so plentiful, nor so significant in people's lives: the railways offered new forms of pleasure-seeking and more accessible entertainment. Old-style attractions were dwindling; mechanisation had yet to make its mark. Perhaps the Walkers decided to get out while they could, although, ironically, 1865 was the year in which the steam-driven roundabout, which would shortly revitalise fairgrounds, made its first appearance.

In Chesterfield, the Walkers met a barber, Joseph Nash, who lived and worked a short distance from the racecourse. Joe's barber's shop may not have run to a striped pole and fancy lotions, but my understanding is that his was a proper shop with a window on to the street. Perhaps Joe's shop was the occasion of his first meeting with Thomas Walker: confidences exchanged during the false intimacy of a friendly lather and clean shave. For whatever reason, and by whatever means the two men met, Joseph agreed to take Thomas's young son.

Joseph and his wife, Mary – with two such names, how could they possibly refuse the Walkers' request? – had a son of their own, though, by the time the Walkers came to Chesterfield, William Nash was seventeen and would shortly take up lodgings in a different part of town, nearer to the colliery that employed him. Mary was some nine years older than Joe, time enough to have a whole other adult life before she met him, but if she did, it can only be guessed at. Their own circumstances were complicated enough. Joe hailed from Hertfordshire; Mary, Worcestershire; their son William was born in Warwickshire at the end of the Hungry Forties. This couple knew about travelling to secure a life, and could surely sympathise with the Walkers in that. But many working-class families of the period were sticking pins in the map, and they weren't all taking on other people's children. Perhaps Mary wanted another child to mother – it was unusual for a woman of her generation to have only one, though she may have had others that did not survive: these were the years in which women spoke in one breath of the children they'd given birth to, versus the number still living – but whatever Mary's feelings on the matter, the actual agreement to take young Richard refers only to Joe.

It seems altogether extraordinary, but this arrangement between a fairground couple and a jobbing barber was written down. Though it may be less extraordinary than I imagine. Genealogy is said to be particularly valued among showmen because of the lack of other continuities in their lives. But, if the Walkers shared this view, they were about to lop off the youngest branch of their family tree.

The consequence of this momentous decision was recorded on a small piece of paper; on the back of black-edged mourning paper, to be precise, which raises further unanswerable questions. Fragile now and long since secured with tape, its spidery handwriting tells a vital story: 'I Thomas Walker, Deliver my Son Richard Darnce in to the hands of Joseph Nash to keep as his Son and I remain your affectionate friend Sarah Walker.'

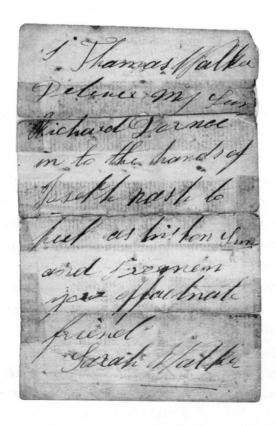

Though precarious by today's standards and with no legal foundation – the Walkers probably did not realise that Richard remained his father's responsibility – the 'adoption' (and I use the word in the loosest sense) was nonetheless a solemn pact.

I hope they loved him. I hope the Walkers left Richard behind because they loved him and felt they were doing the best they could for their son. The fact that the exchange was documented suggests a proper sense of responsibility and thoughtfulness, rather than a desire to get rid. But there is no reference to a loving mother, heartbroken at the thought of surrendering her child. For all the emotion expressed, Sarah might have been an amanuensis recording an everyday transaction on her husband's behalf. But, perhaps I'm being unfair: this was a formal statement in which sentiment had no place: she was setting down the bare bones of their arrangement. Sarah evidently believed that Joe Nash might require some proof of their understanding, although, in the 1860s, children appeared (and disappeared) all the time with very few questions asked.

There were two documents, not just one. The second, a letter, is unfortunately – tantalisingly – incomplete, a veritable dot, dot, dot. Its concluding page or pages no longer exist. Writing from a village on the outskirts of Nottingham, Sarah, who had been ill, hoped that Richard was keeping well, and planned to visit the Nashes the following week; a seemingly casual enquiry, not the sentiments you would expect from a mother who was about to say goodbye for ever. If desperate loving words came afterwards, these have been lost to the ages.

All my great-grandfather was left with – though it is a great deal more than many in his situation – was the evidence of his being handed over to Joseph Nash, and his mother's letter. Richard knew his name, and that he was three years old when he was brought to Chesterfield, but he had no idea of his birthday. He did not even have that date to carry with him into the future.

The Walkers were fortunate in their choice of adopters. Childhood was cheap in the 1860s. Demands for entertainers were not the only advertisements making an appeal in print. Newspapers contained requests from those wishing to adopt small children, some of them genuine, others placed by unscrupulous individuals whose heart-tugging pleas concealed a desire to acquire an infant drudge, or worse. This was an era rife with baby farming: children deposited with kind or careless 'carers' for a fee, babies quietened with one too many teaspoons of Godfrey's Cordial (the widespread use of cordials to quieten babies even had 'Mrs Beeton' counselling her highly respectable readers to ensure that nursemaids did not overdose their infants). Some children were inadvertently left to die, or 'adopted' with that end in mind: the premium pocketed, no questions asked, the baby disappears or fails to thrive; the mother is relieved of an unfortunate burden, the baby farmer makes off with the cash. Indeed, a few years after Dick's adoption, the trial of the Brixton Baby Farmers would attract notoriety and appal the general public with revelations of desperate and unsavoury goings-on among the poor.

The casual attitude displayed towards children at this time is hammered home in a tiny detail in Luke Fildes' *Houseless and Hungry*, an engraving commissioned in 1869 for the first edition of *The Graphic*, a magazine with a mission to convey the brute reality of nineteenth-century life, its poverty and squalor. The subject of the engraving, a disparate group queuing for the workhouse, includes a drunkard, a beggar and a mother with a toddler and a babe in arms. Adjacent posters on the wall behind them offer rewards: £2 for a deserted child; £20 for a lost pug dog.

This was the decade in which Thomas Barnardo first became aware of London's abandoned children: during the 1860s, some 30,000 homeless children were estimated to be living on the streets of the capital city. Had my great-grandfather not been adopted, he could so easily have become a street-urchin himself or been swept into Chesterfield's Scarsdale Workhouse, a building as capable of tormenting the thoughts and empty stomachs of the town's poorer inhabitants as any Poor Law Union institution elsewhere.

NURSE CHILD WANTED, OR TO ADOPT: The Advertiser, a Widow with a little family of her own, and moderate allowance from her late husband's friends, would be glad to accept the charge of a young child. Age no object. If sickly would receive a parent's care. Terms, Fifteen Shillings a month; or would adopt entirely if under two months for the small sum of Twelve Pounds.

– Example of a suspicious 'adoption' advertisement from the 1860s

ADOPTION: A good home, with a mother's love and care, is offered to a respectable person, wishing her child to be entirely adopted. Premium £5 which includes everything. Apply, by letter only, to Mrs Oliver, post office, Goar-place, Brixton.

– An advertisement placed by Sarah Ellis, Brixton Baby Farmer, in *Lloyd's Weekly Paper*, 1870

It was trusting of the Walkers to bequeath their son to Joseph Nash – trusting, foolhardy, or downright careless. Though Sarah signed herself 'your affectionate friend', she and Thomas were not long-standing friends of the Nashes; her letter was not written to 'Mary', but 'Mrs Nash'. The only thing my great-grandfather learned about his parents was his fairground origins; he knew nothing else of their lives and received no letters once they left. When the Walkers disappeared, it was for good.

One day, Richard was a fairground lad; the next, the son of a barber. My great-grandfather's life changed beyond recognition overnight. He also acquired a shorter version of his name. From now on, he was known to his new family as plain 'Dick' – a more serviceable name for the life ahead of him.

There was a new security in having a fixed address and in being protected from the elements by thicker walls, but, at three years old, Dick could talk and knew his Ma and Pa; knew the feel of his mother's skirt clutched in his small fingers, and the familiar smell of her body and hair. I wonder how long it took him to realise his parents were never coming back?

My great-grandfather always spoke fondly of Joe and Mary Nash. He remained in close contact with them until their deaths and became a great favourite among his adopted family, but childhood was brief as well as cheap in the nineteenth century, and all the shorter for those with reason to forget their beginnings.

Dick told only two stories about his childhood years with the Nashes. One was that his new life enabled him to acquire the smatterings of an education. A small dame school stood across the road from the barber's shop; Dick zigzagged his way in and out of passing carts to reach it. The dame swished her cane and pursued her pupils around the room, but she managed to teach my great-grandfather his letters and how to cipher. Throughout his life, Dick read slowly, almost as slowly as when he chalked his first words on a slate under that schoolmarm's watchful eye. But, thanks to Miss Alvey, Dick learned how to read, and for a working-class boy of the time (and a fairground lad at that), this was achievement enough.

His other memory concerned the barber's shop. On dark afternoons when he'd finished school, Dick was required to stand on a crate and hold a candle steady so that Joe could see to shave his customers. Too small to hold the candle aloft without this extra elevation, too young to stop himself from nodding off, he was not the most reliable assistant. When sleep got the better of him and Dick swayed, a friendly shove from Joe revived him and saved them all from going up in flames.

All too soon, a more demanding occupation called him. At the age of twelve, my great-grandfather started work down the pit. The mines had swallowed boys far younger than Dick and just as fearful. When Lord Salisbury produced his 1842 report into working conditions, the Derbyshire coalfields were employing boys as young as five and six, but, by 1860, the legal age was twelve, though that did not mean all colliery owners observed it.

Dick's first job was at the Dunston pit, one of three collieries owned by the Sheepbridge Coal and Iron Company established by William and John Fowler. At its flotation in 1864, the company was also responsible for twenty-eight ironstone pits, twenty-three coke ovens, a calcinating plant, four blast furnaces, a large foundry and a mechanics shop, and was linked to the Midland Railway and to the Chesterfield Canal by eight miles of track. By the 1870s, when my great-grandfather started work, Sheepbridge already employed 2,000 men and boys. This rapid industrial growth was reflected in the outlying village of Whittington, where Dick lived: in the years between 1851 and 1861, its population expanded threefold, and during the next decade almost doubled again, thanks to the industrial might of coal.

Sheepbridge's Dunston pit at Cobnar Wood was a small pit producing 250 tons of coal a day, from two shafts 100 yards deep. Mining was a terrible initiation for a young boy, working as much as a twelve-hour shift, alert always to any unusual shifting of the pit props, his nostrils filled with that close, dark smell with its incipient heat and incendiary dust. Boys of Dick's age, and older, often worked as putters ('putting' wagons into place where a crane could transfer them to trains for delivery to the shaft), a task with its own gang hierarchy and Dickensian job titles, such as 'foals', 'half-marrows' and 'helpers-up'. Putters dragged tubs of coal weighing between six to eight hundredweight along the underground road, some sixty yards, sixty times a day; arduous work, considered by some to be, alongside hewing, the most strenuous in the pit.

My great-grandfather soon had company underground. By the 1880s, Joe Nash had joined him. The barber's shop barely outlasted Dick's childhood. Joe had worked in a colliery before, so the routine came as no shock, but it was far easier to dust off his lamp and find a bait tin than to toughen hands softened by hot water and bend his back into the crippling positions demanded by narrow seams of coal. It must have been particularly difficult for a man in his fifties to return to that life and to hear the familiar squeal of the cage, a sound he'd hoped never to hear again. The devil drives, however. Joe was finding it impossible to make a living as a barber.

*

The world of coal and iron and engineering was continually overhauling Chesterfield and opening up new vistas. A town which, before the advent of the railways, had only 'two societies of note' – one devoted to agriculture, the other to literature and philosophy, which gathered 'on the evening of every Wednesday nearest the full moon' – was transforming itself with all the swank and vigour of a thriving economy. Chesterfield's Institute of Engineers now boasted over 300 members (mostly mining engineers and colliery managers) and, by 1879, the town had erected its Stephenson Memorial Hall – complete with lecture rooms, a free library, billiard rooms and so on – in honour of the pioneering railway engineer, George Stephenson, who had spent his last days looking down on Chesterfield's seething chimneys from the more elevated heights of Tapton House.

Train lines were scoring further criss-crosses of iron and steam in the Derbyshire hillsides, cutting through limestone, sandstone and millstone grit to attach the town and its surrounding collieries to distant places. Market days testified to the fertility of surrounding farms, while the rapacious expansion of the coal and engineering industries predicted a confident future. When, in 1889, the Manchester, Sheffield and Lincolnshire Railway (later the Great Central Railway) further extended its reach, it traversed a coalfield estimated to contain no less than 800 million tons of coal. The landscape that seduced – and still pleases – countless Romantics has always had a solid girth.

My great-grandfather's coming to maturity, as a man and a worker, is part of this industrial story. By the mid 1880s, he was no longer down the mine. Dick was never happy below ground and much preferred to work with industrial engines, tending the iron steeds that sunk shafts, operated pulleys and powered innumerable workshops and foundries. He was good with his hands and with machinery; any work with industrial engines attracted Dick and, at the turn of the century, there was plenty. Industrial engine tender, driver, fitter, mechanic, engineer – over the years, my great-grandfather laid claim to all these occupations – but, at the time of his marriage, in 1885, at the age of twenty-two, Dick described himself as an engineer tender.

Betsy Ward courted someone else before she knew Dick, and I put it that way round because, even as a young woman, Betsy was the one who did the choosing. She gave this impression straightaway. In part, this was due to her stature: she was a big-boned woman and tall – all the Wards were tall – and she carried herself with a dignity beyond her station. Though her father was a collier, her eldest sister Annie had worked as a lady's maid and knew what it meant to be a lady. The lessons in decorum and the occasional cast-offs she brought home gave Betsy and their younger sisters a glimpse of another world and its ladylike ways.

All working-class schooling was haphazard at this time, but my great-grandma's was more haphazard than most. Betsy had not mastered reading and writing before being told to stay away. The height that became an advantage to her as a young woman was a distinct disadvantage as a child: 'You're too big to be at school now,' her schoolmistress informed her. 'Go on home and help your mam,' an instruction so devastating, Betsy still spoke of it seventy years later.

Home was rooms in Speedwell Buildings, Staveley, another of Chesterfield's outlying villages, where Betsy's mother took in sewing and brought up nine children. Much of what Betsy learned was gleaned from home and her mam was extremely grateful for her help. The third child and third daughter, Betsy soon knew

[B]esides the fumes and the gases, every breath of wind at the ironworks carries dust with it, whirling through the air in a wind, dropping through it in a calm, covering the ground, filling the cabins, settling on the clothes of those who are within reach, filling their eyes and their mouths, covering their hands and their faces. The calcined ironstone sends forth red dust, the smoke from the chimneys and furnaces is deposited in white dust, the smoke from the steel-rolling mills falls in black dust; and, most constant difficulty of all, the gases escaping from the furnaces are charged with a fine, impalpable brownish dust, which is shed everywhere, on everything, which clogs the interior of the stoves and of the flues, and whose encroachments have to be constantly fought against. One of the most repellent phenomena at the ironworks to the onlooker is the process of expelling the dust from the stoves...the stove is filled with air at high pressure...and the air is forcibly expelled. A great cloud of red dust rushes out with a roar, covering everything and everybody who stands within reach, with so intolerable a noise and effluvium that it makes itself felt even amidst the incessant reverberations, the constant smells, dust, deposits, that surround the stoves and the furnaces. That strange, grim street formed by the kilns, the furnaces and the bunkers, darkened by the iron platforms overhead between the kilns and the gantry, is a street in which everything is a dull red, is the very heart of the works, the very stronghold of the making of iron, a place unceasingly filled by glare, and clanging, and vapours, from morning till night and from night till morning.

– From Florence Bell, *At the Works: A Study of a Manufacturing Town*, 1907

how to manage the household and her five younger brothers and sisters. She had a fund of common sense and grew into a strong and capable young woman. When her chores were complete, Betsy helped her mother with the dressmaking, although that word gives perhaps too grand an impression of all the unpicking and cobbling together that went on inside their Staveley home. The skills involved were real enough, nonetheless. Betsy learned how to make the best of what was available and how the merest strip of braid could lift a worsted jacket out of the ordinary.

She was only twenty when she married Richard Nash, nineteen when this dark-haired moustachioed young man first caught her eye. (One of the ways in which Dick reckoned his age was by saying he was two years older than Betsy.) The fact that he had turned his back on the colliery where their fathers and many neighbours were employed told Betsy he'd a mind of his own, which was no small thing when you consider how quickly the pit became the warp and weft of a miner's life. She was relieved to meet someone who saw things differently, even if battling in the hell-fire temperatures of a foundry was not exactly dainty work.

They were near neighbours when they started courting, so Betsy already knew something of my great-grandfather's character. He was a quietly spoken, practical man, with skills beyond deft hands and physical strength. Dick was popular with his fellow workers and gained their respect without feeling the need to shout about it – or at them – and his smile could soften any day. Betsy's first young man had had a starchy look about him; there was nothing starchy about Dick.

He and Betsy moved to a cottage in Whittington and settled down to married life. Most of their neighbours had small children running about the yard (and, in many cases, more than they could cope with), but my great-grandparents' circumstances changed far more slowly than either of them envisaged. Five years passed before the birth of their first child. Dick spent his days at the foundry. Betsy washed and baked, and swept and re-swept their stone floor, and waited. Finally, in July 1890, a daughter, Mary Elizabeth Doran Nash, was born.

The relief of her first cry, after all that waiting, and a summer baby too. Betsy felt fortunate to be delivered of a July baby. It was pleasant to sit on the doorstep on warm afternoons, rocking the cradle with her foot while darning and watching the spiders spin their webs. More importantly, a summer birth would give Mary the chance to thrive before harsh weather set in. Like most work-men's cottages in the area, my great-grandparents' house was damp. No matter how wide Betsy flung open the windows, an earthy smell clung to the interior. It was as well to establish a child before winter seeped through the walls. But with the spiders' webs still draping the backyard, Mary contracted bronchitis. She died on 1 October, aged eleven weeks.

Infant mortality was high in the late nineteenth century. In the year Mary died, children aged one and under (who represented barely more than 2 per cent of the population of England and Wales), accounted for nearly a quarter of all deaths, a third of those taking place in the first month of a child's life, and a fifth during the first week. To have raised a child to nearly three months old felt like some kind of milestone, but, in the face of statistics like these, it was a crooked and crumbling one, with poor foundations. Mary Elizabeth was a long awaited, much wanted firstborn and her death was greatly mourned. My great-grandparents were parents for no time at all before they were childless again.

Betsy kept the arrangement of wax lilies that decorated the tiny

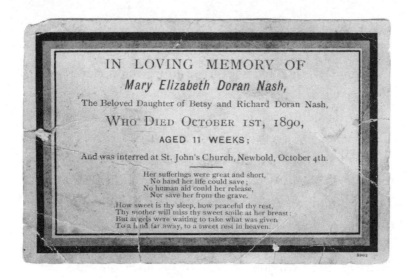

box in which Mary was buried, and the memoriam card they had printed with verses selected from a book. Choosing the verses was especially difficult with Betsy unable to read and Dick a slow reader at best. He read each one out loud, weighing their rhymes so that Betsy could decide which one most closely represented her feelings, but they were all much the same: sentimental posies and too pretty by far. In the end, they had to settle on something.

Neither of my great-grandparents were church-goers, although Dick regularly knelt to say his prayers, a gentle murmur rising from the bedside as he did so. The Lord Giveth and the Lord Taketh Away. These were just words, as far as Betsy was concerned. Religion offered her scant consolation.

Two years later, my great-grandparents were living on the opposite side of Chesterfield. Dick was tending engines still, currently employed at a brickyard, literally helping to build the town. Two years is no time at all, but an eternity if, like Betsy, you are

twenty-eight years old, mourning a child and watching your neighbours' children grow. Dick's new job brought a new address, but,
most importantly, 1892 was the year my grandma was born.

Betsy wanted the very best for her new daughter and so she
was christened Annie, after her ladylike aunt. She had Richard's
birth name too, or a version of it, at least, as had Mary, to keep
the name Dorance in the family. A photograph taken some years
later shows them: Betsy, dark hair, dark blouse; twenty pearl
buttons counting down to her slim waist, standing proud and
erect in the doorway of their home, though it's merely another
workman's cottage (one of several they came to know), with rough
shutters at the window, a dank privy down the yard and no
running water, which only underlines how hard Betsy worked to
maintain their snowy window nets and dress Annie in her white
lawn frock fashioned with a dark ribbon sash. Dick sits beside

them. Whatever his day has been up to this point, he looks polished clean, and rests his foot on a kerbstone as easily as his daughter places her small, trusting hand on his knee. Their Jack Russell is alert in the foreground (there was always a small dog about somewhere).

Betsy's cinched waist and Annie's lace look out of place in their humble surroundings, but this was a best-dress occasion – a birthday, perhaps – posed for the camera, for keeps. And if Annie's ribbon sash was broader than was strictly necessary and her bodice comprised the most complicated lacework Betsy's fingers could achieve, then behind my grandma, always, was the ghost of the child who had not survived.

Annie had her mother's nose, 'the Ward nose' as it was known within the family, though it was not especially prominent. She had her father's thick brown hair. She inherited her composure from them both. Even as a small child (a solemn child in photographs), Annie appeared self-contained, as sure of herself as of her two small feet planted firmly on the ground in the new button boots in which she started school. No clutching at a toy boat or rag doll, like some of her classmates, or making an appeal with her smile. My grandma always knew who she was.

By the early 1900s, Dick was appointed foreman of the men constructing Chesterfield's third and final reservoir at Linacre, with some twenty workers under him. Far better to be a foreman directing men and overseeing machinery than tackling the back-breaking work of digging out the new reservoir and excavating tons of earth. Parched and exhausted at the end of their long shift, Dick's men headed for the Crispin Inn. Beer was downed in enormous quantities, eight pints a night being not uncommon for labourers who'd worked up a thirst. Dick became such a good customer himself that the landlord gave him a kissing cup, one of three silver tankards discovered in the cellar. He hoped it would bring Dick luck (and many more return trips to his pub).

My great-grandfather's job came with a cottage at the edge of the woodland site; their only near neighbour was the town's bailiff and his family. Annie played games of tag-and-chase with his young sons and idled with them on the way to school. On summer days, they walked down narrow lanes where overlapping branches made a dappled canopy. Come winter mornings, Annie was bundled into a thick woollen shawl which criss-crossed her chest and held her fast as she tried to balance on the spangled paving stones.

In 1933, 'Chesterfield's D. H. Lawrence', novelist and poet, F. C. Boden, wrote lovingly of the beauty of 'wood, water and sky' at the Linacre reservoirs. You could 'lie at the top of the Linacre wood watching the sinking sun burn on the stretch of water… listening to the sweet chiming of the Old Brampton bells'. This undisturbed haven became a place to escape from the town's industrial clamour. Though less glorious during the construction of the reservoirs, to walk through the deserted woods in the early morning, especially during springtime, when bluebells crouched in the long grass, or at late evening, when your footfalls released the scent of wild garlic, was to enter a perfect green world. My great-grandfather loved it.

It was a beautiful spot, but an isolated one in which to bring up a child and Betsy missed the sound of children's games and women's voices ricocheting around backyards. It was hard to have just one neighbour, however reliable and well-liked, and Betsy missed her sisters being nearby. Five miles might as well have been the other side of the county, given the number of times they managed to meet.

And Betsy wanted to be doing something herself. A few years earlier, an industrial accident, a blow to the head, had put Dick in the Sheffield Infirmary. She could still picture his workmate, standing, breathless, ashen-faced, looking anywhere but at her, while he explained where they'd taken Mr Nash. Neither Dick nor Betsy spoke of that desperate time: the worry of it all and of the state he would be in, if he survived; his long, slow, painful recovery, with no money coming in except a pittance from the insurance. Amazingly, Dick recovered fully, a dent in his forehead the only legacy of those dreadful months, but its presence served as a reminder of what might have been and could still be. Industrial accidents happened daily.

Betsy was busy with the chores for which there were no short cuts then, but she still had time enough to make plans. At night, while she sat threading the ribbons that edged Annie's petticoats, nightdresses and bodices, and which had to be rethreaded with each wash, her mind considered all the possibilities before her.

She was nearly forty now and wanted an occupation, but not one at someone else's bidding. Betsy hankered after a shop, Her sister Annie, a widow now, ran a beer-off (not the most ladylike of activities) and seemed to manage by herself pretty well. If Betsy ran a shop while Dick was working, they'd have two incomes coming in and she'd have a role that would suit her. She asked sister Annie to keep an eye open for somewhere close by, though not on Annie's doorstep, which Betsy could inspect for herself. And, around 1905, she found it: the corner shop at Wheeldon Mill.

2

Brasso and Dolly Blue

Only one photograph of Wheeldon Mill appears to have been taken during all the years my great-grandparents lived there, its singular status confirmation of the area's insignificance. The picture shows an overcast day, circa 1908, and does the place few favours, the photographer keener to foreground the man crossing the canal bridge with his decrepit donkey and handcart than the surrounding houses. Its most prominent feature is the poorly surfaced road the hawker stands on. Unless you know that the tiny white slab, barely visible through the trees, is a doorstep, you may not even realise the corner shop is there. The picture was sold as a postcard but would hardly encourage visitors. It looks a pretty dismal spot. Wheeldon Mill: the last place God created.

My great-grandparents' new address was 150 Station Road, Brimington, but, as anyone who walks the mile uphill into Brimington proper knows, Wheeldon Mill and Brimington are not one and the same. For all the years my family lived at or visited 'the Mill' – those in the know tended to drop the 'Wheeldon' – a distinction was made between the two. Wheeldon Mill, as described to me, was the little clutch of houses at the bottom of and either side of Station Road, a short stride from the Chesterfield Canal, just above the Sheepbridge and Brimington Railway Station with its pastry-cutter edging and wooden stairs. It comprised no more than forty houses and stood about a mile north-east of Chesterfield town centre, and a quarter of a mile from the racecourse.

The area grew up piecemeal, a handful of stone cottages probably dating back to the eighteenth-century water-powered mill for which the place is named, others to the opening up of the canal and railway. Its brighter redbrick terraces, including that with the corner shop, came later, in celebration of Queen Victoria's Jubilee. There was nothing twee about these two-up two-downs, with their night-soil middens, communal backyards and strips of front garden. They were not, however, the tight back-to-backs of industrial legend, but short, stubby rows, bordering the road or canal, some comprising no more than half a dozen houses.

Today, summer visitors are drawn to the pub beside the refurbished Chesterfield Canal. This seems about right: for as long as my family was connected with the area, beer played a vital role in this small community. Church and schools were higher up the hill; how much more convenient to have the Great Central Hotel – an ordinary pub – on your doorstep. Corner shop and pub stood at right angles to one another, the rough ground between them serving as a makeshift playground for local children.

The uppermost limit of Wheeldon Mill was its Plantation – a grandiose name for a small copse. There was a brickyard nearby, a sewerage plant (odourless by the 1930s, but historically more iffy), and a small colliery, whose seams were worked for a short time during the 1900s and again in the late thirties. Numerous

small open mines and footrills showed how the immediate area had been mined for coal and ironstone intermittently since the nineteenth century. Some two miles north-west stood the Sheepbridge Company, that bulwark of industry (and sometime employer of my great-grandfather) whose fortunes and enterprises expanded year on year. Two miles north-east, with its own collieries and ironworks, and interlinked activities with Sheepbridge (plus houses built for its clerks on Gentleman's Row), the Staveley Coal & Iron Company reigned supreme. Beyond these dark chimneys and stark colliery wheels, in the distance always, and close at hand, lay the deep green folds of the Derbyshire hillside. Industry might scour and plunder, but harvest reports continued to appear alongside accounts of mining accidents and fatalities.

Like most of its neighbours, 150 Station Road was a two-up two-down, one of the 'downs', in this instance, comprising the shop with its katy-cornered door on to the street. A contemporary trade directory lists 'Richard Nash, grocer', though everyone knew the corner shop was Betsy's. Dick was still at Linacre when they secured the tenancy; his working life always happened elsewhere. The corner shop was definitely hers.

Its windows were smeared with dust when she first set eyes on the shop, and the shelves and floorboards needed a good fettle, but it did not take Betsy long to set the place to rights. Sweeping brush and mop chivvied every corner, the large wooden counter was thoroughly scrubbed and oiled, and the panes rubbed with damp newspaper and a splash of vinegar. By the time she turned the 'Open' sign on the shop door, my great-grandma had everything organised.

A bank of tiny drawers concealed all manner of things such as matches and gas mantles, clay pipes, nit combs and string. Floor-to-ceiling shelves held every tin and packet you could think of, from mustard powder, pickling spice and candied peel, to Horlick's Malted Milk and Brasso. Bags of poultry spice and pig powders stood near a vinegar barrel fastened beneath a thick, heavy lid; cans of paraffin were grouped nearby, out of the way of sacks containing potatoes, sugar and flour. Cheeses cooled on a marble slab behind the counter, next to the bottles of Pikanti and A1 Sauce.

Betsy opened the door each morning wearing a starched white apron which, like her skirts, practically brushed the floor. Though the apron was often grubby by the end of a long day – in the early years of business, the shop stayed open until ten or eleven p.m. – its crisp white linen was part of her authority: 'I run this shop,' was the message it conveyed. 'The corner shop doesn't run me.'

There were generally two or three people in the shop at any one time (more, at weekends): neighbours like Florrie Stokes, who came with her toddler and new baby while her other four were at school, or Kathleen Driver, who wanted to inspect the new shop-keeper and pick up a loaf while she was there.

Bread came high on every woman's shopping list. For some of Betsy's customers, bread provided breakfast and tea: bread and jam, bread and scrape, bread and dripping, bread and treacle, bread-and-you-just-be-thankful, if that's all there was to eat. My great-grandma traded in half loaves as well as whole ones, stale bread as well as fresh and, sometimes, reluctantly, if someone was particularly desperate, two or three slices at a time.

Potatoes were also a priority, and the only vegetable the corner shop sold. Aside from an onion to provide flavouring, potatoes were the sole vegetable in some Edwardian diets. Other quanti-ties might rise and fall or be crossed off a shopping list altogether, but the pounds of potatoes usually remained secure. Other frequent purchases were tea, sugar, biscuits, currants, flour. Bottled relishes added spice to a grocery list as well as to a husband's plate, a spoonful of mustard pickle enlivening a nice piece of ham.

Boiled ham, brawn and hazlett, plus bacon by the slice, were delivered by the butcher, and stored in a meat safe which did not exactly keep meat fresh, but at least kept the flies off. The butcher also supplied ha'penny 'ducks': pieces of chopped liver and other intestines stewed in a seasoned gravy. These arrived as a dark, not-quite-solid rectangle faintly quivering on a tray, and were cut into wedges by Betsy, a task she accomplished while holding her breath. (My great-grandma might sell 'ducks', but she couldn't bring herself to eat one.) As with the relishes and boiled ham, bacon was usually destined for the man of the house, his wife and chil-dren making do with bread and dip: the fat that had fried the bacon, mopped up with a slice of bread.

The women of Wheeldon Mill were Betsy's chief customers,

their purchases revealing both the pattern and the detail of their lives, their days determined by the occupations of husbands and sons. The majority of the men were manual labourers, many employed as miners. Mining accounted for the largest portion of Chesterfield's workforce, but there was also a whole vocabulary of skilled and unskilled foundry men, plus general labourers, railwaymen and brickies. Whatever their occupation, the result was the same: most of the men were engaged in filthy work; collar-and-tie chaps were the exception.

Wives fought a constant battle against dirt, not just the dirt in poorly ventilated houses but the muck their men brought home. Betsy's stock described their unequal struggle. Borax, Rub-a-Dub, Dolly Blue, Carbosil, Fairy Flakes, Sunlight Soap, Reckitt's Blue, Robin Starch, Persil – she sold every brand of laundry soap and washing soda you could think of, plus donkey stone for whitening sills and doorsteps, and peggy legs for pummelling wet clothes.

Coal dust was particularly pernicious. These were the days well before pithead baths, when men came straight from the mine. There was kettle after kettle of hot water to boil and heavy clothes to dry for the next day. Even the moleskin trousers miners wore were stiff with perspiration by the close of a long shift, sweat and dust intermingling, each rearrangement of their steaming bulk, as they dried before the fire, releasing further coal dust into the room. It was impossible to keep a baby clean with a collier in the house and, no matter how hard you scrubbed them, there was no such thing as clean sheets. Coal dust ground its way into the very grain of the cloth.

Colliers' wives were as wedded to the pit as their menfolk, the timing of colliery shifts setting the rhythm of domestic life: one steel cage descending as another ascended towards daylight, with the expectation of hot water at the ready and the stew pan simmering nicely regardless of the hour. Those with husbands and sons working opposite shifts could be on their feet from dawn till nightfall, a coat pulled over their nightdress at both ends of the day when they stumbled out of bed to stoke the fire.

Betsy's neighbour Nora Parks had four sons follow their father down the pit. Five loads of pit clothes to darn, wash and dry; five colliers working a mix of shifts, five men requiring hot baths and food; Nora sluicing water into the tub (and out again, once the bathers were through), her skirt and apron splashed with filthy water, perspiration running down her face; the whole room steaming and condensation puddling on the sills. If they were in from school, her daughters Lil and Edna were called upon to swill their brothers' backs, in anticipation of a future like their mother's.

In the early years of the corner shop, at least until the First World War, most wages kept purchasing to a minimum: 3s 3d was the going daily rate for a foundry labourer, while skilled foundry-men might earn the same as a curate or junior clerk. In 1906, the average coalface worker earned £112 a year, approximately £2 a week, though there were frequent slips and stoppages. The majority of shopping lists varied little from one week to the next. Requests for two ounces – of cheese, butter or flour – were commonplace: most customers bought food in small quantities. Many women shopped daily, especially those whose husbands were paid by the day. Weekly wages were easier to manage, but with basic foodstuffs sold loose and weighed out by hand, it was easy for Betsy to adjust quantities to reflect people's needs, or, rather, their purses. 'Just do me that corner of hazlett, Mrs Nash, and a mouse-size piece of cheese.'

Trade was conducted in pennies and halfpennies more often

It must be remembered by those who are convinced that the working man can live well and easily on 3d a day, because middle-class people have tried the experiment and found it possible, that the well-to-do man who may spend no more than 1s 9d a week on food for a month or more has not also all his other expenses cut down to their very lowest limit. The well-to-do man sleeps in a quiet, airy room with sufficient and sanitary bedding. He has every facility for luxurious bathing and personal cleanliness. He has light and hygienic clothing; he has warmth in the winter and a change of air in the summer. He can rest when he is in; he has good cooking at his command, with a sufficiency of storage, utensils, and fuel. Above all, he can always stop living on 3d a day if it does not suit him, or if his family get anxious. When his daughter needs a pair of 6s 6d boots he does not have to arrange an overdraft with his banker in order to meet the crisis, as the poor man does with his pawnbroker. He does not feel that all his family, well or ill, warm or cold, overworked or not, are also bound to live on 3d a day, and are only too thankful if it does not drop to 2½d or 2d, or even less, should under-employment or unemployment come his way. It is impossible to compare the living on 3d a day of a person all of whose other requirements are amply and sufficiently satisfied, with the living of people whose every need is thwarted and starved.

– From Maud Pember Reeves, *Round About a Pound a Week*, a survey of working-class wives in Lambeth, by the Fabian Women's Group, 1909–1913

than shillings; a half sovereign was something to change down into more useful coinage. You could buy a surprising amount with small coins: a quartern loaf cost approximately 6d, a pound of tea one shilling; a halfpenny could buy quite a lot. Even so, it was impossible to run a corner shop without offering credit; several neighbours relied on tick by the end of the week. But there was nearly always someone willing to risk a little splurge and, for the better-off, temptation came round each Saturday in the form of the few iced fancies Betsy displayed on a tray.

Inevitably, those in straitened circumstances made more of an impression on my great-grandma. Hunger presented a needier face at the shop door, often a woman with young children, like Florrie Stokes. Florrie's daughter, Ethel, ran errands whenever she could, which brought in the odd ha'penny, but the only wage coming into the house was her husband's and him too lippy to keep any job long: a short spell as a hewer, a stint of labouring here and there, some fetching and carrying, while Florrie struggled to raise a family of six. 'You wouldn't believe it, Mrs Nash,' she said, 'but my long hair,' (now scrunched into a bun) 'was once as bright as a new thrupenny bit.'

Several neighbours had to fend for lodgers as well as husbands and sons: young men squeezing into rooms whose table could scarcely accommodate a growing family, let alone another pair of elbows. One lodger after another (and sometimes more than one at once); a nephew or other relative, perhaps; a stranger, quite often; someone sharing the same shift as husband or son (and complicating matters even further, if not). There was talk of lodgers breaking up families – and probably some did – but a boarder whose inky bathwater you threw across the yard and whose chamber pot you emptied soon took the shine off temptation.

December 7, 1910

Rent (of which 2s is back payment) 10s 0d

Boot club 6d

Burial Insurance 7d

Mangling 2d

Coal 1s 4d

Gas 9d

Wood 1d

Soap, soda 4d

Linseed meal 1d

Pinafore and bonnet 8d

Total 14s 6d

Left for food 11s 6d

20 Loaves 4s 2d

Meat 2s 10½d

2 Tins of milk 6d

Sugar 4d

Margarine 1s

Potatoes 9d

Tea 8d

Fish 4 ½d

Vegetables 6d

Pepper, salt 1d

Jam 3d

Example of Mrs E's weekly household budget. Mrs E had no idea what her husband earned. She received 22s a week in summertime and what he could give in winter; never less than 20s when in work. Her eldest daughter had just started work in a soda-water factory and was allowing 4s a week. Owing to a period of almost entire unemployment in the previous winter, £3 4s was owed in rent when the Fabian Group's visits began. There were seven children alive; three dead. One son had left home.

– From Maud Pember Reeves, *Round About a Pound a Week*, a survey of working-class wives in Lambeth, London, by the Fabian Women's Group, 1909–1913

Some of Betsy's customers accomplished their near-impossible feats of hard household labour while living in part-houses, their landlord having divided the property into two. Other households comprised several generations, widows (or, less often, widowers) sharing their home with married daughters or sons. With this shifting mix of family, lodgers and shared houses, plus neighbours moving to find new employment, better accommodation or cheaper rent, as my great-grandparents had done until now, the population of Wheeldon Mill was, in part, itinerant. There were frequent comings and goings, all of which Betsy had to be aware of, along with people's names: corner-shopkeepers needed to know their customers (and who might be tempted to do a moonlight flit).

Not everyone in the vicinity used the corner shop. The little knot of houses comprising Wheeldon Mill was its mainstay; those living higher up Station Road had grocers of their own, though many of them called in occasionally. There were Sunday strollers too, rounding off canalside walks with a drink in the Great Central Hotel and some cigarettes from the shop; plus passing trade from those using the railway station, or cutting along the towpath from Newbridge Lane. Larger properties in the neighbourhood, further up the social scale as well as higher up the hill, moved in a different sphere and had their groceries delivered, though the Brimington House slavey was partial to an ounce of pear drops on her half day.

The room behind the shop was known as the house, an appropriately all-encompassing word, as everything bar sleep went on there. Its black-leaded range provided all heat and hot water – there was no hot tap in the house: water for cooking or the weekly bath came from the one cold tap and was heated in a saucepan or kettle.

Clothes were boiled in a gas-fired copper concealed beneath a cloth when not in use. Gas mantles cast a subdued light across all rooms (and shop); Wee-Willie-Winkie candlesticks or candles on saucers were on hand for trips to the privy. Rugs overlaid the floors, several overlapping rag rugs made from oddments and cast-off clothing. As the years went by and fashions changed, these became more colourful, but when Betsy made her first rugs for the house, their fronds were mostly brown or black.

Though separated by a different class of rug (older versus new), kitchen sink and sofa were merely yards apart. The sink had plates and tea cups on shelves rising above it, whereas framed photographs hung from the picture rail above the horsehair sofa, emphasising their distinct roles. The pictures were a veritable family gallery: Betsy's father looking stern and decidedly Victorian, Dick and Betsy's own head-and-shoulder portraits, blown up in size, and a hand-tinted photograph of Annie looking like a young Lady of Shallot, her long, loose tresses tumbling on to a rose-coloured gown.

The house lacked a scullery or larder, but the area at the top of the cellar steps was roomy enough for the shelves housing Betsy's home-made jam, bottled fruit and pickled eggs, plus the pancheon where she kept her loaves, teacakes, baps and balm cakes. I can't imagine where Betsy found the time for baking or preserving. The room held one armchair (albeit a stiff-backed Windsor) – not surprisingly, this was Dick's.

Though the furnishings were plain, my great-grandma loved strong colour and introduced a vibrant note wherever she could. One of her passions was cranberry glass – the ruby world glimpsed through it always gave her pleasure. Brass ornaments were also prized and polished to a ruddy sheen; a Staffordshire boy and girl

clutched matching pottery tulips at either end of the mantel shelf.
Brasses, china, treadle machine; heavy cast-iron saucepans – the
house held the usual mix of function and decoration in a room
required to provide almost all things. It was a comfortable space
nonetheless, its many purposes blending, and its surfaces, wherever
possible, overlaid with lace – thanks, yet again, to Betsy: scalloped
runners in drawn thread-work, cobweb-fine doilies, broderie
anglaise mats. It was incredible what could be achieved with a
willing pair of hands and a ready supply of Dolly Blue.

The focal point of the house (room and dwelling both) was the
table. Baking, eating, reading, family chat and, shortly, Annie's
homework: practically everything was accomplished here. A door
to the right led into the shared yard with its coal houses and privies;
to the table's immediate left was the door opening into the shop,
the rattle of its curtain signifying the beginning and end of each
day. The door itself was generally kept closed, but it was a small

matter to serve someone late into the evening, summoned to the counter by the shop bell. This connecting door also confirmed Betsy as queen of her territory, making an entrance, stepping from the wings on to the stage.

She was always Mrs Nash to her customers. That never changed; to the majority of her customers, my great-grandma was Mrs Nash until she died, though she learned most of their first names soon enough – some on her first day. Several on that first morning just wanted to be neighbourly, others wished to ingratiate themselves in the hope of obtaining tick on favourable terms; some, like Florrie Stokes, fell into both categories.

For the first few months of the tenancy, Betsy and her customers exchanged little more than general greetings and replies to requests for a box of Atora Suet or a ha'porth of cheese. In addition to being a novice shopkeeper, with suppliers to establish and deliveries to arrange, my great-grandma was on trial herself. Was she mean or generous with her portions? Did she lean against the scales when weighing out? Did she tittle-tattle or have favourites?

These tests passed, neighbours started to linger. Brief comments across the counter grew into extended conversations and, at quiet times, customers took to sitting on the sack of potatoes by the door or perching on the long thin crate of minerals that gave on to the shady window with its sweets. The crate or 'the box', as it became known, could accommodate a couple of people at any one time and was the best place to pause for a chat, with the sweet window a vantage point for seeing who might be coming up or down Station Road. ('I see Polly Bly has a new hat. I wonder what she did to get that?'... 'There goes Elsie Needham. She looks like death warmed up. A daughter of twenty and a new baby; she'd thought she was through with that caper.') Some of these flinty women had a flinty turn of phrase.

Back-door living with a communal yard meant life lived in sight of your neighbours, whether headed for the privy or the coal house, the corner shop or train; lines of washing (theirs as well as yours) flapping in your face, and buckets of dirty water shot through open doorways. If you stood at the window with an eye on your neighbour, chances were your neighbour also had her eye on you. Very little went unobserved; some of it was passed on to Betsy. Her role was to listen, not join in.

A woman's world was entirely separate from that of her husband's with his pub and penny bets and exhaustion after a day's rigorous physical labour – not that these women weren't exhausted themselves. Men learned to shrug off bruises and aching bones, deal with the loss of workmates, and to handle themselves in all situations. Tough lives bred tough attitudes, some of them taken out on wives and children.

Whatever their status in the outside world, most men were lord and master in their own homes. Betsy saw what that sometimes came down to: thick leather belts with heavy buckles slid from trousers and wrapped around a fist. 'You bloody well shut up. You'll damn well do as you're told.' Some who let their fists fly did not care who knew it; others surprised her. Harold Driver was one of the quietest of men, apparently. Betsy knew different. She saw Kathleen's arms when she came in search of arnica for her bruises. A thick-set woman who could dish out a few salty phrases, Mrs Driver was still no match for her husband's fists. When Harold took himself home after a Saturday-night skinful, Betsy knew Kathleen would be waiting to see which face he presented at the door. If Harold came whistling along Drake Terrace, all was well, but if the first thing she heard was his hand upon the latch, heaven help her.

'What would you do, Mrs Nash?' Kathleen leaned into the counter. 'What do you think I should do?' This was a plea my great-grandma heard many times over, although rarely with other customers present. Keeping face mattered: not letting your neighbours see your desperation, even if those living in the houses either side heard the row that preceded the blow.

Requests for advice came in all kinds of situations, not just from women leading cat-and-dog lives with their husbands. Whatever the problem – be it blackclocks beneath the sink or insufficient money to pay the insurance, my great-grandma did her best to help. The only situation in which she refused to give advice was

'Families too large, more than they could afford to keep, tempers rising and quite a lot of cruelty on the part of their husbands, through frustration and irritation with conditions. Now, if this got unbearable, and the wife had the courage to summons her husband for cruelty...there was a time to wait before she had to appear in court. A lot of the injuries was fading, [but] there was no woman magistrates allowed, no women solicitors allowed. That woman stood in a court alone, in a man's world and got man's sense of justice.'

– Elizabeth Dean, interviewed aged 101, in Angela Holdsworth, *Out of the Doll's House: The Story of Women in the Twentieth Century*, 1988

when faced with skirmishes between neighbours. The most Betsy allowed herself on these occasions was a sympathetic, soothing, 'Oh dear.'

Like the majority of corner shops, Betsy's was also an unofficial dispensary. Doctors cost sixpence most neighbours could not afford, and with poor diets and exhaustion undermining general health, the shop was well stocked with all kinds of laxatives, general soothers and old faithfuls: Seidlitz Powders, Blood-and-Stomach Pills, Bile Beans, Senna Pods, Scott's Emulsion, Indian Brandy – neighbour heal thyself. My great-grandma knew who was buying peppermint to stave off morning sickness and who placed their faith in the digestive properties of liver salts, but some ills could not be cured with corner-shop medicaments. Clara Tissington had lost a much-loved daughter. Nine years old, old enough to hope she might pull through but, though each year ticked off the calendar meant a greater chance of reaching adulthood, pneumonia (like diphtheria, bronchitis, scarlatina and every other multi-syllable killer of the time), made nonsense of Clara's prayers.

It is hard to think of my grandma in the push and shove of Wheeldon Mill, though it's where Annie spent many years. She was no more than twelve when the family moved there. There were new friends to make and another new school to attend. Fortunately, Annie was befriended by Florrie Stokes' daughter, Ethel. Ethel saw this new and solemn child, with her clean pinafore and shiny hair, standing at the edge of the playground, waiting to be asked to join in. 'Come on, then,' Ethel said, and that was that.

Unlike Annie, who was more of an observer, Ethel would dive into any game, take up the skipping rope and start turning. A big supple girl whose swing of the rope described an arc as easily as she turned a mangle, Ethel took ready pleasure in the short periods she was allowed out to play, just as she knew to grab a slice of bread before one of her brothers snatched it. She was full of fun, would do anything for a dare, and avenged any wrong with her fists. You thought twice about challenging Ethel Stokes – you and whose army?

Protecting herself in childhood scuffles was not something my grandma was good at. If someone pulled Annie's hair, she stood still. Thankfully, whenever swift blows or sharp elbows were needed, Ethel was there to defend her. 'I'd gi' em a crack,' she explained years later, 'Well, Annie always was a lady.'

Whenever my grandma told me about her childhood, she always mentioned poverty and hunger – though not hers. She had jam spread on her bread (and butter, if she wanted it, though some considered butter *and* jam an extravagance), and as many slices as she could eat. She had stout boots that Dick mended when their soles became too thin, and, after she had washed her hair, it was spread across her shoulders to help it dry while Betsy brushed it, if not quite one hundred times, then sufficient times for Annie to lose count.

The poverty and hunger were Ethel's, though hers was not the only family going without. If she called for Annie on the way to school, Betsy would ask if she'd had breakfast, and it was often evident from Ethel's face that she had not. Time and again, my great-grandma placed a hunk of bread and jam in her hands. One morning, Ethel appeared with bare feet. The soles of her shoes had worn right through and even the cardboard stuffed inside them had disintegrated. A new pair of boots cost around six shillings. There was no point in Betsy asking when Ethel's would be replaced, when Florrie did not have sufficient money to feed her family, let alone the penny for the boot club. That afternoon, when Dick came off shift, my great-grandma walked down to Whittington Moor and returned with a brown-paper parcel. When Ethel appeared the following day, a pair of shoes was passed across the counter with a smile and a shushing finger.

Annie's other childhood friend, Zoe Graham, was the publican's daughter, whose circumstances could not have been more different. She wore nice clothes, like Annie, and shared Annie's disinclination for rough games. With most games played on the spare ground between their houses, they sometimes gauged the general mood before venturing out to play. Quieter, rhyming games were more to their liking: 'The farmer wants a wife, the wife wants a child...' Each time their respective doors opened, sweet young voices drifted into the shop and the pub.

My grandma was not stuck up, but she was indulged. Even those who loved her dearly (including Ethel) said she was not allowed to soil her hands in any way. Annie was not to wash a single pot, peel a potato or lift a sweeping brush, but to sit with her school books or her sewing. At a time when girls like Ethel had one sibling on their hip, others at their heels and a long list of chores to complete, my grandma was having crochet lessons, learning the piano and perfecting her embroidery. Dick and Betsy greatly regretted their own poor schooling and wanted her to have an education in all the things they lacked, and as many extras as they could afford. Dick's income was reasonably stable, with a foreman's wage, and the shop was beginning to pay its way. Their own needs were relatively minimal. And unlike the majority of their neighbours, my great-grandparents had only one child to provide for. They could not afford to raise a lady of leisure – Annie would have to work until she married – but the better her education, the more chances she would have. Her hands would be smooth, unlike theirs.

It was probably Dick and Betsy's friendship with the publican that helped determine my great-grandma's schooling. Zoe Graham was a paying pupil at the Netherthorpe Grammar School, Staveley (tradesmen's daughters were often fee-paying pupils). In 1907, Annie joined her. She had to pass an entrance exam in Reading, Writing and the First Four Rules of Arithmetic, but with that achieved, was accepted. School fees were £1 13s 4d a term; dinner in the School House a further 9d a day – most pupils came from too far away to return home at lunchtime (though, this being the north of England, no one ate 'lunch'). Students were required to provide their own books and stationery; there was also a sports fee of 2s 6d a term, although my great-grandparents could have spared themselves that cost: it paid for the hockey lessons Annie hated. My grandma could think of nothing worse than pounding up and down a muddy field.

Staveley Netherthorpe Grammar School had a long pedigree stretching back to the sixteenth century and had recently resisted attempts to deprive it of its grammar-school status. Shortly before my grandma became a pupil, the school had sixty-six day boys, one boarder, and forty-one girls. Over the next few years, an influx of those wishing to train as elementary school teachers at its newly established Pupil-Teacher Centre further increased student numbers. As befitted a co-educational establishment, the staff was mixed, its female members inspirational New Women in college gowns, teaching their young charges to think for themselves, a lesson my grandma absorbed.

The school syllabus included Latin, Euclid, Trigonometry and Science. Pupils were encouraged to perform their own experiments in the chemistry and physics' labs and to 'attack problems with confidence'. Additionally, girls were taught housewifery, dressmaking and cookery; and boys woodwork, to introduce 'ideas of economy, thrift and careful attention to detail'. Annie's favourite subjects were English and History – she relished Dickens and Longfellow and devoured Walter Scott; the Kings and Queens of England; the little Princes in the Tower; Alfred burning the Cakes. Aside from the dreaded hockey, my grandma loved her Netherthorpe years.

There were more new friends to make at the grammar school, boys as well as girls, who were just as interested in reading Shakespeare as she was: Maurice Unwin, who had views on most subjects; and a quietly spoken boy, George Walter Hardcastle, who kept his opinions to himself, but generally had something interesting to say. There was slim, fair-haired Gwennie Peat, and, of course, Zoe was a classmate too. Just as Ethel had defended my grandma, now Annie stuck up for Zoe. Whereas Annie had needed a champion to fight with slaps and fists, Zoe was a diffident pupil. Words did not frighten Annie; she knew and enjoyed their power, and spoke up for Zoe whenever she could. Though no fists flew at the grammar school, there were other ways of wounding with intent.

It was quite a performance to walk the five miles to school and back again at the end of the day, and so, for her fifteenth birthday, Dick and Betsy bought Annie a dark green bicycle from Flint's on Whittington Moor, with dress guards to protect her coat and skirt from splashes. The bike had to be pushed uphill for the first leg of the journey, but Annie could cycle on through Brimington, into Staveley and on again to Netherthorpe.

My great-grandparents were so proud of their grammar-school girl, they had a new studio portrait taken and mounted on the wall, where it joined the panorama of family photographs. The new picture showed Annie in her grammar-school cap and uniform, hair flowing free, trusty bike in the foreground – the independent young scholar cycling into the future. Framed in gilt, with a slim green velvet border, the picture had pride of place on the wall. The first thing you saw when you opened the house door was young Annie.

She and Ethel saw less of one another when my grandma became a grammar-school pupil. Ethel left school the minute she could – she couldn't have stayed even if she'd wanted – and

was soon stacking newly pressed glass at the bottle factory on Coronation Road. Faced with a choice of the sticky, scalding sweetness of the jam factory, fettling crocks at Pearson's Pottery, the yes/no servility of domestic service, or lugging bottles and crates, Ethel plumped for the latter. Cut fingers and an aching back were preferable to scalded hands and forearms, lungfuls of dust or mountains of some old biddy's pots. While Annie was walking out in a dress so new its velvet shimmered, Ethel was collecting her first wage and tipping all but thru'pence up to her mam.

Now that she was working, Ethel had more of a voice in her household. Having her say did not make family life any easier, however. If Ethel had a view, she expressed it. She was sick to death of her father's aggravating ways, his leathering the younger ones, bullying her mam and pouring half his wages down his throat. She put food on the table just as he did. One night, during yet another furious altercation, he lunged at Ethel who lunged straight back at him. Immediately, she was thrown out of the house.

Ethel was tearful and trembling, though defiant still, when she landed on my great-grandparents' doorstep. Of course she could stay, Betsy reassured her, and made up a bed in the attic, which, until now, had housed assorted sacks of grain, but there was a small table in one corner, an upright chair and a hook on the back of the door which would do for her things. It had a sunny aspect too, with stairs that came right into the room.

Ethel stayed with my great-grandparents for several months, returning home when she knew her father would be out, and washing pots and generally helping Betsy while Annie did her homework. She had always been grateful for the kindness they showed her, now she could not thank them enough. But Ethel could not stay at the corner shop for ever. Eventually, she and her father called a truce. They'd been passing in the street without acknowledging one another, but Ethel had enough of that game, and wanted to be at home for her mam. Which was just as well, because life at the corner shop was set to change. Annie was about to get a sister.

Part Two

3

Pick Me

ON 2 FEBRUARY 1901, QUEEN VICTORIA WAS BURIED WITH state ceremony and full military honours. On the same day, a baby came into the world with no fanfare whatsoever, a daughter born to Emily and Thomas Martin. At least, that's what the birth certificate says. In fact, although they lived together for some seven years and he gave his name to their four daughters, Emily Ball and Thomas Martin never married, though that's less unusual for the time than some might think.

Thomas was a colliery hand, a hewer. By 1901, he and Emily were living in the Derbyshire town of Eckington, having had as many houses as they had children, and in as many years, just about. Life looked set to be the same for Emily as for her own mother, who gave birth to eleven children, her youngest born when Emily was already a mother herself; at one point, mother and daughter were pregnant at the same time. Thomas was also one of eleven children, born to Irish parents living on the outskirts of Chesterfield.

In 1903, Emily was pregnant again, a pregnancy she did not survive. A fifth pregnancy in seven years was not that unusual for a working-class woman of her day, nor was death in childbirth: maternal mortality was a major cause of death among married women. In October of that year, at the age of twenty-seven, Emily haemorrhaged following her confinement. There is no record of what happened to the baby she was carrying.

The tragedy of Emily's short life was not quite over. The following day, Thomas went to register the death and, as is the custom, was required to state his own name along with hers and define his relationship to the deceased. There are two ways of interpreting what happened next. A sense of propriety, a need for truthfulness at the end; shock or exhaustion, or perhaps a combination of all these, made Thomas give her correct name: Emily Ball, and not the surname, 'Martin', which she had given on recent documents and for the purpose of the census two years earlier. A less generous

'My mother died at thirty-eight. She left six of us. I was only six years old. She died with childbirth... There was no information at all on birth control. If it happened, which it did very, very often in my younger days, that a woman went into hospital for her confinement and the doctors said if there was a recurrence of pregnancy the woman would die, that woman was sent out without any information as to how to avoid that. The law forbade them to give information on birth control...'

– Elizabeth Dean, interviewed aged 101, in Angela Holdsworth, *Out of the Doll's House: The Story of Women in the Twentieth Century*, 1988.

interpretation is that by giving her correct name, Thomas not only told the truth but also distanced himself from further responsibility for their young children. This naming left him with a problem: how was he to account for his relationship with Emily? Faced with the recording authority, Thomas chose the term sometimes used to acknowledge a settled but unsanctioned relationship. And so the mother of his children, with whom he had lived for at least seven years and who, twenty-four hours earlier, had bled to death in childbirth, is defined on her death certificate as: 'Housekeeper'.

It was almost impossible (though not unheard of) for a man to bring up four daughters by himself. These were the days before welfare provision and Thomas had to work to survive. He had sisters who could have helped him, however, and I suspect that one of them did, because his eldest daughter was separated from the other three and disappears from this story. Not so Kitty (aged four), Margaret (three) and Annie (three months off her third birthday). For whatever reason, Thomas Martin could not or did not provide for his youngest girls.

These three little girls lost their mother in desperate circumstances (and may well have been in the house when Emily died). They were about to lose their father and their oldest sister too, who, despite her youth, had probably taken on the mantle of protector. Their births were registered as 'Martin', but they now acquired their mother's surname, Ball. However, Emily Ball was dead and could not help them. They were about to become nobody's children; children of the Poor Law Union.

A long straight path led from wrought-iron gates to the doorway of Chesterfield's Industrial School on Ashgate Road. A broad straight line, from which there was no deviation. I can see Kitty, Margaret and Annie walking down that long, hard path, Annie too young to walk the distance unaided; three little girls holding hands, as fragile as a string of paper dolls. Annie had no idea what they were walking towards, but Kitty knew: the Industrial School, coming closer and closer.

Industrial Schools were instruments of the Poor Law, designed to house destitute and vulnerable children. The majority of their young charges were removed from their parents because of neglect (though the death of a mother could constitute 'neglect' in itself, the children being left to their own devices). Those admitted to the Schools were to be trained in 'suitable occupations' and so steered from the bad influences that might lead them to be a continuing drain on the public purse when they grew up. Children in the care of Poor Law Guardians were to learn to become 'useful' members of the community, not paupers. Much was made of this intention when, in 1881, the Chesterfield Industrial School – one of the first in the country, second only to St Pancras, a local newspaper was pleased to announce – opened its doors. 'A boy trained not only in ordinary learning of a rudimentary character, but in such trades as tailoring or boot-making, and also in the rudiments of agriculture and gardening, and a girl able to read, write and cipher, and also to wash, iron, get up linen, cook and sew, need hardly re-enter a Union poor-house again.'

A report of the opening ceremony described the buildings as well as their purpose. A central administrative block separated the girls' wing from the boys'; the ground floor held classrooms, teachers' apartments, an infants' dining room, bathrooms and lavatories, while, on the floors above, dormitories, accessible via stone staircases, extended the full length of both wings. Each child

had their own bed, a fact considered noteworthy – as, indeed, it was. For many children, including little Annie Ball, this would be the first time they'd had a bed to themselves, recipients not of comfort, but of the adamantine care of the Union.

The emphasis on the lack of ornamentation, 'the utmost care taken to secure good ventilation' – ventilation is stressed more than once – and the insistence that no unnecessary money had been spent, conjures as grim an admonishment as any Poor Law Union could wish for. And translated into plain walls, plain fare, plain everything; draughty corridors, insufficient heating, icy water and blasts of cold air. At least one orphanage matron of the period favoured wide-open windows, regardless of the snow drifting on to the beds.

Methods softened over the years; labels softened with them. By the time my great-aunt walked through its vast iron gates, the Industrial School had been renamed the Chesterfield Children's Homes. Within a few years, the new title had stuck, but, for now, the name recorded in the Committee's monthly meetings depended on which member was taking the minutes. For all the renaming of the Industrial School, 'shades of the workhouse' were never far away. However well-intentioned individual committee members, they were working within the constraints of the Poor Law and answerable to the local Board of Guardians. Dietary regulations (which determined which foods the children and staff ate, and in what quantity) were those of the workhouse; the workhouse Master and Matron took charge during the School Matron's annual leave. The workhouse by any other name… there was only a thin veneer between them. Regardless of which title officialdom preferred, as far as my great-aunt was concerned, she spent her childhood in The Orphanage. Another picture keeps coming to me, although it's one I'd prefer not to see, of a little girl not yet three years old, sent to that drab institution, with its scratchy frocks, strict regime, echoing stone corridors and ever-present discipline – Walk, Don't Run; Stand Straight.

The Orphanage could accommodate 124 children. Numbers fluctuated, but in the 1900s, it held around 100 'inmates', including my great-aunt and her sisters. They were fortunate, apparently. Around 1903, the institution came under the care of the Madins, a married couple who were complimented on the marked improvement in the children since their appointment as Superintendent and Matron. True, questions were asked, in Mr Madin's first year, about his severe use of corporal punishment, but these concerns were quickly brushed aside. The Committee expressed its full confidence in his judgement and authority: the Superintendent should administer discipline as he thought fit. Some may think it even more fortunate that Mr Madin died three years later, leaving his wife in sole charge.

Other residential staff included a Labour Master (for the boys), an Industrial Trainer (for girls) and a Girls' Attendant and Infants Teacher (one post). There were some half a dozen Girls' Attendants in four years. Miss Turner, Miss Berrington, Rose Church, Alice Butler, Mrs Blagdon, Marion Shawson – one after another, they traipse across the Minutes. One attendant lasted only three months, another was dismissed for insubordination after five days. These were the women responsible for the welfare of the youngest girls, the women my great-aunt should have known best, and felt able to turn to. One face after another departing: no mother, and no motherly figure to rely on (although at least the careless and cruel attendants departed as swiftly as the kind ones).

My great-aunt said she was neither happy nor unhappy during her orphanage years – both states seeming too extreme for the kind of nothingness she lived in, which was neither one thing nor another, but just Tuesday following Monday and her left foot following her right in the slim crocodile heading to and from the Catholic Church on Spencer Street on Sunday mornings. As Catholics, she and her sisters were in a minority; theirs was a longer walk to church, more fresh air and a longer time away from Ashgate Road, but greater opportunities for chapped hands and chilblained feet. Her cuffs never quite reached her wrists, no matter how hard she tugged them; her boots were generally too large or too small, with the rare pair that fitted shaped by someone else's feet before hers. She was never quite warm enough and there was never quite enough to eat. She had known it for so long, my great-aunt did not even recognise that the stone in the pit of her stomach was hunger.

Friday breakfasts consisted of 6 oz of bread, a pint of milk and a pint of porridge – glutinous, thick grey porridge that stuck to the bowl and made her gag. With the children struggling to swallow this tepid mess without the sugar that would have helped to make it edible, much of the ration was wasted. Orders were issued that Friday porridge be replaced with three-quarters of an ounce of jam. Friday's stone became even larger. Though, however much she loathed the inedible porridge, my great-aunt was lucky to be given fresh milk and in such quantity – a splash of condensed was a more frequent offering for most working-class children at this time.

For all the ghastly food and insufficient everything, attempts were made to humanise institutional life. There were fireworks on

Guy Fawkes' Night (costing a sum not to exceed £2), annual trips to the seaside, plus the 'usual extras' at Christmas. Benefactors donated greenery, crackers, oranges, sweets, figs and – on one occasion – dolls, though there were not enough dolls to go round, and some little girls had no idea how to play with a doll, having never had the chance until now. Figs and oranges, though appropriately festive and a vast improvement on the usual fare, disappeared with the season and were, anyway, not things you could play with. And even figs and oranges could not be relied on. Nothing nice was guaranteed. It is impossible not to consider the following year, when the youngest girls wanted dolls and none appeared.

For anything out of the ordinary, the children were dependent on someone's generosity: on upstanding citizen and committee member Miss Swanwick providing shuttlecocks and three dozen tennis balls, or the Reverend Templeman supplying footballs, a cricket bat, magic lantern slides, and so on. People living nearby sometimes donated a shilling or two for sweets, or brought in magazines they'd done with. One year, the Mayor gave £1 for Christmas games, prompting the Committee Chairman to dig into his own pocket and match it.

Christmas entertainments provided by church and chapel were gradually supplemented by more colourful treats: a trip to the dress rehearsal of *The Mikado* one year; a rehearsal of *The Gondoliers* the next, to watch Chesterfield's Amateur Dramatics Society do its finest. In 1907, the children were invited to the pantomime at the town's Corporation Theatre (no mere dress rehearsal on that occasion). At the end of the performance, when the lights went up, each Industrial School child was presented with an orange.

But these were the high days and holidays. Weekdays saw a

plainer regime in every sense: junior children attended lessons at the local elementary school and, as they approached thirteen or fourteen, began to be prepared for work. Boys could volunteer for naval training; some became farm workers, or were apprenticed in tailoring, shoe-making and other trades. For young women, as in all Poor Law Union schools, only one option was considered suitable: domestic service. (Domestic service was the largest form of employment for single women at this time.)

Industrial School girls were destined to become general servants or lowly kitchen maids doing 'the rough': staggering with pans of scalding water; manoeuvring heavy terracotta pancheons; carrying coal – a full hod of coal weighed around thirty pounds; emptying and scouring cast-iron stew pots they could scarcely lift when empty, let alone full. The School had its own laundry where girls learned the intricacies of goffering and starching collars and cuffs. In 1907, the institution needed a new servant of its own – its lower-ranking servants rarely stayed long, though one or two were promoted within the School itself: kitchen maid one year, seamstress the next. One young woman who accomplished this feat, asked if her sister could replace her in the kitchen. Within a month, her sister resigned, unable to cope with the heavy lifting. When the Matron found a further replacement in a girl who had just left school, she could not manage the work either, being 'rather young and scarcely strong enough'. Yet this was the role for which the Matron's school-leavers were being trained. Never mind frilly aprons and lace caps; most of these girls were destined to do the donkey work. And my great-aunt looked set to join them.

Thinking about it now, I can see the beginnings of this training in the way she polished shoes. She was a dab hand at cleaning shoes, could polish them to a shine no one else in the family could muster – 'I'll do them, Pidge,' she'd say, when school shoes loomed on Sunday evenings. (We were always 'Pidge', my brother and me, to Auntie.) 'You leave them.' It saddens me to remember this now. I want her to have had a different childhood.

Month after month, the townswomen of Chesterfield applied to the School for domestic servants. If the enquiring household was deemed 'satisfactory' – these young women would be living in, surrendering themselves to their employers – girls were sent for a month's trial and, all being well, supplied with a uniform at the month's end. Except that, all was not always well. Girls (and boys) were returned for impertinence and insubordination; some were sent to a second household and returned yet again. Institutional life did not fit girls to become accomplished servants. It was hard to be careful with your mistress's things if you had never handled nice teacups, and some of those taking on orphanage girls merely wanted cheap and easily exploitable labour.

Committee reports of girls (they were barely young women) returned to the School due to insolence or because they were 'unsuitable' – a word covering many unspecified misdemeanours, including wetting the bed – conceal a host of private miseries. Sometimes girls were deemed 'unsatisfactory', a word which, like its opposite, runs like a dark seam through institutional life. Some poor girls were sampled and rejected, like shoddy goods returned to a shop.

Thankfully, rejection was not all one-way: some requests for servants were refused, though the enquirer was generally soft-soaped and told there were no girls old enough at present. One employer was threatened with legal proceedings for failing to pay a weekly wage of 1s 3d (though the poor girl had worked for more than twelve months in receipt of only twelve weeks' wages before this abuse came to light).

Committee minutes provide bald statements and resolutions but, occasionally, stories like these seep through, offering glimpses of the realities behind formal words: not just the young girl who worked without wages (and in who knows what atrocious conditions), but the father sentenced to six months' hard labour for cruelty (consider how cruelty was defined in an era when

'Meet Eddie 7.30 Midland Station,' announced the telegram received by Chesterfield's Corporation Theatre. Six-year-old Eddie made the twelve-hour journey to Chesterfield alone, with a luggage label tied to his neck. He'd come to join his Daddy at the Theatre. The woman looking after him in Bromley had tired of the child (or else the money had run out) and put him on the Chesterfield train, the town chosen because a paragraph in a theatrical newspaper said his father's company was playing there. But when Eddie arrived in Chesterfield, there was no theatrical company and no father.

The Theatre's lessees met the young boy and looked after him while they made desperate enquiries. The father was tracked down to Seacombe, near Liverpool: a change of booking meant the company was playing there instead. Eddie reached Chesterfield on Monday evening. It was Thursday before his father was found.

– Based on a report in the *Derbyshire Times*, 2 November 1910

corporal punishment was widely accepted); the letters withheld from children because of their mother's intemperate behaviour; or the girl whose mother, should she ever succeed in freeing herself from the workhouse, was judged totally unfit to care for her child. One poor boy who absconded from the School twice in one day was immediately dispatched to the workhouse. (That'll learn 'im.) But there were success stories too, although, admittedly, fewer of these: women whose children were returned to them when, on re-inspection, their homes were judged 'satisfactory', plus reports of grandparents and other relatives taking children out of the Homes.

No relative came to rescue Emily Ball's daughters. In years to come, my great-aunt would have no recollection of her parents. She remembered, however, a tall man who visited one day and gave her an apple, a rare treat. She thought he may have been her father. If so, what love and regret in one apple.

My great-aunt had been at the Orphanage for some six years when all the girls were instructed to join a line-up in the yard. Back straight, eyes forward, as she had been drilled, she watched a short stocky 'gentleman' with a moustache and kindly eyes and a tall 'posh lady' walk towards them. The lady would select a child and take her home, the Matron informed the waiting girls.

'Pick me,' Annie Ball pleaded silently. 'Pick me.' This is how, years later, she described the experience, not an invention of mine. How terrible to know, at the age of eight, and with her sisters at the school – her only remaining family as far as Annie was concerned – that this was the place to escape from. She was in luck. The 'posh lady and gentleman' were my great-grandparents, Betsy and Dick.

I've known this story for years, but had no expectation of finding any reference to it when I consulted the Industrial School archives. I simply wanted to know what daily life was like for Annie Ball. My great-grandparents had walked past the School when they lived at Linacre and pitied its poor wretches. Dick knew better than most how chancy life could be; were he of a different generation, he could easily have ended up in an Industrial School himself. Instead, my great-grandparents took a child away from one and gave her a fresh start, just as Dick had been given a new beginning.

It is written in beautiful copperplate. On 13 April 1909, it was minuted that Mrs Nash desired to adopt a little girl, between five and six years old. The Relieving Officer for the district was required to inspect my great-grandparents' home and on pronouncing it satisfactory – that word again – the Committee granted the request. How quickly and how easily this was accomplished; how appalling that the inspection procedure seems to have been the same whether you applied to adopt a child or employ a servant.

Individual Poor Law authorities took their own view on the 're-adoption' of children in their care, which does not seem to have been that common. Some authorities preferred fostering arrangements with the children remaining their overall responsibility; others gave up on the idea altogether because youngsters were returned too many times. Although Chesterfield's Guardians were clearly in favour of 'adoption', there were far more requests for servants than for children to adopt during this period (and, as with requests for servants, not all were granted). My great-grandma's enquiry was one of the very few. Imagine my delight when I found it. The decision is recorded in crisp black ink and, like all resolutions in that Committee minute book, partially underlined in red. And so it should be. 10 May 1909: 'Resolved that the application in question be granted.'

Both my great-grandparents walked along the rows, inspecting those desperate young girls who were all busily arranging their faces into the kind of look they hoped would free them. She conferred with Dick, but Betsy did the actual choosing. And she did not choose a child aged five or six as she'd intended, but a girl of eight, who was small for her age and might have seemed indistinguishable from all the other girls lined up in coarse pinafores that day were it not for the appeal in her smile. Something about it won them over. I know that smile. It's recorded on the photograph taken shortly after Dick and Betsy took her home to the corner shop. I know a stronger, brighter version too. It belonged to my much-loved great-aunt.

4

Eva Nash, 1909

ANNIE BALL WOKE THAT MORNING IN A DRAUGHTY dormitory but went to sleep that night beneath one of Betsy's warm plump weighties, in her new sister's bed. Far better, everyone agreed, that the little girl should not be by herself at first.

My great-grandparents could not have two daughters sharing a first name and so Annie Ball became Eva and began a new life with her brand new parents and new sister (though, aged sixteen, my grandma was twice Eva's age, and so was almost as much of a grown-up as a sister). It was impressed upon Eva that she now had a home and a family, with parents who would always care for her.

The Industrial School's lack of ornamentation and excess of fresh air were now exchanged for the warm clutter of the back room, with its vases wafting peacock feathers, decorative cranberry glass, and lace runners covering every surface. And the bustle of the grocer's shop out front. There were new dresses for Eva – dresses whose patterns she could choose – and cotton pinafores, and hair ribbons instead of rough braid, and lots of underclothes, and all of them just for Eva, who had never had any things to call her own. And there were toys for Eva too, who would never again have to hope for a charitable doll.

Shortly after her arrival, the new sisters posed for their first photograph. Annie towers above young Eva, who looks especially small and both pleased and overwhelmed by her new circumstances. An enlargement was made of Eva and hung on the wall, where it joined the other family portraits in gilt frames. At Christmas, Dick and Betsy sent their friends a festive card displaying a further photograph of Annie and Eva: winter princesses in corresponding outfits of dark velvet. That year, Eva was given her own money box in blue enamelled stoneware stamped with strong black flowers. Strongest of all was the lettering: Eva Nash, 1909.

*

The more my great-aunt heard the name, the easier it became to absorb, but it was strange, all the same, becoming a new person overnight, even if her old identity had little to recommend it. It was not just that Eva had a new name, but that her new sister had her old one. Sometimes, when they were walking together up Station Road, a neighbour called out, 'Annie', and both sisters turned round. My great-aunt practised saying 'Eva' aloud and writing her new name in the new books her new parents bought her. In her large, round hand, in the corner of each first page, she declaimed, in descending steps: Eva Nash, 150 Station Road, Brimington, Chesterfield, each short line a building block towards her new identity.

Had she known any bedtime stories, my great-aunt might have wondered if she'd stepped into one. It was a sign of the life Eva had been used to that, at first sight, she'd thought Dick and Betsy posh. She had gone from nothing to plenty, not the fantastical plenty of unattainable make-believe, but the more realistic daydream of a home and family, and no more cold and hunger. Eva found herself in the kind of home she'd wished for when the dormitory floorboards made ridges in her knees from kneeling to thank God for her lot.

For a while, at least, God remained in the picture. The Spencer Street priest called at the shop on several occasions – Betsy could see him coming along the road well before he saw her – but was quietly but firmly told that Eva was no longer a Catholic. All God's creatures were equal in His eyes and you had no need to attend church to learn that. Eventually, worn out by my great-grandma's obduracy, the priest retreated.

Not every aspect of my great-aunt's former life was discarded.

She was to stay in touch with her sisters, Kitty and Margaret. Eva was delighted to know that, though they remained in the orphanage on the other side of town, her new family did not want them forgotten. Kitty and Margaret were now eleven and ten, still very young themselves. There was barely any difference in the three girls' ages, but the contrast in their lives was now immense.

One thing Eva had not pictured in her daydreams was a shop – with everlasting strips of toffee, gobstoppers and licorice bootlaces, humbugs and bullseyes. There were huge jars of currants, raisins and sultanas that required both hands to lift them from the shelf. She could take a handful of dried fruit whenever she wanted, as long as she asked first. And there was jam in enormous quantity, doled out from great big pots; large boxes of biscuits (Eva was allowed to eat the broken Rich Teas) and bottles describing things she did not know existed, such as tomato ketchup and Daddies Sauce. There were squat drawers for money and metal scoops in graduated sizes which slid silently into the bran tub but crunched into the sacks of lentils and dried peas. Sugar came wrapped in solid rolls of dark-blue tissue paper that Betsy sliced through with a knife, or in thick bags marked 'Granulated' or 'Demerara'. Every bit as good as sweets, biscuits and raisins was the slice of bread and butter liberally sprinkled with sugar Betsy gave Eva to eat while she tackled the lugs in her hair.

Dick took to calling her 'My Ava'. ('My Nancy' was his pet name for Annie.) He showed her where red chandeliers bloomed on the scraggy currant bush in the strip of earth that passed for their garden, and took her for long walks where they nibbled 'bread and cheese' (hawthorn) from the hedgerows and plucked handfuls of watercress from a stream. Dick taught her the names of birds and wild flowers, and how to make sharp blades of grass whistle between her thumbs. Betsy showed Eva how to create pastry leaves to decorate pie crusts, and how to turn a dish on raised fingers while slicing excess pastry from the rim. Together, she and Eva gathered the rose hips, blackberries and damsons my great-grandma used for making jam. Betsy taught Eva to pick only the berries that left the stem willingly, not the ones that resisted, and always to leave some behind for the birds and the next gatherer. Moments like these had a gentling quality, a belated release into childhood.

Eva made friends quickly among the children of the Mill; she was used to pitching in, and fast at games of run-and-tag, but she also discovered the entirely new pleasure of being by herself. She could dawdle or stamp in puddles if she wanted, or set out to walk nowhere in particular, and even stay outside till dusk, if she liked. She could wander along the towpath up to and beyond Wheeldon Lock, and out towards Bluebank Wood, and run or skip all the way home if that was what she wanted to do. Sometimes, Eva ran for the sheer joy of running, stopping only when the back of her throat burned and the wind took away all her breath. Whatever happened to her now, she would never have to go back there.

Everything about my great-aunt's new life felt different, with one exception – school. There was little to choose between one elementary-school regime and another except the schoolmarm, and Eva's was particularly sour. Miss West's full-length apron and elbow-length cuffs suggested a nursing matron rather than a teacher of healthy girls; she ruled her class with matronly authority and was furious if her cuffs became soiled. Tall and thin, with a nose as sharp as her elbows, she looked to Eva like someone who'd just swallowed a spoonful of raspberry vinegar. Adults were reassured by Miss West's strong pious face but she had long bony fingers with which to prod her pupils in the back.

There were thirty girls in Eva's class, though one was a mere ghost of a child who did not look long for this world. Several wore dresses large enough to grow into, with deep bulky hems for turning down, and one had shorn hair that had been hacked at with a knife because of nits, but Eva was the only Orphanage Girl.

Most of her classmates lived higher up the hill, in Brimington, but Eva walked to school with near neighbour Maud Evans, whose mother would shortly teach her piano, and sat next to Carrie Rice. Carrie, Eva discovered on her very first day, had rough and tumble brothers who liked to tease her; she could sympathise when some of the other girls called Eva names.

Under Dick and Betsy's care, Eva lost her look of vulnerability and learned to feel proud of herself. Their message was simple: though no better than anyone else, she was just as good. She should be well mannered and kind but, if picked on, retaliate, and by blows, if necessary (though not strike first). Unlike Annie, Eva needed no instruction in fighting back: you couldn't survive an orphanage without meeting an assortment of bullies and pinchers.

Miss West was more difficult to subdue. Eva's friend, Carrie, was slight, like Eva, which made her an easy target for their teacher's prodding finger. One day Miss West was particularly provoking, bullying Carrie while Eva sat beside her. Their shared desk had inkwells which could be eased out of position from beneath, and so, leaning forward while seeming to be engrossed in her sums, Eva worked her fingers round the inkwell and gradually, then forcefully, pushed. Bullseye: Miss West's blouse was splattered with

ink. For once, she was completely speechless. It was worth six 'stripes' of the cane to see her face. The blouse was parcelled up and dispatched to Betsy for starching, but Eva had made her point.

Unfortunately Miss West had other ways of asserting her authority, which Eva was equally determined to resist. Their war of nerves continued. Miss West insisted that Eva bring extra ingredients for the domestic science class – her mother had a shop: they could afford it. Flour, butter, sugar: quite a list. Eva said nothing to Betsy. She wanted to resolve this herself. It did not matter how often Miss West waved her cane, the request offended Eva's sense of justice. This particular stand-off was eventually won by Eva continuing to bring the same quantities to the class as the other girls, but the cane was her teacher's answer to most things. The intakes of breath my great-aunt produced when describing these stripes to me more than fifty years later showed how much they bit into her skin.

Not everything about school was purgatorial, however. Eva developed a strong sense of mischief. One especially vexing girl, conscious that her hair was her best feature, was constantly tossing her head. The ends of her long plaits repeatedly struck the edge of Eva's desk, until Eva stopped that lark by tying the girl's hair ribbons to her chair. Eva discovered she could run fast and win races. She also enjoyed recitations and declaiming aloud in class; one rhyme particularly appealed: 'Curly locks, curly locks, wilt thou be mine?/ Thou shalt not wash dishes nor yet feed the swine,/ But sit on a cushion and sew a fine seam,/ And feed upon strawberries and sugar and cream.' It reminded Eva of Annie.

My grandma decided to stay on at Staveley Netherthorpe Grammar School and train as a pupil teacher (the option for those whose parents could not afford college fees). For three years, she combined taking classes in its Pupil-Teacher Centre with teaching at Brimington's Princess Street Infants' School. By now, Zoe had left Netherthorpe and was keeping her mam company at home, but Gwennie Peat, George Hardcastle and Maurice Unwin were still classmates, and all planned on teaching in elementary schools.

George was the kind of boy mothers described as 'a nice young lad'. He had a way of looking at you as if uncertain how much space he should occupy, and of brushing his hand across his hair when he felt nervous. But he was clever and kind, and could be funny too, and he was certain about one thing – his feelings for Annie. One afternoon, George slid a picture-postcard on to her desk. On the back were scrawled four pencil words, 'I love you Annie,' sealed with a tentative kiss.

Annie was fond of George and enjoyed their conversations, but her school crush was Maurice Unwin, with his straight blond hair and slightly curling lip. He had a rather nice way with him, or so Annie thought, until she met Willie Thompson.

He was laughing the first time she saw him, his head thrown back as if taking a deep drink of laughter. That was the thing about Willie: he generally had a smile on his face. A baker at his brother's firm on Whittington Moor, Willie did the occasional Saturday delivery, managing to hand Betsy her box of cakes as if conveying precious jewels across the counter.

There was something about Willie Thompson – an assurance, an ease – that immediately distinguished him from the other young men Annie knew. Her classmates were courteous and polite, and destined for positions of respect and authority. Already they were developing the quiet consideration and balanced views they'd be required to demonstrate in the future. Even Maurice Unwin, who liked to think himself debonair, talked to Annie as if he'd read up on how to do it. The Wheeldon Mill lads didn't have much to say for themselves in front of Annie, although she'd known some since they were scab-kneed boys. Long before her education came between them, there was always an unspoken reserve. The fact that she was the shopkeeper's daughter established a barrier; grammar school erected a high wall.

Willie Thompson was different. Everything about him seemed fresh, newly minted. He was not much of a reader, he'd admit, but he loved a good music-hall turn and seemed to know all the popular tunes. Annie heard him whistling them while he unpacked their bread. He was not daunted by her schooling either, but joked about lady teachers being bossy. Should he mind his Ps and Qs?

The corner shop was one of Willie's last deliveries, so he and

Annie generally found time to exchange a few words, though she had to walk at quite a clip to ensure she did not miss him when returning from her Saturday-morning class. Then just when she was becoming accustomed to her heart leaping at the sight of the baker's horse and cart, Willie announced he was leaving. He had a passage booked for New York, Philadelphia, on to Pittsburgh. His brother Jim, the baker, was paying his fare.

Their older brother Harry had made his home in America, having sailed two years earlier: an expedient departure, if you believed what you heard. Several irate husbands were rumoured to be on Harry's tail. Oh, he was doing fine now, in Pittsburgh: Harry always came up smelling of roses. And now young Willie was off to join him.

'Is that it, then, lad?' Dick asked when Willie delivered their Saturday cakes for the last time. America was the end of things, as far as my great-grandfather was concerned, the place where people disappeared off the map. 'Who knows, Mr Nash?' said Willie, answering Dick, but looking at Annie.

He sailed on 18 January 1911, a few days short of his eighteenth birthday, but gave his age as twenty-one. Sometimes, you had to tell a story to get by.

Will Willie write or won't he? This question vexed my grandma; it also vexed her mother, who was none too keen on the thought of Willie Thompson writing from America. Betsy hoped Annie would forget him once the Atlantic Ocean was between them. Willie was not the young man she had in mind for her daughter, though Betsy knew better than to interfere. The lad's gone now. Let it rest.

'*What Are Your Views? Do you think boys and girls ought to be*

stopped by their parents from talking to one another or correspon-
ding?' Annie cut this article from a newspaper and pasted it into
her commonplace book. '*Do you think a boy of 16 years ought to
be stopped speaking to a girl of 16 years if there has been nothing
said about their conduct? Don't you think a father and mother of a
girl ought to let her speak to boys if she be under 21?'*

The editor asked his readers for their opinions on 'this delicate
subject'. Annie awaited their replies. '*We don't know much about
the "ought" of the matter, but we should rather like to meet the parents
who can.'* Snip, snip, snip went her scissors.

It was difficult to conceal correspondence when there were three
posts a day and you were not in the habit of receiving letters.
Whether Willie was forewarned of my great-grandma's views and
judged circumspection the best course, or was too busy enjoying
America, he appears to have been silent for much of the time, but
he did not want my grandma to forget him. One May morning,
a picture-postcard of the Commonwealth Building, Pittsburgh,
landed on the corner shop's mat. Though addressed to Miss Annie
Nash, it contained no greeting whatsoever, nor any indication of
the sender, yet Willie's silent postcard reads like a declaration of
intent.

5

Turn and Turn-about

LIFE AT THE CORNER SHOP HAD SETTLED INTO A ROUTINE – the family woken by the sound of workmen's boots striking cobbles on their way to early shifts at pit and foundry; deliveries from butcher, baker and wholesaler; the shunt and exhalation of trains pulling into the branch-line station, and the frequent rumble of passing trucks and coal carts. The rag-and-bone man and knife sharpener cried their wares from the top of the canal bridge, where the muffin man also stopped to ring his bell. A far less appealing sound was the lowing of cattle taking their last desperate stumble up to the slaughterhouse off Brimington High Street.

One of the more attractive sights to be seen from the sweet window was the bunting fluttering around the station for the Coronation of George V, and the neighbourhood parading its Sunday finest (and the power of Betsy's laundry soap). More entertaining still were the crowds emerging from excursion trains on Race Days, the local station being the closest to the Chesterfield course.

As in years gone by, race-goers were a mixture of pleasure seekers and ne'er-do-wells, all parties dressed to the nines. These days, many more revellers travelled by train, and were as likely to be lured by the swing boats, roundabouts and helter-skelter as the actual races. Theirs was a procession to watch. It was well worth kneeling on the box to glimpse the effusive confections some of the women wore on their heads, a profusion of feathers, bows, silk flowers and birds; sometimes, a whole nest. ('Isn't she the bobby dazzler. She must have raided Jenkins' window.')

There was a lot going on at the back door too. The family were seeing more of their neighbours via the house door as well as in the shop. There was always someone calling; if the shop was closed, they came round to the back. There were those who stood on the threshold, others who were invited into the room and a further select few, such as Mrs Graham, the publican's wife, and Dick's friend, colliery foreman Bob Britt, who were asked to sit down and talk.

No such hierarchy existed within the shop itself. Anyone could claim a seat on the box. Mildred Taylor was a frequent visitor. A hefty woman, whose bulk made Betsy fear for the sides of the crate, she walked to the shop via the canalside path and felt she'd earned a good chat when she got there. Her three sons were pit-pony drivers, whipping their charges along the underground road; a coveted job as well as a dangerous one, seven shillings and sixpence the weekly rate, though her lads did not say as much to her. They were becoming as close as their father, a collier himself, though too old for their daredevil game. Mildred's was a house full of swagger, the three young drivers as proud and fiery as the ponies they subdued. Looking at them now, it was extraordinary to think she'd dandled each one on her knee.

For all their bravado, the young men of the neighbourhood were slower than their mothers to linger and talk to Betsy. Once

they became accustomed to her, however, they were just as happy to stop and chat. Shorter working hours from 1908 meant young colliers had more time to themselves, a chance to kick a can or a football about outside (though, as often as not, their ball was screwed up paper). Some kept ferrets and liked to go ratting – 1d a tail – and describe their successes to Betsy. Slapping their hard-earned pennies on to the counter, they'd tell her about their day. Those buying cigarettes with their first wage handed over the coins with particular pleasure. Arnie Cresswell, Thomas Jobb, Isaac Dance and Joseph Braithwaite, friends since schooldays and now young foundrymen together, liked to share a packet of Wood-bines and sit on the causey edge to divide them: one passed between the four while they sat talking, the remainder tucked behind their ears for safekeeping. Betsy heard them divvying up their spoils and making plans for the following day.

By 1911, my great-grandfather was foreman of the brickyard just below the Wheeldon Mill Plantation, with a motley crew of ten beneath him, men and boys; Dick, the collar-and-tie man with a watch chain spread across his chest, they, hoisting up their oldest clothes with leather belts or knotted rope. Come Tuesday evenings, a fresh collar was needed, plus braided cuffs and ceremonial apron. My great-grandfather's 'elevation' to grocer (a silent title if ever there was one) led to him joining the Buffs. For more than forty years, Dick was a member of the Royal Antediluvian Order of Buffaloes, being admitted to the organisation shortly after leasing the shop. Tuesday night was Buffs' night. Rain or shine, he picked up the attaché case containing his regalia and walked to his lodge meeting at the Angel Inn.

Sometimes, Annie and Eva accompanied him, on their way to see the latest extravaganza at the picture palace, Whittington Moor's first. It was all a bit makeshift, really – literally, a hole in the corner affair – in the clubroom above the stables for the Queen's Hotel. A bedroom held the projector, with a gap knocked through the wall into 'the auditorium', its rough and ready nature and flickering screen part of the excitement of the new. Until the cinema's premier status was usurped by the Lyceum, Annie regularly took Eva (she eighteen to my great-aunt's ten), the Nash girls clipping up the steps in their ankle boots, with their chosen sweets for the evening – a handful of mint humbugs, toffees, or whatever else they fancied from the shop. They chatted to the publican's young son, Joe, who liked to assist the projectionist (an early exercise in hand-eye coordination that may have come in useful: Joe Davis was later World Snooker Champion.)

This new-fangled world was all very well, but Betsy much preferred Variety: frock coats, moleskin titfers and all that frothy colour; young girls strutting across the stage, or else picking their way daintily like cats. Some women claimed they only liked the ballads, but Betsy enjoyed the stronger numbers too: the Marie Lloyd imitators, hand on hip and winking – oh, the sauce they got away with in those songs.

It was a case of either muck or nettles for the corner shop in the years before the First World War: if there wasn't a slump, there was a strike. Everyone in the neighbourhood suffered. Some strikes were more memorable than others, and in the hot sticky summer of 1911, with temperatures soaring higher than at any time during the previous century, one set of workers after another withdrew their labour: dockers, carters, miners; on and on…'It Is War,' the headline boomed when railwaymen stopped work in August. By the end of the month, the Derbyshire *Courier* had even stronger news to report: the Chesterfield Riot.

The Battle of Chesterfield, a brief but bitter skirmish, started when a Saturday-night crowd surged from the Market Square down to the town's Midland Railway Station and overwhelmed the handful of policemen posted there in the aftermath of the strike. The shriek of police whistles and sound of truncheons cracking heads preceded the arrival of Mayor (and industrialist) Charles Paxton Markham to read the Riot Act to those hurling bottles, bricks and stones. Megaphone authority got him nowhere – Markham was forced to take cover behind a fence – and police reinforcements were helpless before a crowd of some 2,000 (5,000 according to one enthusiastic observer). The whole town was said to be in the grip of the mob. A crescendo of breaking glass all the way up Corporation Street and on to Stephenson Place announced the destruction of plate-glass windows in some of its department stores.

The fight was still raging at midnight, but, shortly after one a.m., the *Courier*'s reporter spotted 'glints of steel': fifty men from the Second West Yorkshire Regiment advancing on the crowd with fixed bayonets. The following week, in answer to Keir Hardie's criticism of the Home Secretary positioning troops in strike districts, MP Sir Arthur Markham, who had accompanied his brother the Mayor to the scene, gave a vivid account to the House of Commons of the pandemonium outside the Midland Station.

The Battle of Chesterfield was discussed locally with relish as well as shock – at one point, the town's main Great Central Station was also in possession of the mob: imagine if they'd taken the station at Wheeldon Mill? Strikes were much more than talking points and newspaper headlines, however. No work meant no food beyond the small amounts relief committees could organise. Without their husbands' wages, Betsy's customers could neither buy groceries nor settle their existing debts.

The following year brought another miners' strike – even more working days were lost to industrial unrest during 1912 than in 1911. No coal: no cages lowered down pit shafts; no greedy raging furnaces; nearly everyone in the district was affected. Florrie Stokes, Nora Parks, Mildred Taylor… one after another, women came into the shop and shook their heads in disbelief. Never was a newspaper twist of tea or sugar, or a spoonful of jam more welcome. The Sheepbridge Company established a soup kitchen and issued tickets for groceries that could be repaid once the men were back at work. There was nothing to do but wait.

Some said they knew 1912 would be a bad 'un, given the wicked start to that year: the funerals of five young girls due to perform in a Christmas performance at the town's Picture Palace. Waiting in the nearby cottage that served as a dressing room, one of the young performers threw something on to the fire. A spark leapt the fire guard and caught her dance dress. In terror and blind panic, she dashed about the room, igniting one gauzy Eskimo after another. Their burns were so bad that one father, hurrying to the cottage upon hearing of the fire, asked his own daughter, 'Whose little girl are you?'

By 1912, Annie was in her third year of training at the Princess Street Infants' School and had much more to occupy her time than keeping an eye out for the postman. She loved teaching small children, but mere enjoyment was not enough: in order to obtain a good reference at the close of her apprenticeship, she needed to make a good impression on the headmistress, Mabel Doughty. Annie worked alongside Miss Doughty as a classroom assistant and was allowed to take charge of some lessons, with Miss Doughty observing her work: Composition one week, History the next, and so on, all the way through the lengthy syllabus. Each plan and scheme of work had to be submitted to the headmistress, and every faltering command and imprecise instruction dissected and discussed. When Annie looked about the room to take in her pupils' faces, there was Miss Doughty, straight-backed, solemn-faced, an irritant in the corner of her eye. Night after night, Annie was tormented by the thought of her sharp observations and the way she had of saying, 'I wonder, Miss Nash...' before slicing into some new failure of hers.

There were also exams to revise for. In 1912, Annie passed the Oxford Local, enabling her to work in schools outside the borough. She could now teach Arithmetic, History, English Language and Literature, including Composition, Geography and Needlework. Betsy and Dick were delighted: another gilt frame for the wall.

Q. What illustrious lady did [Queen] Elizabeth imprison?

A. Her cousin Mary, Queen of Scotland, was kept many years in prison by Elizabeth.

Q. What became of her?

A. Elizabeth at last ordered her to be beheaded. This is one of the worst acts of her reign. Mary was very beautiful.

Q. What great fleet was fitted out for the conquest of England in this reign?

A. One was fitted out by Philip II of Spain, and it was blessed by the Pope, and called by the King the 'Invincible Armada.'

Q. What became of this Invincible Armada?

A. Many of the ships were broken by violent storms; others were defeated by the English, and with the rest the Spaniards were very glad to go back to Spain.

– From *Mrs Gibbon's Simple Catechism of the History of England, from the Invasion of the Romans to the Present Time, Adapted to the Capacities of Young Children*, 1890

That summer, my grandma applied for her first post as an elementary school teacher; Miss Doughty was one of her referees. Amazingly, Annie looked set to make a good disciplinarian ('looked set', mind, Miss Doughty would not go too far in praising her); the manager of Arthur Shentall's grocery business confirmed her

good character and that she came from a respectable home. Miall Spencer, headmaster of Staveley Netherthorpe Grammar School, also testified to her suitability. Annie's destination was a school in Bolsover, a village some three miles east of the corner shop. Her classmate and admirer, George, found a teaching post near Wheeldon Mill. They both needed lodgings; their mothers agreed the two of them should swap homes.

For the next twelve months, it was turn and turn-about. On weekdays, Annie lodged with George's family, and George occupied the attic room above the shop. It was strange to inhabit one another's houses, to be inside his family but not of it, to come to recognise the brand of furniture polish his mother favoured and how she liked her tea, and to get to know his sisters, especially the youngest, who blushed whenever George's name was mentioned in front of Annie. And it was strange to sleep in the room beside his, a peculiar intimacy, even though George himself was never there. Annie enjoyed his admiration and his company but this was too much like becoming one of the family. It was as if she was there on approval, with no one saying the one thing on everyone's mind; a foretaste of married life, although Annie was still a guest to be entertained and made welcome, not yet a daughter-in-law.

For George, the exchange was just what he wanted, and my great-grandparents loved having him to stay. Eva was fond of George, too, and he of 'Kiddie', as he called her. He came to love them all. It was the easiest thing to call Betsy and Dick, Mam and Dad, but there was no reciprocal gesture from Annie. His mother may have found this reticence pleasing and entirely appropriate behaviour in a young woman, but there was more to it than that. If George's vocabulary staked a claim for his future, so did Annie's. And things were about to get more complicated. In 1913, Willie came back.

6

A Garden Party and a Wedding Invitation

IF WILLIE WAS FULL OF STORIES BEFORE LEAVING FOR AMERICA, he had plenty to tell on his return. Two years in Pittsburgh: his first weeks working alongside his brother Harry until he found a bakery job; and the highways, the buildings, and the cars – oh, the cars. He'd seen New York and the Statue of Liberty; he could spin a dollar like a true American. The picture Willie painted of himself, sitting on the quayside on the day he arrived, sounded like something out of the films. But, despite his adventures, he was glad to be home and especially pleased to reach dry land. His ship docked in Liverpool a year and a day after the sinking of the *Titanic*.

Annie was not entirely sure why Willie had come back. If she asked outright, Willie would say was she fishing for a compliment, or simply shrug his shoulders and smile. And Willie only had to smile, and she was done for. If Annie had to find one word to describe the effect Willie Thompson had on her it would be 'dazzled'. His smile, his eyes, his hair: the number of times she mentioned his forget-me-not blue eyes and corn-coloured hair, you would think him the most handsome man on earth, and so he was to Annie soon enough.

'Who's Willie Thompson when he's at home?' her father teased her, though Dick knew perfectly well who Willie Thompson was, and only asked to watch Annie blush. Betsy said very little about Willie's reappearance, but the fact that she said little, made her opinion clear enough. She could not fathom what her daughter saw in him, compared with good, kind, reliable George.

Are School Teachers Stuck Up? This question, being asked about 'lady teachers', now that there were even more of them in evidence, was the title of another article that found its way into Annie's commonplace book, and had a particular piquancy for her around this time. '*The constant quick speaking as she instructs her class… is apt to give her conversation a dictatorial tone [but] when a school teacher has the good sense and good feeling to make the most of her opportunities, then indeed a man may search the whole world over before he finds a more delightful person… the woman with a trained intelligence is able not only to rule her household wisely and well, but be a good companion for her husband.*'

Willie Thompson's education could not compare with Annie's or that of his rival, George (just as theirs suffered in comparison with college-educated teachers). Willie had left school at the age of twelve, dragged away from classes by his father who obtained an exemption to get him into work as soon as possible. What did a lad want with school? Joiner, farmer, coffin-maker, *master* builder, or so he claimed, in later years ('Oh ay?' I hear my great-grandma say), William Thompson senior had never put much faith in learning, or in idealistic dreams, come to that. A taciturn man with enormous pride in his own achievements, he was nevertheless curmudgeonly with his eight children. Though he helped with deliveries in the bakery's early days, he watched his eldest son build the business in silence – and worse. When Jim earned his first hundred pounds, he bought himself a pair of shoes, the first leather shoes – proper lace-up shoes, not working boots – he'd ever owned, with a pattern pricked out on their perfect toes. His mother shared his pride at what they represented. When she'd finished admiring them, Jim left them on the hearth, where he found them the next day, chopped into half a dozen pieces. His father had taken an axe to their smooth black leather. It didn't do to flaunt your hopes before William Thompson senior. Whatever dreams young Willie had, he made damn sure he kept them to himself.

Willie was working for his brother once again, and paying court with smiles and songs and fancy cakes and scones. He was winning rosettes and national medals too. He could bake enormous loaves shaped like sheaves of wheat or corn, and decorate cakes with elaborate icing that carried off first prizes in competitions. His skills helped put Jim's business on the map. Thompson's became a 'gold medal' bakery, a thriving, expanding concern. Their baby brother Bernard also joined the firm; as soon as he left school, he took over the deliveries from their father.

Jim Thompson had political ambitions and was already learning that connections are made and influence wielded via social engagements and conversations with the right people. Shortly after his return, Willie invited Annie to a garden party held by Jim and his wife, Edith, where tea was served in fine china cups and women with lace parasols ate strawberries from little glass dishes. Afternoon tea and parasols, and tales of Willie's American adventure – Annie felt quite giddy.

In the summer of 1915, Jim was appointed to Chesterfield's Urban District Council. Never one to do things by halves, he hired a tram to drive along Whittington Moor and stood on the platform, the man of the day, thanking all those who'd cast their vote for him. Annie and Willie were among the half dozen invited to make up the party. She spent hours trimming her hat (shaped like a giant upturned soup plate, as was the fashion then) with an abundance of silk flowers in order to look her best for the occasion. Standing on the open deck beside Jim and Edith and their close friends, Annie and Willie leaned against the rail and waved to the pedestrians below. There was something faintly regal about their progress along the Moor in their own special car with its chocolate and yellow livery, its windows plastered with can-do posters of Jim. For all that it was wartime, the day had a holiday atmosphere: it was a relief to have something to celebrate.

George was still around – George was always around – and knowable in a way Willie was not. He asked Annie out on two or three occasions and was a dear, kind friend, but he did not make her heart leap or her fingers stutter over the buttons on her gloves when his sleeve brushed against hers, as Willie's had on the open deck of the tram. George invited Annie to accompany him to a wedding. Which was all very nice, but when the photographer required the guests to position themselves, Annie hung back. She was the only one who was not part of the family.

In case she needed reminding of *his* interest, Willie sent Annie another silent card. This one, dashed into the post with stamp askew, came from nearby Stavelcy, and showed a picture of the Thompson's bakery cart. Though more prosaic than a Pittsburgh scene, its message was loud enough.

But this was 1915, and there was a larger story taking place. All over the country, fit young men were deciding whether to do their bit and volunteer. In July, George enlisted.

7

Goodbyes, 1914–16

AT THE CORNER SHOP, THE GREAT WAR STARTED WITH A scramble for food. Everyone anticipated shortages. Anyone with any pennies to spare bought extra tea and sugar; Mrs Graham wanted the largest tin of golden syrup my great-grandma could supply.

Eva was chosen to be Britannia and lead a fund-raising parade which wound through Brimington, down into Wheeldon Mill and back up the hill again, following the colliery band. Neighbours stood on their doorsteps and Betsy left the shop to see Eva enthroned, with helmet, shield and trident (garden fork), in a dress made over especially for the occasion. Her float was festooned with Union Jacks and garden flowers and accompanied by half a dozen younger children in assorted national dress – handmaidens from Wales, Scotland, Ireland, India, the Colonies. One young lad, intended to represent the globe, looked stuffed to bursting, showing off all the pink bits on the map. 'John Bull', 'Peace' and Red Cross nurses marched behind them.

Gradually, the local landscape changed. Men still worked the pit – coal was essential – but anyone travelling into Chesterfield

saw the khaki tide transforming its pavements. The Brimington
Parish Magazine published its own Roll of Honour, listing local
heroes who joined the Colours. Some were in a great hurry to join
up, others harried into it by recruiting sergeants. Young Rolly
Cook signed his papers before August 1914 was through, and
came into the shop to announce that he was a soldier.

Kathleen Driver would have packed her husband off in a jiffy
if she could, but as a winder at the colliery, he was secure. Instead,
she bought a cake of laundry soap and rubbed it across the stairs
and along the edge of each tread. 'The bugger's still standing,
though,' she told Betsy. She'd hoped the brute would slip and
break his neck. The next time Betsy saw Harold he was wearing
his weekend suit and Sunday muffler, and heading for the Great
Central Hotel. He raised his cap, as usual: 'Afternoon, Mrs.' You
would think that butter wouldn't melt.

Ethel's younger brother Sid, her nearest in age, had his portrait
taken in uniform and presented a copy to Betsy, practising a confident air his eyes disputed. Jimmy Frith did the same, his cheeky
smile captured for ever in black and white. Someone gave Betsy
a small album for these and other photographs neighbours' sons
started bringing in to the shop. There they all were in their caps
and insignia, looking like they'd borrowed their fathers' clothes.
Most managed a smile, some looked wary; one, completely petri-
fied. His under-exposed image seemed bleached with fear. The
album was so discreet it could be tucked into a pocket, safe from
harm, which was more than could be said for the lads themselves.

Eva turned fourteen during the First World War and started working alongside Betsy. She was quick at mental arithmetic, deft at
transferring flour and sugar from the sacks on the floor to the

SUNLIGHT SOAP

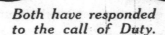

Both have responded to the call of Duty.

THE proverb says that "many hands make light work"—but at Port Sunlight the hands of every woman worker are making light work even of those tasks which, before the war, were judged beyond their strength.

But nearly 3,000 Sunlight men have joined the colours, and the girls who have taken their places in the ranks of industry are demonstrating to the world that heavy tasks can be done with light hearts, where loyalty and devotion to duty are the order of the day.

In our photograph, Sunlight girls are seen stacking long bars of Sunlight Soap to dry, so that the Soap may be thoroughly mature before it is stamped, wrapped and packed ready for dispatch to the grocer.

£1,000 GUARANTEE OF PURITY
on every Bar.

The name Lever on Soap is a Guarantee of Purity and Excellence.

LEVER BROTHERS LIMITED, PORT SUNLIGHT.

small bags on the counter (blue bags for sugar, white for flour). Standing all day was tiring, and shifting sacks of chicken feed heavy work, but she loved greeting customers and was much happier serving behind the counter than reciting the Rivers of England for Miss West.

The stock acquired a patriotic flavour: *Bovril gives strength to win... Don't Forget the Man at the Front. Post him Oxo Cubes. They Warm, Invigorate and Sustain in a Moment.* Shopping lists began to include little extras that could be parcelled up and sent to France: a bar of Cadbury's or Five Boys; a packet of shortbread; a Christmas tin of Doncaster Toffee; plus liberal quantities of Keating's Powder and Hawley's I.K: Destroys Insects, Vermin & Body Parasites.

Uniformed portraits notwithstanding, there was still the tramp of boots to the pit. Derbyshire farmers complained of the number of colliery workers exempt from soldiering compared with those drawn from the land. The nation needed food as much as coal: what was the point of decimating the farms?

George was granted embarkation leave and came to the house to say his farewells. He looked broader in uniform, as if he'd grown into himself; the war put meat on his bones. Before leaving to catch his train, George also presented Dick and Betsy with a photograph. It was a much larger picture than those of local lads, and a fitting image of the young man my great-grandparents regarded so highly. There are no comparable portraits of Willie.

There is a photograph of Willie from around this time, however. He's in mufti still and is looking quite the dandy, with a centre parting in his hair. The gold watch chain clipped to a waistcoat button grins twice over and almost as broadly as Willie. His hands

are in his pockets and he's lolling in his chair (two counts of etiquette dashed in one go). Annie stands beside him, her hand on his left shoulder. She looks as if she is claiming a prize.

George wrote from France, sending Eva the lace-fronted postcards she requested. Commonwealth flags flit across most greetings, their cheery colouring and delicate lace as much at odds with the place they have come from as his anodyne words. Some are sentimental tokens, like the sweet briar rose in palest pink, with 'forget me not' stitched beside it, a postcard written to Eva,

with a larger message intended for Annie. Eva returned the favour with parcels of socks and cigarettes and news of Wheeldon Mill. But she did not tell George everything. One of his pencil-written cards makes poignant reading: 'Is it correct that Annie has married? Why did you not write and tell me?'

When Annie and Willie married on 1 January 1916, they hoped the New Year would hold all the right promises, despite atrocious weather and the continuing war. Eva and Willie's younger brother Nelson stood witness at the ceremony and accompanied the couple to church, arm in arm, so as not to slip on the ice. Annie wore a

new hat, though not one she had trimmed herself. This one was made especially by a local milliner and had an under-brim of pleated silk. Despite snow carpeting the ground that day, she looked a picture of spring elegance. Annie was handsome before Willie Thompson came along, but on the day my grandma signed a photograph, 'your ever loving wife', she was beautiful.

The attic room was rearranged to make it 'new' for the young couple with the addition of a little bamboo table and a cushioned wicker chair. It was a sunny room for Willie to come back to after a day at the bakehouse, though not his to enjoy for very long. In no time at all – or so it seemed to Annie – he was conscripted.

The talk in the corner shop was nearly always of goodbyes. The number of lads departing for the Front was soon joined by that of lasses engaged in war work. Sheepbridge Works converted to munitions, enticing young women from their pre-war jobs. Fast and alert workers were needed; wages and camaraderie were good. They disappeared into vast hangars each morning and spilled out again at night, linked arms and singing, nobody seeming to mind the twelve-hour shifts.

Ethel Stokes was one of them, a 'canary' (so-called because of the cordite staining their faces), working in an overall and cap; no hairpins, no corsets – 'Oh, Annie, the blessed relief,' – no metal of any kind allowed on site. Ethel spent her days twisting something that looked remarkably like macaroni into a lethal dish. Though wages were high, so were the risks. An explosion at a nearby gunpowder factory permanently scarred a number of women. Patriotism was all very well, but they had not reckoned on displaying theirs for life.

Patriotism had other ugly moments. Bricks were hurled through the windows of German butcher, F. Stünder, on Sheffield Road, in retaliation for the sinking of the *Lusitania*, and windows smashed in Haag's butcher on the High Street. 'Whoever would do a senseless thing like that?' asked Betsy. 'German or not, they're all some mother's sons.'

Quietly at first, but gathering momentum, news starts coming in. Soon, it's a weekly dispatch. The vantage point of the sweet window is shunned nowadays, when the clear view it affords could be that of the telegraph boy crossing the canal bridge on his bike. It takes such an age for him to pass the shop it is like waiting in slow motion. All conversation stops until he rides by.

Carefree youths, who liked to hang around outside the shop are picked off, one by one. Eva's friend Carrie loses the big brother who used to grab her hands and swing her off her feet on payday. She has four brothers in all, and a stepbrother too, but that does not mean she has a brother to spare. Lads Annie knows from grammar school, some of whom she vied with over their position in class, join the list of dead and wounded. One former assistant master, presumed killed, is discovered to be a prisoner of war. By the time the war is through with them, nineteen 'old boys' will be dead. Betsy learns to read her customers' faces. How do you greet a woman who has lost both sons?

It is not just neighbours and school friends who suffer. Annie's cousin Jack survives only one month at the Front. Nineteen years old – and what's the good of that, his mam asks Betsy. There is nothing ladylike about Aunt Annie's grief. Her young Jack had a fund of stories always, and liked pulling everyone's leg; now his jokes rot with him in France. Jack's brother Charlie is wounded three times before finally being invalided out. The photograph he sends from his convalescent home is supposed to reassure them, but he's lost so much weight his clothes hang off him. Betsy wonders how much else of Charlie has gone.

But there is good news too, or what passes for good news in wartime: Willie is posted to the Middle East as a dispatch rider, and will surely be safer there than in France; and George has a commission, which is exactly what everyone expected. On the Home Front, there is the very best news of all: Annie is expecting a baby.

The baby was due in the autumn. She was born in November, a beautiful little girl, but the pregnancy was disturbing and the birth itself a terrible shock. Betsy had told my grandma nothing, just as, years before, Annie had been left to discover menstruation by herself, retreating to the privy feeling frightened and ashamed, wondering if she'd bleed to death. The pain, the indignity, the whole bloody mess of childbirth offended Annie's fastidious nature. Worst of all was her fear, not knowing what would happen next, or if she would survive the delivery. Just two years earlier, Willie's sister Nellie had died giving birth to a boy. Poor Nellie, Willie's childhood playmate (and every bit as mischievous), was dead, aged twenty-five, and Annie only one year younger.

Like most women then, my grandma gave birth at home, which in her case meant the attic room, two flights upstairs, the shop bell marking time between contractions. But, in the end, it would all be worthwhile. Except that it was not: Annie's baby was stillborn.

If you look for my grandma's baby in the General Register, you will not find her. Stillbirths were not required to be registered nationally until 1927, although from 1915 all had to be notified locally. In 1916, the year my grandma gave birth to a stillborn child, Chesterfield's Medical Officer of Health (MOH) reported

In the early twentieth century, stillborn babies were cheaper to bury than other infants, a crude but telling fact for poor families. The poorest might avoid cemetery fees altogether by asking a grave digger to tuck the child into a newly prepared grave. (This was perfectly legal, providing the burial was reported.)

One young woman recalled taking her mother's stillborn baby to be buried when she was but a small child herself. She collected a soap box from the grocer and prepared the baby for burial by wrapping the body in the lining of her father's coat – it was like dressing 'a little doll', she said. She padded the soap box with cotton wadding and laid the baby down, as if tucking up her doll for sleep, then carried the lidded box to the churchyard, where she gave it to the grave digger with a letter from her father.

'That's all right, my lass,' the grave digger said. 'You see the church there?… Well, in the far corner, you'll see a heap of boxes and packets.' Other stillborns awaiting burial.

– Based on the recollections of Rose Ashton, in Angela Holdsworth, *Out of the Doll's House: The Story of Women in the Twentieth Century*, 1988

forty-one stillbirths in the borough, though it is likely that, even then, some slipped through the net. All those notified were investigated to ensure there was no foul play, a stillbirth not always being what it seemed in the years when many women were overburdened with children.

That year, Chesterfield's MOH also recorded an increase in

infant mortality and condemned the unhealthy environments in which some expectant mothers and their infants were required to live, especially those in working-class neighbourhoods with 'insanitary privy-middens' – night-soil lavatories like the ones at Wheeldon Mill. This may have had a bearing on my grandma's situation, though I doubt it: the family was scrupulously clean. (It is almost impossible to contemplate how all their white lace petticoats and blouses, starched aprons and shirts, linen sheets and pillowcases, lace runners, damask tablecloths, handkerchiefs, napkins and doilies issued from a house whose plumbing ran to one cold tap and a privy-midden.) Infant mortality was generally high in Chesterfield: only three years earlier, its MOH had reported that the district's figures were higher than any elsewhere in England: one child in five, between the age of one and five, was born to die.

All over Britain, women like my grandma lost babies they'd longed for. All over Britain, women gave birth to babies they could ill afford to keep or did not want to begin with. When the first soldiers marched out of Chesterfield in 1914, they were trailed by weeping women clutching babies. Wartime births caused distress and consternation in equal measure. Illegitimacy was on the increase. 'War Babies', newspapers screeched, with some head-lines preceding the actual rise in the illegitimate birth rate. Figures rose from 1916 and, by the end of the war, were up by 30 per cent. Chesterfield's own illegitimate birth rate rose to a record high of seventy-two in 1916, although the actual number of women conceiving children out of wedlock was probably disguised by the number who managed to convert their panic into confetti. Other pregnant women found desperate solutions. A VAD nurse working in a poor area of London spent her wartime service on a babies' ward at a hospital near Waterloo, presumably St Thomas's: 'All I did was lay out dead babies like little birds… babies… left on doorsteps to die.'

My grandma knew that babies died, of course she did, but not her baby, and not with Willie so far away. Though my great-grandparents knew what it was to lose a child and could support her, it was not the same as having Willie there, and Annie's grief recalled their loss from all those years ago – and what desperate memories did it revive for Eva? Theirs was a household fastened tight in mourning. A year of beginnings and promises became a year of endings and loss.

There would be no cotton daisies for Annie to stitch on small silk bodices, no ribbons to thread through impossibly fine woollen shawls, no baby to bathe and pat with the large powder puff, like a giant pale dahlia my grandma had bought for her first child. The swansdown puff was pushed into a drawer, where I came upon it many years later: 'That was for my baby, who died.'

I did not know my grandma's baby was stillborn, nor did my mother. Annie never said. We thought she lived for a few days and was called Mary, like Dick and Betsy's first child. During the nineteenth century, even a baby who breathed for a few hours

---

'It is more dangerous to be a baby in Britain than it is to be a soldier.'

– Slogan for the UK's first National Baby Week, 1917

might casually be termed a stillborn. With the local notification of stillbirths and improved training for midwives, the likelihood of this misrepresentation was greatly reduced (and finally ceased altogether), but I wonder if Annie's baby lived for a few hours? This may be a mere fancy of mine; there is no way of knowing, but, if so, it would account for her words. Either my grandma gave birth to a child she yearned for, who was as real to her as any who drew breath, or else she held her first child and lost her, all in one day. Neither version bears contemplation, though each has been the fate of many women and continues to be today.

The Brimington Cemetery records give neither name nor gender for Mrs Thompson's 'stillborn', who is listed among the others buried there, tucked into a corner of the churchyard. No christening, no gravestone, though never forgotten by Annie. My grandma's child, not child, her lovely daughter, Mary, lies buried beneath the trees.

There was snow on the ground that December. The trees became frosted sketches, the flowering currant bush bloomed falsely white; the streets round about were iced over, but few enjoyed a picture-book Christmas in the winter of 1916.

8

Oh Dear! What a Dreadful War

FOR ALL THE TALK IN THE TAPROOM OF THE GREAT CENTRAL Hotel, of what they'd do to Fritz if they caught him, no civilian expected to come face to face with a German soldier. Yet that's precisely what happened in Brimington in 1917. In no time at all, the story was the talk of the neighbourhood and the Derbyshire press. The local bobby liked to call at the corner shop for a cup of tea; I expect Betsy and Eva heard the tale first-hand.

One Sunday lunchtime in late September, William Darkin and George Fretwell were walking in Bluebank Wood when they spotted four men up ahead. Darkin and Fretwell had permission to walk the wood and, these being the days before public right of way, had not expected to encounter anyone else. As the two men approached, they saw that the group had obviously made some efforts to conceal their presence: they were lying half shrouded in the undergrowth, their bags jutting out of the bracken.

Suspicions were further aroused when, in reply to a cheery greeting, 'there was not the Derbyshire ring in the voice, a foreign accent striking the ear'. What happened next seems ludicrous.

The strangers commented on the volume of traffic on the nearby railway and, as if reading from an espionage handbook, displayed a keen interest in the large industrial works in the distance – Sheepbridge. This was too much for Darkin and Fretwell who quickly retraced their steps and alerted Mr Stott, the man who had given them permission to walk the woodland path. Stott hastened to the spot, greeted the suspects, and then – as in the best detective fiction – made as if to leave, but doubled back, while keeping the group under observation. Meanwhile, Darkin went in search of a policeman. It was the kind of moment village bobbies dream of.

The strangers offered no resistance when confronted by Sergeant Parnham, and admitted they were prisoners of war who'd escaped from a Nottinghamshire camp some days earlier. 'The game is up,' their spokesman conceded, as if quoting again from his espionage handbook.

'News of the capture spread like wildfire.' By the time a car had been located and commandeered (no instant matter in Brimington in 1917), 'the prisoners were the centre of a large and excited crowd'. Here was a chance for women with sons and husbands at the Front to harangue and abuse real-live Germans. Amid much jostling and shouting, the prisoners were bundled into the car and conveyed to Chesterfield Police Station.

The *Derbyshire Times* was tickled pink and delighted in unfolding all aspects of the story. Particularly fascinating were the contents of the fugitives' kitbags. The prisoners had amassed sufficient tinned food to last a fortnight – which was more than could be said for Betsy's customers – plus cigarettes, tobacco, mackintoshes, bottles of tea, a pair of tiny handmade compasses and several maps said to have been drawn with such precision that even the smallest hamlets were included. A portmanteau they were carrying weighed 'fully a hundredweight'; it was extraordinary the men had managed to travel as far as they did. Their fellow escapees had been picked off fairly easily; the last of them to be recaptured, an ace pilot, was spotted by a group of schoolchildren, crouching in a ditch.

The final intrepid four had spent their last day of freedom in the Derbyshire village of Ashover, crossing further into the county as darkness fell and making their way towards the mail train. Missing the train by just three minutes, they had decamped to Bluebank Wood where they spent several hours before their discovery. Their chances of getting further in broad daylight were slim, to say the least, but, with luck, and without drawing attention to themselves by lighting a fire, they could have remained hidden until the next mail train the following day.

A grateful Sheepbridge Company issued specially minted gold medals to Darkin and Fretwell; my grandma kept a report of the private ceremony. The pair were fêted as heroes – drinks on the house – though when they first reported their suspicions to their fellow drinkers on that fateful Sunday in the bar of the Red Lion, they'd been greeted with typical Derbyshire candour and disbelief.

For a few short weeks, the Bluebank Wood incident bolstered morale. People felt their own small contributions to the war were of value, albeit that night-time fears – and taproom jokes – acquired a new edge: the bogeyman behind the coal house really might be the Hun.

This morale boost was timely. By now, everyone knew a handful of people who'd been killed or injured. Annie's friend, Ethel, was widowed. Earlier in the war, she had married a local lad, Henry

Dec 25th 1917

Xmas Day and such a sad one. My dear lad Tony was missing from the family circle first time in 20 years. Oh Dear! What a dreadful war and what awfully sad homes there are this Xmas. The worst I have ever known. No joy. No singing Xmas hymns. No decorations. The singing will be in Church... Anthony and I have no heart for anything, only grief for our dear lost lad; and poor John and Louisa, how sad they must feel, as [their] poor Anthony was with them as our dear boy was with us this time last year...

Dec 26th

Cold and dull at times. Young Billy Twelves went back tonight on his way to France again where he has spent nearly 3 years. We do not seem to be getting any nearer the end of this terrible war. The Russians are nothing to be depended on and the Italians are having a severe struggle to hold back the Huns. I am afraid there will be a famine before long as there seems to be no getting things for money and people are standing by thousands outside the shops in the large towns... We have nothing to sell, only minerals and very few of them are left.

– Maria Gyte, farmer's wife and publican, lived in the Derbyshire village of Sheldon, and kept a diary 1913–20. Her son Tony was killed at Passchendaele.

Marsden. One of seven children, he was keen to see the recruiting officer, pleased to get fixed rations, and proud to put 'soldier' on his wedding certificate. They were married barely two years before Henry died of wounds. 'I never really knew him, Mrs Nash,' Ethel said. 'Not really.' In her heart, she knew the marriage had been expedient. They'd both had reasons to escape. She bought a black hat and wore it for a month or so, but she was only twenty-four. Ethel Marsden, widow, did not suit her.

The *Derbyshire Times* offered 'In Memoriam' cards, two shillings and sixpence a dozen, two bob for three dozen or more: everyone wanted a card and a last photograph, including those the dead had fought alongside. What with the grief and the weather and the shortages, one day seeped into the next, shaming those who, in 1914, had regretted being out of the fun.

Neighbours who lost husbands and sons hadn't the heart (or the shoe leather) to scour the shops for the tea, butter, sugar, currants and jam that were rapidly disappearing, and cared nothing that eggs were twice the price of two years earlier, or that flour – if you could get it – was nowadays measly stuff that needed bulking out with potatoes. Who needed eggs and flour to make a batter pudding when the lovely boy who liked to eat it would never taste a pudding again?

From late February 1918, rationing evened things out and reduced the interminable queues. There were coupons for Betsy and Eva to check and collect and customers were obliged to register with the corner shop as their chosen supplier for grocery staples. But there were still mouths to feed from shelves still half empty and with everything increasingly dear. The fourth year dragged

---

WHITTINGTON OFFICER KILLED

Killed in action only a few hours before the signing of the Armistice is the untimely end of sub. Lieut. Harry Young, of the R.N.V.R, youngest son of Mr and Mrs Chas. Young... The sad news reached his parents on Monday evening to the effect that he was killed on the 10th Inst. Deceased was 24 years of age, and joined up in the early stages of the war. At the time he was an assistant schoolmaster at the Brimington Schools, and after a period of training with A.S.C. he was sent to Salonica, where he stayed a little over two years. Later he was given a commission in the R.N.V.R. and went out to France in August last... On Tuesday morning of this week his parents received the usual letter saying he was quite well.

– 1918 obituary [unattributed] pasted into Annie's commonplace book

---

on, rubbing out hope and picking at everyone's wounds. When, at last, there was talk of peace and neighbours dared to contemplate the future, news came of a grand lad Annie knew, killed the day before the Armistice.

1918 had not quite finished with indiscriminate deaths. Next came the influenza, killing those the war could not reach. In no time at all, the Spanish 'flu claimed local man Charles Inns and, five days later, his son. Young Charles, a fit man of twenty-six, with a wife and a son of his own, contracted pneumonia following the 'flu and was buried with the flowers still fresh on his father's grave. Poor Charles, poor Constance, and their poor young son, who was barely more than a baby. Constance often used the shop; Eva and Annie always chatted with her. She and the baby were so ill themselves that the funeral service was conducted at their home.

But the greatest shock for my grandma was the death of Elsie Phipps, headmistress of the Princess Street Girls' School, the companion school to the Infants' where Annie taught as a pupil teacher and to which she returned following her baby's death. With all her hopes unravelling, Annie needed something to occupy her thoughts and distract her. Though a married woman now and, by rights, no longer needed – like most local authorities, Derbyshire expected married women to give up teaching – regulations were relaxed during the war. Annie took herself back to her old classroom and her old adversary Miss Doughty, and also got to know Elsie Phipps.

Less formidable than Mabel Doughty, Miss Phipps was popular with both colleagues and pupils. Barely a month earlier she and Annie had sat in the church hall, pricing goods for a Red Cross Fancy Fair. 'And what would you give for this?' Miss Phipps had asked, lifting a misshapen muffler, 'or these?' – a pair of gloves – before writing exorbitant sums on the price tags.

But the date intended for the Fair turned into the day of Elsie's funeral. The Phipps were well respected in the neighbourhood – Elsie's father was a committee-man and High Street grocer – and many neighbours as well as colleagues turned out for the church. My grandma joined the procession but, even as she walked in that cold black line, the occasion made no sense. It was incomprehensible how someone she had laughed with, had liked and admired, and expected to go on seeing over the years, could be alive and well one week, and dead the next. She knew Miss Phipps was ill, but she was strong and would recover. Expecting to hear that Elsie was sitting up in bed, making light of her scare and wanting visitors, Annie was told she was dead.

My grandma kept one of the price tags from the Fancy Fair. '6/6', it said, in thick red ink. 'Written by E. Phipps Oct 9 1918, died Nov 5,' she wrote underneath those vivid strokes, the insignificant memento underscoring the preposterousness of the death. Some weeks later, the delayed Fair went ahead. Everyone agreed that was what Miss Phipps would have wanted (and what else would they have done with the contributions?). The church hall was filled with stalls and there was the usual raffle and prizes, but though the Armistice had been signed some weeks earlier, few could muster much enthusiasm for the event.

The year was not quite over, nor the difficulties experienced in the aftermath of the 'flu. There were still parcels to make up – with Glaxo, bread, butter, tea, sugar – and deliver to frail neighbours. On Christmas Eve, Clara Tissington sent Annie ('Mrs Thompson') small gifts for herself and Eva, with a card expressing 'kindest regards to your Mother and yourself and thanking you for all you did to help me'. She enclosed a recent photograph of herself and hoped that 'when your husband comes home, you will be very happy'. Mrs Tissington's picture joined the others in my great-grandma's tiny album: snapshots of a small community, 1914–18.

9

Tea for Two

WILLIE HAD BEEN HAVING A DIFFERENT KIND OF WAR. PACKED off to France with the rest of them in 1916, he learned that though roses might bloom in Picardy, none grew in the trenches. He considered his posting to the Middle East a stroke of immense good fortune.

His new role as a dispatch rider suited him much better. Willie was not the sort of man to stand in line and much preferred to be a lone adventurer. The job enabled him to drive through the desert on a motorcycle, delivering communiqués both urgent and mundane, kicking up sand in unknown, open spaces. He was proud of his service-issue rifle and prouder still to handle a revolver.

Willie was curious about the world in which he found himself and jotted down some 'Hindoo' words and phrases: common commands – yes, no, stop, come here – and a smattering of other useful nouns: porridge, paper, bucket, meat; a frugal (and Imperial) vocabulary, just enough to get by with supplementary signs and gestures. He was interested to know more about the culture he observed. 'Caron,' Willie wrote: 'a book or bible composed of 104

books, split into 30 portions, and Arabs must read 1 portion each day…' He photographed a Sheik's sons and a young Arab boy to show Annie, and collected postcards of the far-flung places he visited and others he hoped he might see one day: general views of Aden, Basra, Cairo; majestic tombs and pyramids trapped in grainy images. But he was also a card-playing private who liked to place a bet and enjoyed the camaraderie of his fellow soldiers and their boasts about the number of pints they could sink. He was only twenty-three, after all.

Willie must have worked quite hard to remain a private during the First World War, though this was easier in the Middle East than in France, where, with mortality rates rising as fast as the mud men drowned in, and an officer's life expectancy down to a matter of weeks, it required tenacity to remain on the bottom rung. Head down and get on with it: that was Willie's mission; anything that enabled him to survive the thing and spend time astride his beloved motorcycle.

The Middle East was not an entirely cushy billet, what with the sun and the flies, and the way his guts churned daily. On the journey down to Basra, the heat was so thick you could have cut it with a knife. At some point, Willie developed malaria which wrapped him in rank sweats and made him long for Blighty, but a Middle East posting made home-leave nigh on impossible and letters took for ever to arrive. Until the envelope was put into his hands, he'd been picturing Annie with their new baby. The baby's death demolished the images Willie had built of his wife and child running to greet him as he walked back up Station Road with his kitbag. Sometimes Willie had pictured a babe in arms, at other moments, a toddler stumbling towards him – but it was all so far away, it was hard to make the image stick. With time, he hoped there would be other children for him and Annie. Meanwhile,

there was the war, and years of it at that, eating up his future and other people's lives. It was at least 1921 by the time Willie was demobbed. He still had a good while to wait.

Peace and quiet was what most returning soldiers longed for, the monotony of the everyday: Clem Stokes and Jimmy Frith wanted to sit on their back steps and see a patchwork of green fields and moorland on the skyline, not cruciform trees, blasted bodies, seething mud. Even colliery wheels and smoking chimneys were preferable to the images bombarding their vision.

A trip down the aisle was an efficient way to eradicate bad memories. Some slow-burning courtships outlasted the war; others were whirlwind romances or marriages made catch-as-catch-can. Survivors grabbed happiness where they found it.

One after another, Edna, Liza, Ellen marched into the shop. I'm getting married tomorrow, Mrs Nash. I'll be Mrs Stokes (or Frith or Taylor) they informed her, as if Betsy had not witnessed the burgeoning courtship (and heard their mother's opinion of the match). Another generation of young couples, set to live similar lives to their parents. Some faced greater obstacles before they even started: Clem Stokes came home with a badly smashed jaw; Jimmy Frith was shell-shocked.

Rolly Cook returned wearing a taut leather glove, a second skin to conceal his disabled hand, damaged when a shell exploded near him. He had also injured his leg and, for the first few months, walked with the aid of a stick. The effect was not so much of an impediment, but of a permanently raffish air. He looked more dapper gent than wounded soldier. 'Nice stick, Rolly,' Ethel said, the first time she saw him coming along Station Road.

'Yes, I'll use it to hook the ladies.'

'If you think you're quick enough to catch one.'

They were married the following spring.

Meanwhile, Annie waited and made plans. All over the country, women like my grandma were busily shaping homes for returning heroes. Annie waited longer than most and so had time to make her plans more elaborate. By 1921, the war was mostly the stuff of mourning and of newly erected memorials, not a living, breathing, longing for a husband who would finally be coming home.

Home. The mark of a good home was its furnishings. Annie had some five years in which to squirrel away her wages and save towards the home she and Willie would have on his return. Betsy encouraged her to put away as much as possible while she was still teaching. Each month, Annie strained to extend the amount she saved by another sixpence or shilling; she lost count of the number of times she caught the train into Chesterfield and gazed through Eyres' window – 'Eyre & Son's: **the** thoroughly up-to-date dependable firm… Designers and Manufacturers of Artistic Furniture' – huddled in her winter coat, disappearing into her turned-up collar, attempting to warm herself on her own breath, while she contemplated the Denmark Suite in solid satin walnut (three bedroom pieces plus two cane chairs) for £9 5s 0d. In the end, she chose a suite whose dressing table had slim legs and a swing mirror. While Annie was breathing frosted air on to a plate-glass window and doing rapid sums, Willie was checking his hand beneath the palm trees and wondering whether to play his Jack of Hearts.

Next, she bought a dining suite in varnished wood, another Eyres' purchase, and some second-hand silver to show off the sideboard: a Georgian teapot, a filigree bun tray and an ornamental tree that sprouted cranberry-glass cones for single blooms. The minute Annie got the tricksy thing home, she wondered when on earth she would use it, but the silver was so dainty she had not felt able to resist. In time, she bought a dressing-table set with a pattern reminiscent of a spring garden. Though her evenings were spent at Station Road with her parents and sister, all Annie's thoughts were directed towards the future.

EYRE & SON'S LTD

Palm Stands

Music Cabinets

Smokers' Cabinets

Luxurious Easy Chairs

Oak & Japanese Trays

Occasional Cabinets

Music Stools

Coal vases & cabinets

Tea Sets

Plant Pots

Rose Bowls

Silk lampshades with plain or beaded trimmings

Pouffe cushions

Carpets in the Newest Styles

– A selection of tempting furnishings from a *Derbyshire Times* advertisement, 5 January 1916

In the picture she had of Willie, he was standing in a garden, throwing a laughing child into the air. She was smiling at them both and pouring tea through a delicate Georgian spout. Sometimes the image changed and she and Willie were walking along the canal path with the corner shop behind them, each holding a small hand in one of theirs. There was always a child in view. A married friend in whom she confided lent Annie a book which explained many facts about pregnancy (and sex) a young woman ought to know, and of which she'd had no idea until now. She would not feel so helpless next time round.

My grandma saved the pattern for the baby's petticoat she wanted to crochet, though resisted the urge to buy the yarn or practise butterfly edging straightaway. Instead, she embroidered a large silk handkerchief with tulips and curling leaves, to put in a frame on the wall. While she stitched, Annie tried to close her mind to all the months and years that were disappearing. She

was already twenty-six when the Armistice was signed. It was impossible not to realise how much time was slipping away, even though it seemed to pass so slowly.

One of my grandma's treasured possessions was a silver pen-wipe in the shape of swan, a perfect choice for her in many ways, but this elegant creature was not bought by Annie, but by Dick, and probably came from his country-house foraging. My great-grandfather's liking for country-house sales began during the First World War and gathered momentum thereafter, when high taxation and death duties left the gentry and upper-middle classes strapped for cash. One after another, homes were advertised for let in *Country Life*. Some landowners sold up entirely; auction houses acquired a new zeal.

Sales in Derbyshire were as plentiful as elsewhere. In March 1920, the Duke of Rutland auctioned part of his estate. Land

stretching diagonally from Sheffield to below Matlock, and from Buxton into Chesterfield, was auctioned, together with farms, smallholdings and cottages, some of them going to sitting tenants, the rest to speculators as 'parcels of property', while the auction of 13,300 acres of the Duke's Belvoir Estate realised a total of £489,780, the equivalent of some £14.5 million today. (A farm worker kept his family on 15s a week.) Later that year, Major Philip Hunloke sold the Wingerworth Estate on the edge of Chesterfield. The sale raised just £32,300 on land that had been in his family more than three centuries.

It was not only large estates that came on to the market. In 1915, the 'valuable household furniture and effects' of Brimington's Sutton Lodge were auctioned over the course of two days. Motor buses delivered prospective buyers (and nosey parkers) to the house, where everything from burr walnut suites and a grand piano, to bonbon dishes and a soup ladle was up for sale, not forgetting the 'art border carpet' from the maids' bedroom. Two years later, Brimington Hall was similarly denuded, the whole of its furnishings plus a 'single brougham in perfect order' and a dog cart coming under the hammer. Pockets of land and property elsewhere in the neighbourhood were broken into lots and sold to the highest bidder. For some families, money and influence were trickling away.

Their losses were my great-grandfather's gain. Dick loved to visit big-house sales – beanos he called them. Whenever he could, Dick took himself off for the day to see houses stripped of their furnishings – everything from tapestries to the contents of their larders laid out on the grass; mangles set out on once exclusive parkland, meat-mincers and nests of basins arranged on trestle tables like some early twentieth-century boot sale. For the price of a thrupenny catalogue and a short walk, or a lift hitched on a farm cart, Dick could have himself a real fuddle.

Sales like these gave outsiders like my great-grandfather – and no one could be more of an outsider – a chance to glimpse the workings of a different social class: to see, if not their dirty linen, then their clean linen, at least (and piles of it, at that), and the reduction of a way of life that had persisted for centuries. But Dick was not just looking, he was buying. This fairground lad had a good eye. (He wasn't cowed by his 'betters' either. Years later, Lord Andrew Cavendish, soon to become the 11th Duke of Devonshire, came to the shop as a prospective Tory candidate and was invited through to the house. 'Sit y'sen down lad, and have some bread and jam,' said Dick, who was eating his tea.)

My great-grandfather's booty included two huge mirrors of the size that nowadays occupy the walls of dance studios – on the occasions she left the house, Betsy liked to check that she looked 'right' – hefty chests of drawers, an overmantel mirror; shell-like silver salt cellars and their minuscule spoons, and a china dressing-table set for Eva, its Art Nouveau shape splashed with poppies. Even the household bible was picked up at a country-house sale. And a sale was surely responsible for an improbable shawl that belonged to my great-aunt, its geometric patterns and metallic sheen promising a sophisticated evening and a full dance card. I doubt that the shawl was ever worn; Eva did not go dancing. For much of her life, it glittered in a drawer.

My great-grandfather's big-house jaunts continued well into my mother's childhood (death duties carried on climbing and, by 1934, had reached 50 per cent). At one such sale, he found a musical box, a relic of some child's nursery, with a sentimental watercolour decorating its lid and a halting rendition of 'Pussy

Cat, Pussy Cat…' in its windings. From then on, it played its plaintive tune for my mum and, later, me.

Country-house sales were as much a sign of the times as the advertisements being produced for products sold by the corner shop – 'A word to the wise coquette and cocktail drinker: drink Enos Fruit Salts'; 'Icilma Face Cream (essential for the female pillion rider)' – and the felt cloche hats, like tight spring buds, that were beginning to decorate Whit Walks. With the end of the war and, gradually, rationing, the new decade offered a sense of possibility even industrial unrest could not diminish. But the past refused to be erased entirely. Jimmy Frith still trembled with shell-shock and was jolted by sudden bangs; a motorcycle or car backfiring were enough to set him off, while Ethel's brother, Clem, was left literally propping up his jaw. Each day was a reminder of the injuries you could sustain and have to live with, though God knows how some people did. Not everyone succeeded: one Staveley man killed

DR WILLIAMS' PINK PILLS

When Girls Grow Thin

When girls grow deathly pale, weak and miserable then is the
time for parents to take prompt steps, for delay means danger

– Dr Williams' Pink Pills

(there is no medicine that can compare)

Advertisement, *Derbyshire Times*, 1910

DR WILLIAMS' PINK PILLS

When Your Nerves Fail – Beware of Neurasthenia

Pitiful is the cry that comes from men and women, victims
of this 'twentieth-century complaint' which arises out of
the competition, speed and striving of the age

– Dr Williams' Pink Pills, 3s 0d a box – nothing else will do

Advertisement, *Derbyshire Times*, 1926

his mother and injured his brother and wife, before turning his
war-issue gun on himself. Newspaper reports like this one were
grist to the 1920s, when nearly every out-of-work serviceman had
a row of medals on his chest and every door-to-door salesman
with a suitcase full of brushes seemed to be missing a limb.

When Willie finally returned, in the early 1920s, he and Annie
took themselves off to Sheffield, where Willie found himself a job

in a city bakery. It was the furthest my grandma had been from Chesterfield and the longest time she had spent away from the family, but it gave her and Willie the chance to get to know one another again, and less self-consciously than if they'd remained at the shop. Perhaps this was the reason Willie did not immediately start working again for his brother Jim. Maybe he and Annie wanted some time to themselves.

Willie had gone off to war as C. W. Thompson. He had too much gumption (and too long a memory of schoolyard ribbing) to enter the army with his correct initials. While in Sheffield, he was William C. Thompson and sometimes reverted to plain W.C. He and Annie had two or three addresses during their short stay; each new street came with a small adjustment to his name. Willie was still working out who he wanted to be.

That first summer was as hot as Hades. A home from home, after the Middle East, someone said. All people wanted to hear from Willie were exotic details like those described on the bangle he'd brought back for Annie: a Mesopotamian circle of elephants, crocodiles and palm trees.

Though he and Annie had been married six years, they'd spent so much time apart and in such different circumstances, they might as well have been married six weeks. They were still tentative with one another, circling each other, discovering themselves all over again. Willie's corn-coloured curls were just as angelic as they'd always been and his eyes just as blue, but his face looked different somehow, though no less handsome for that. Annie liked to watch him smoke. She was fascinated by Willie's hands and the long, fine fingers he kept spotlessly clean because of the bakery. She loved the way he smoked, seeming to inhale a sense of himself with each fresh drag of tobacco.

They were only perching in Sheffield, marking time in rented rooms. They knew they'd be back in Chesterfield before long and so did not try to put down roots. The best thing about the city was its theatres: Variety shows at the Empire, and plays and musicals at the Lyceum, where they saw *The Maid of the Mountains* twice in one week so that Willie could learn the best songs. Years before, he had copied his favourite lyrics into an exercise book; he was too old for that lark now, but he still wanted to sing all the tunes. They were frequent visitors to the Star Picture House on Ecclesall Road where they saw 'the Kid' lean against street corners in his oversize cap and trews and held their breath as Pearl White managed to free herself from the railway line as an express train hurtled towards her.

Sometimes, at a loose end on a weekday afternoon – my grandma knew no one else in Sheffield and couldn't teach with the marriage bar resurrected – Annie took herself back to the Picture House and slipped into a seat in the semi-darkness. All around her, women like Annie were sitting in their own private worlds being charmed by Ramon Navarro or appalled when Lillian Gish was cast into the snow, a fallen woman. Annie saw *The Kid* a second time and marvelled at Charlie Chaplin and Jackie Coogan all over again, but her heart snagged on the mother's note: 'please love and care for this orphan child.'

Coming out of the cinema with Willie one evening, Annie had her arm through his and was thinking how good it was to have him home, and to be a married woman out with her husband. They paused at the window of a department store and joined another young couple peering at the display. Absorbed by the china tea sets, Annie followed the curve of the glass round the corner of the street until tea sets gave way to jardinières, but when she turned to ask Willie his opinion, he'd disappeared. He was already halfway up the street, looking for all the world as if he were out by himself, with no one else's views to consider. Feeling awkward and a bit of a fool at being left stranded like that, and in front of the other couple, Annie fussed with her coat and hurried to catch him up. She was perfectly capable of walking by herself or of running after Willie, but that was not how things were done. Not back then. It was one of those incidents that should have been entirely insignificant but which, in time, came to suggest something else.

There were jobs for each of them on their return to Chesterfield. Willie went back to Jim's bakery and Annie – the young woman who was never meant to stand behind a counter – was to manage Jim's cake shop on Whittington Moor, an arrangement which would finally mean a proper beginning to their married life: their jobs came with the house above the shop. Jim no longer lived on the doorstep, but in a seventeenth-century house, Hill House (Hell House, he called it affectionately), a mile or so away.

Living above the cake shop meant a downstairs arrangement of shop front, living room and scullery, plus two bedrooms upstairs. The front bedroom was designated for Willie's small but growing collection of budgerigars and canaries, their acid yellows, sky blues and apple greens contributing a vibrant note to the street. People out for a Sunday stroll were sometimes startled by the unexpected cadences of birdsong. The birds competed with the gramophone: Willie, his caged birds and Ivor Novello serenading sunny afternoons.

The front room was the birds' domain because my grandma preferred the back bedroom, which was quieter and a greater distance from the road, with its six-day rattle and hum of trolley buses, wagons, carts and drays heading uphill to the Whittington collieries, trundling west towards the Sheepbridge Works, or to and from Chesterfield town centre; and the brewery men endlessly rolling barrels of beer into the Sir Colin Campbell and the Travellers' Rest across the road. And, perhaps, by occupying the smaller bedroom, Annie was less likely to think of the child who might have slept there.

Willie liked his own colourful plumage – a gold tiepin with a ruby eye for best-dress occasions, the fob on his gold watch chain polished to a sheen his old colour sergeant would be proud of. He had a gold tooth, too, visible when he threw back his head for the final bars of 'The Desert Song'. For Christmas and birthdays, Annie contributed to the gleam, dipping into her savings to buy Willie cufflinks with their own ruby specks and a gold case that gave a satisfying retort when tamped with a cigarette: Woodbines on regular workdays, Black Cats when Willie was feeling flush. They made a dapper pair in the 1920s: Annie in tam-o'-shanter secured with a large globe pin, Willie sporting a ribboned boater.

J. W. Thompson's 'Hygienic' Bakery was now well established. Everything at the bakehouse was spotless – the large pine table at which the two brothers worked was scrubbed until the grain showed almost as white as their uniforms. Willie was as meticulous with his bakery whites as with his Sunday clothes and neatly manicured hands. The cleanliness of the operation was one of the boasts of the business.

Now that he was back at the table where he'd learned his trade, Willie was able to reprise old favourites and secure further medals

with competition loaves and cakes with elaborate icing. Most days, however, required the usual teatime fare: Lady cake, raspberry buns, Bakewell tarts, Vienna bread, slab cake, gridle scones, Grantham gingerbread, and so on, a surprisingly large repertoire for a small provincial firm. They baked rock cakes by the thousand and everything from penny tarts and a 'cheap sandwich' (a sponge cake with one layer of jam), to cherry Genoas priced two shillings. Jim was extremely pleased with the way things were going. There was talk of Willie becoming a partner in the firm.

Willie noted all ingredients in his bakery book, a professional tool, a list of proportions only. There are no instructions to encourage the uninitiated to beat or knead or sieve. Sometimes, in the evenings, Wilie baked at home and taught Annie some of the tricks of his trade, such as how to make vanilla slices with melting flaky pastry and perfect crème anglaise, and how to bake the

COCONUT PYRAMIDS

Half pound of loaf sugar
Half a gill of water
Two ounces of desiccated coconut
One ounce of butter
Half teaspoonful of cream of tartar

Dissolve the sugar slowly in the water, stirring over a low gas. Boil till it forms a fairly hard ball when dropped in water (time 20 to 25 minutes). Stir in the butter (with the pan off the gas), then add the coconut and cream of tartar. Beat and mix well, and place teaspoonfuls of the mixture on small heaps of greaseproof paper.

– From 'All Things Nice: An ABC of Sweet-Making', *Woman's Weekly, Supplement of Sweet-Making*, 1920s

lightest savoury tarts. Occasionally, he made sweets, borrowing recipes for coconut pyramids and marzipan fruits from Annie's *Woman's Weekly*. Anyone calling at the end of a summer's day might find them relaxing in the yard, sweet smells emerging from the house, Willie changed out of his bakery whites and smoking a cigarette, Annie relaxing in a wicker chair, her legs stretched before her in stockings as pale as the water icing Willie drizzled across his fairy cakes.

10

Modern Times

In 1922, Eva turned twenty-one. Though not considered pretty, she had expressive brown eyes, thick dark hair twisted into the nape of her neck and lips always twitching to smile. There was a natural mischievousness about her. Even some solemn occasions would find Eva suppressing laughter. One of her straight looks could puncture any trumped-up solemnity or inflated ego.

From her earliest days behind the counter, Eva wrote all the orders for the shop, both for customers and their own deliveries. For all Betsy's ready reckoning and organisational skills, it was impossible to run a shop without signatures. Dick still signed all legal documents but Eva working with Betsy simplified matters. In her hands, writing was much more than a necessary skill. Grocery lists acquired attractive embellishments; Eva's capital letters were a calligrapher's delight. She made great efforts with notices for the windows – Lux Soap 3d, Colman's Starch 1d – and wrote Betsy's signature on a slip of card in case Betsy needed to sign for something while Eva was away from the shop. My great-grandma kept the template in her apron pocket (and, later, her spectacle case). The card was renewed from time to time, but the writing never changed: always the same distinctive flourishes.

Eva introduced a system of cash books for customers wanting groceries on tick, each purchase recorded in a small red book and totted up at the end of the week. Her command of mental arithmetic enabled her to calculate running totals and grant or withhold credit without keeping customers waiting, not that many would have been embarrassed by the wait. When the sum owing became risky and the ledger overfull, neighbours attempted different tactics. Requests that strained credulity mostly came from children sent in their mother's stead. Mrs Vine was a particular caution, always contriving to get that bit extra, stretching ingenuity to barefaced cheek.

They made a good team, Betsy and Eva. With Eva doing all the writing connected with the shop, Betsy probably did more fetching and carrying, so there was no sense of her being in charge. If Mrs Parks wanted soap, suet, tea and yeast, Eva started jotting down the quantities while Betsy put the items on to the counter. By the time she reached for the tea, Eva would be weighing out the yeast. If Mrs Tissington came in with an order to be collected later – Lyon's Jam Roll, Jacob's Rich Tea, 3 Gunstons' loaves, 6lbs potatoes, a bottle of lemonade, 2lbs Bourneville Cocoa, 1 packet Sankey's Soda – Betsy was as likely as Eva to stand on the steps to reach for the lemonade, or dig deep into the sack of potatoes. She was in her fifties when Eva started working with her, but even well into her seventies had no desire to reduce her working hours. Betsy liked hard work and preferred vigorous tasks, like scrubbing floors and fettling corners, to shining brasses, washing china or the other fiddly jobs Eva enjoyed.

Whatever else was happening, great or small, they were always behind their counter. Neighbours moved into and out of the area; the corner shop stayed put, and Betsy and Eva with it. Their constant presence made them available to women who were otherwise alone all day or to children whose mothers had no time to chat. It was easy to tell Eva, when you came for a licorice stick, that you were swinging on the rope by the canal, or were wearing a new hair ribbon that day. My great-grandma and great-aunt were as permanent a fixture as the shop.

Women came to Betsy for advice, but if someone was in a panic or needed practical help, they turned to Eva. Young men joked

with her when they called for their bootlaces and cigs. Her easy manner meant Eva was well liked; there was a fearlessness about her too. She was proficient at lighting fires, and reckless with it (or so it seemed to me during my childhood). She could force a blaze out of any fire with the aid of a taut sheet of newspaper and would cast quantities of sugar on to recalcitrant coals with a casualness shared only by those who had lived at a grocery store and knew there was more sugar in the jar. Close neighbours presented her with lids they struggled to unfasten. This slim, small woman had surprising strength.

It was probably this combination of strength and unflappability that gave Eva her distinctive role. The same young men who showed off and joked with Eva, came to her with splinters in their fingers and even allowed themselves to wince while she dug at the blighter with a sewing needle. Most surprisingly, she pulled teeth. Few at Wheeldon Mill could afford the dentist.

My great-aunt, thin as a sprite and barely five foot nought, extracted teeth from colliers who could handle several hundred-weights of coal. She pulled teeth for women and children too, but that was less remarkable than the burly men who needed her help. Thick-set miners who had just sloughed off their pit-muck came moaning to the house, 'Oh Eva, can you help me?' And she'd tackle the offending tooth with her fingers or else tie a piece of string around it and the nearest door handle, then slam the door.

It was impossible to look your best standing behind a counter in an apron dusty with grain and flour, and your hair coming loose from its pins (Eva's hair was constantly shedding pins; there was always a handful behind the counter and two or three on the mantelpiece) but, on gala days, Eva swapped her pinny for a dress and jewellery – a brooch for formal moods, her long French beads (a homecoming gift from George on his safe return from the Front) if she felt like cutting a dash.

Galas were occasions to hear the colliery band, guess the number of split peas in a jar and cheer on an egg-and-spoon race – once won by Eva aged ten. On gala days, she picked her way across the hummocky grass of the Brimington field, selling sweets from a tray suspended from her shoulders. Walking daintily so as not to soil her shoes, Eva looked as stately as an usherette, but could move just as fast as any youngster tempted to grab a choco-late bar and run. While she walked, her fine French beads clacked against the edge of her tray, shiny clusters of blackcurrant and purple, and a crimson as rich as Cherry Lips. Plenty of people stopped to chat; everyone in the neighbourhood knew Eva.

It wasn't long before young men came calling, joshingly at first, although one or two were brave enough to ask her out. Eva agreed to meet one young hopeful 'neath the clock' on Whittington Moor, the usual rendezvous for courting couples. Come eight o'clock, however, it was not Eva who walked towards him, but Dick. He and Betsy were firmly of the view that this puppy-faced swain was nowhere near good enough for their daughter. Eva was persuaded to stay at home while Dick walked down to the Moor and advised her admirer to clear off.

My great-aunt was merely curious about this suitor; he was not someone she was particularly sweet on, so it was not too hard for Eva to do as she was told. Dick and Betsy knew more about the world than she did; far better stay at home with Mam and Dad and play the piano beside a crackling fire than traipse off with some gangly lad.

*

Costumes of Distinction
Showing the New Autumn Effects and Textures

Distinctive Velour
Costume with new Fur
Trimmed Collar, lined
self Merve, banded shape
fastened by 3 self buttons

PRICE **£4 18 6**

It is not
generally
known that :

The cane seats of chairs
that are limp and baggy
but not broken can be
tightened by being
washed in very hot
water and soda and
then allowed to dry in a
strong current of air.
If the chairs are much
soiled this treatment
should be repeated.

Cheviot Velour Costume,
Cotton floral lining, Fur
Collar, banded shape,
fastened 1 button.

PRICE **£4 10 0**

The Gentlemen's and Boys'
Outfitting Dept. is always
full of interest, and replete
with large selections.

Excellent Quality Navy
Gab Costume, braided and
banded style, lined grey
silk.

PRICE **£5 15 6**

SWALLOW'S OF CHESTERFIELD

The gap between Annie and Eva narrowed over the years, the differences in their ages becoming irrelevant once they were both adults and had interests in common. They each liked clothes and dressed as well as their purses allowed. Both sisters sewed, but Annie's dressmaking skills were an additional boon. My grandma had taken a course in tailoring towards the end of the war and learned to make full dress suits for men as well as women; what Annie couldn't do with a needle was not worth knowing. She and Eva looked out sewing patterns in the *Daily Express*, 'How to Make Your Summer Frock for 3/6,' and discussed the latest shades: apricot fizz, tango, mole or almond green?

In some working-class districts, shopkeepers' daughters (having more money than most of their neighbours) set the fashion. I doubt that Annie and Eva's clothes were ever the latest word, but

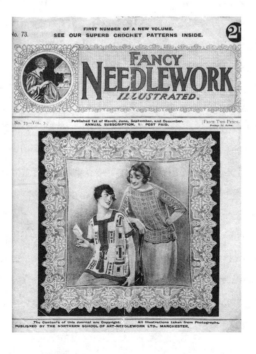

they liked to keep abreast of the times. They enjoyed shopping together, visiting Chesterfield's town-centre emporiums, Swallow's and Turner's, and Eyres' brand-new arcade. Occasionally, they duplicated their purchases or chose complementary styles – the same handbags but with different clasps; necklaces in mother-of-pearl (Annie's, pale discs; Eva's, leaves). They each bought a brooch saying 'Carolina Moon', slivers of lemon enamel, celebrating the popular tune; and, copying a fashion in Bohemian circles (not that Bohemia reached Chesterfield), drew attention to their slim arms by each wearing a slave bangle above their right elbow.

When Annie moved to the cake shop, the sisters saw each other twice a week. Wheeldon Mill and Whittington Moor were half an hour's walk apart. On Tuesday evenings, Eva visited Annie; on Sundays, Annie returned the visit. For the next thirty years, until her parents died, my grandma spent her Sundays with the family and, for a few years, at least, Willie generally appeared at teatime.

Typically, Annie arrived mid-morning to find Dick in the yard, cleaning and repairing his weekday boots, Eva preparing vegetables for dinner or mixing a sponge cake for tea (this was another division of labour: Betsy baked bread and pastry; Eva, cakes); and her mother grating nutmeg over a milk pudding, Dick's staple request. The smell of dubbing caught up with that of stewing meat and nutmeg; a hint of Brasso in the background suggested an earlier chore.

Dinner over, Betsy settled to patch Dick's heavy work trousers – by the 1920s, my great-grandfather was tending industrial engines at Sheepbridge; he was still in charge of several men, and still a collar-and-tie man. While Betsy sewed, Annie and Eva rolled small sheets of white waxy paper into the cones in which the shop sold sweets, and selected advertisements to stand in the sunny window. Betsy favoured sheaves of corn: in her estimation, drawings of golden wheat fields made the most attractive display. Jobs like these, or stripping newspaper into squares for the you-know-what (making sure to avoid the King and Queen), passed quickly while the sisters talked.

They were riveted by the trial of Annie's namesake, Mrs Thompson, and followed each development as closely as those who queued round the block at the Old Bailey. Had she plotted with her young lover to kill her husband, or was his murder the terrible shock she maintained? Throughout the trial, and for some time after she and Frederick Bywaters were sentenced to hang, people commented on the fact that she and my grandma shared a name. Men, in particular, liked to speak of that 'temptress' and jest: 'No connection with *the* Mrs Thompson, I trust?' though Annie couldn't see that there was anything amusing in Edith Thompson's plight. Jim's wife, poor Edith, shared a first name as well as a surname: even more remarks were made to her, though no one could have dreamt any resemblance between the two women.

If ever a daughter was like her mam, it was Annie, and although that was evident in all kinds of ways, an obvious one was her enjoyment of the cake shop. Annie liked being her own boss and took pride in her appearance: you had to look presentable if you were handling bread and cakes. Annie always wore a dress and was never without a string of beads (even when doing the housework). She took care arranging the cakes on doilies to make an attractive display, but, most of all, she enjoyed dealing with customers, especially those who stopped for a cup of tea.

The decision to serve tea and cakes was Annie's. Tea was served on a lace cloth whose scalloped edges dipped and rose around a small table tucked behind a painted screen shielding the tea drinker from view. Women who shopped on Whittington Moor might pause for a cup of tea and a walnut slice after visiting the milliner's or haberdashery, but Annie's regular tea drinkers were commercial travellers. Men who spent their days tramping from one store to the next were grateful for the chance to take the weight off their feet. Some told Annie about the wife and kiddies; the Singer salesman, hearing of her liking for sewing, showed her how, with a pair of sharp scissors and a confident hand, six yards of voile could be transformed into a Paris Mode.

Though things were going well at the cake shop, they were not looking good at Wheeldon Mill. One foggy night, walking back from work along what was colloquially known as the Coal Road, my great-grandfather was hit by a car. Few cars travelled through that neighbourhood in the evening; it was Dick's great misfortune to meet one, although the accident was not his fault. Someone at

the scene was dispatched to run up to the shop and tell Betsy. At the sight of this unknown man standing in the doorway, struggling over his words, my great-grandma's thoughts went straight back to 1901 and the grey-faced lad who'd stood before her, describing Dick's head injury. And, even with all the terror she had felt on that occasion, Dick had been a much younger man then, and Betsy a much younger woman.

The car crushed my great-grandfather's right foot. He was hospitalised for months and underwent at least two operations. The damage to Dick's ankle was so severe, his right leg had to be shortened. It was weeks before he was allowed out of bed and, when he was, he had to learn how to walk all over again, and while wearing a heavy built-up shoe. Left foot forward, swing the right leg round. Dot one and carry one, he said.

Dick was like a child discovering his mobility, inching his way around the table, and from the table to the piano to his chair. A long time passed before he felt able to tackle stairs. As soon as he could, the back bedroom was made over for his use and Eva went in with Betsy. He could not bear to have anything or anyone pressing on his injured foot. Neighbours said it was just as well the accident had happened now, and not years earlier, which was true in many respects – Dick was in his sixties and nearing retirement – but of insufficient comfort. Dick would never be fit enough to work again and would limp for the rest of his life. The future appeared to be shrinking.

The timing of my great-grandfather's accident was particularly unfortunate, sandwiched as it was between the miners' lock-outs of 1921 and '26, two of several stoppages over pay and working conditions during that decade. With each dispute, miners' wives held their breath and wondered how long their men could hold out – three weeks in 1920; three months and more in 1921; six months in 1926, following on from the May General Strike.

As in previous strikes, lean times for the neighbourhood meant lean times for the corner shop. By 1926, Betsy felt she had managed a whole calendar of stoppages but, this time round, Dick's ill health made the family's own circumstances more precarious. The money paid from sick clubs did not stretch that far, and there were now three adults to feed. At least with Eva working alongside Betsy, they could assess the situation together. Now, more than ever, they needed to hold their nerve.

For some, the General Strike was a nine-day wonder, the sight of volunteers driving buses and carts recalling the Great War and a sense of pitching in, but for miners and their employers the strike reopened bitter arguments and old wounds.

'Not a penny off the pay, not a second on the day,' colliers insisted. Associated trades were quickly affected. Within a week, the Staveley Coal & Iron Company shut down its Devonshire Works, putting nearly 1,300 men on to the streets. The closure of the Sheepbridge Works added another 1,000 to their number. By

---

'Big strong men cried like babies for sheer want and frustration. The women didn't cry. They suffered in silence. But what silence! It cut through a man sometimes.'

– Veteran Collier, Coalville, Leicestershire, quoted in Gerard Noel's *The Great Lock-Out of 1926*

the end of the first month, some 5,000 miners had sought relief from Chesterfield's Board of Guardians. In response to a delegation protesting at its slow distribution, the Mayor went to the Guardians' offices to see things for himself and found some three to four hundred men standing in line. Most had been waiting a long time; some had fainted. The strike still had six months to run.

Mildred Taylor and Nora Parks had seen it all before. Their whole married lives had been punctuated with stoppages, albeit shorter ones than this. Now, they watched the strike from the sidelines and from the perspective of their sons. Men whose earliest experiences of a strike had been as a lark and a skive – a welcome glimpse of life without school or work – were now married with young children. By 1926, Mildred's son, Albie, a pit man still, though no longer a daredevil pony driver, had six and another on the way. His wife looked heavier and more exhausted by the month. 'I might as well sit on these, Mrs Nash,' Ellen said, coming into the shop and sinking on to the sack of potatoes. 'I don't know how I'm supposed to buy them.' She was asking the same questions her mother-in-law had asked years before.

According to Mildred, who liked to make her opinions known, her daughter-in-law was a good lass, though a lass was something Ellen had barely had the chance to be. She'd been her mother's unpaid housemaid, nursemaid, and the rest, well before she reached fourteen. Now she had children at two-year intervals (and sometimes with a shorter gap), the fruits of a marriage made in the immediacy of wartime and endured ever since, her husband expecting his due in all things and food on the table the minute he came home. 'I mustn't stop, Mrs Nash. I'll have Albie doing the great-I-am.'

Some women grumbled about men getting under their feet,

the smaller complaint going some way to alleviate the tension of how to make two ha'p'orth of nothing feed a growing family, other neighbours complained that their husbands were down by the canal, a favoured spot for gambling. Crouched over a game of pitch-and-toss in the half-light cast by the bridge, with someone posted up above as lookout, it was easy to lose a hour or two, and their remaining coins. Betting in all forms was a constant source of anxiety. 'He's gone to put a bet on,' – conveyed to Betsy in a hushed voice by many a woman at the end of her tether. With money scarcer than usual, parcels went in and out of pawn so fast they were hardly worth unwrapping. Mrs Driver joked that, if she'd nothing left to pawn, would Johnny Dodd pay out on brown paper and string?

Miners' children rode Chesterfield's buses for free; collections were made to alleviate hunger. Men swapped home-grown vegetables for shoes soled or a haircut, women exchanged half a cup of sugar for half of flour. The backdrop to these long days and even longer months was the weather. The summer of 1926 was glorious, heat stretching into the autumn. Boys released from dank service underground swam in the River Rother; neighbours stood on their back steps, drawn to the door by nothing more than the balmy evening.

Neither strikers nor the authorities wished to be regarded as weak. When an angry group of colliers smashed the windscreen of a lorry carrying slack, the Mayor sentenced the ringleader to two months' hard labour. Two witnesses, fellow strikers called in the man's defence, found themselves marched out of the courtroom and straight back in again, and this time, placed in the dock. Admitting their own presence in the mob earned them a month's hard labour apiece.

Outbreaks of violence continued throughout the summer and grew even uglier when, following an approach by the Nottingham-shire and Derbyshire pit owners, some colliers went back to work. By the end of August, most Derbyshire mines had re-opened; extra police were drafted in to protect the returning men. During one court session the following month, magistrates dealt with forty-four charges of strike-related incidents at one sitting.

Miners and colliery owners finally came to terms in November. ('It was not a fair deal,' was one miner's understated response.) The Staveley Coal & Iron Company began preparations to re-open, though, in a pattern repeated elsewhere, not all workers were immediately re-employed. Some men never returned to the pit; some miners were completely broken by the strike. At least one Chesterfield collier committed suicide.

In some mining districts, even wholly unrelated trades collapsed under the weight of industrial action. Small shops went under, dragged down by customers unable to buy goods or repay old debts. Thankfully, the corner shop survived. My great-aunt always found the sound of boots striking cobbles reassuring. Now, I understand why.

The 1926 strike may have helped my great-grandfather reach a decision. The accident that looked like a catastrophe was actually his salvation. Some eighty yards up the hill from the corner shop stood the Wheeldon Mill Plantation, the small copse you could see from the house. This four-acre wood was private property and therefore inaccessible, but Dick had walked past the entrance so many times, he could describe the trees nearest the road with his eyes closed. Oak, ash, elm, silver birch. He had seen them grow in stature, knew the spreading green of their branches and the

beauty of their winter silhouettes. For almost twenty years, he'd heard birds sing in trees he could see but was forbidden to sit beneath, and watched the woodland floor flush mauve with violets whose scent he could never get close enough to catch. If Dick rented the wood, he could raise chickens and sell their eggs. He could also sit beneath those sheltering leaves.

My great-grandfather had spent his earliest days outdoors; he did not have to think for very long. He approached the owner, a retired farmer, and a deal was struck. Keeping poultry satisfied a practical need; the wood took Dick back to his beginnings.

By the 1920s, a cat's cradle of relationships criss-crossed Station Road and its adjacent terraces. Married siblings were raising families a short stride from one another; cousins' games stretched across their neighbours' doorways; an aunt was close in age to her niece; a brother and his wife were bringing up his sister's sons. Grandmas took in grandchildren; older children came and went. Courtships flourished in doorways, setting up new allegiances between families. Unlike earlier generations at Wheeldon Mill, these families were mostly Derbyshire-born, one man's nickname 'Sheff' (as in Sheffield), branding him forever as a foreigner, an outsider. But not everyone lived hugger-mugger with their neighbours. Some kept themselves apart, called for their groceries, said 'Good Day', and went away again; others brought the smallest details of their lives into the shop.

Maud Cartwright and her family, newcomers before the First World War, were now firmly ensconced in the neighbourhood, and Maud a regular back-door visitor as well as a customer via the front. Though now in her fifties, she had a late-born daughter at home. Ten-year-old Pearl was her darling. Everything Pearl said and did was worth repeating; her clothes were a matter of particular pride. Maud took great care with her own appearance too. Unlike those neighbours who shopped in their pinny, with a coat pulled over the top, this small, trim woman ventured out in nothing less than a skirt and blouse. Maud's appearance was secondary to Pearl's, however. With her older children now in work or off her hands, Maud had time to lavish attention on her youngest daughter, and long tales of Pearl's achievements to relate to Betsy.

Back-door visiting was now such a strong part of life at the corner shop that a hard chair was permanently positioned on the threshold. Activity in the house was frequently overlaid with neighbours' talk, whether brief interruptions for a forgotten packet of rice or tin of peas, or a tale that was long in the telling. Even the voices of those who remained standing carried into the room. Evenings and Sunday afternoons were especially liable to interruption; Sunday was also the day when friends and relatives visited, sometimes all arriving at once.

Zoe Graham, a mother now, living higher up the hill, brought little Georgie to see them, and Eva's friend Carrie walked five-year-old Harold round from Newbridge Lane. Ethel visited too, catching two buses from the other side of the town to show off young Rolly, the spitting image of his dad and just as much of a handful, she said. When Ethel walked through the door, it was as if she had never left. She'd throw off her coat and start clearing the table or tackling the pots straightaway. 'Oh, you make me feel starved,' Betsy would say, shivering at the sight of Ethel's sleeveless cotton frock. This less upholstered generation only had to stand in front of my great-grandma to raise her goose bumps.

Cousin Charlie visited with his doting wife Edie and their young children. Though fleshed out since his wartime convalescence, Charlie was an invalid nonetheless, his rasping breath the legacy of the gas attack that finally brought him home; Edie was constantly alert to any alteration in his breathing while trying to pass it off as of no consequence.

There was a regular parade of Betsy's sisters, including stately Auntie Annie and Betsy's youngest sister, Liza, with her dry turn of phrase and even drier tales of her married daughters, Emily and Annie, who might be sisters but were as alike as chalk and cheese. Dick's family called too: Uncle Dick was a great favourite among them. His nephew Will, an army regular, had fought in the Boer War and could still spin suspenseful tales of Ladysmith and the Relief of Mafeking. Annie could remember Union Jacks fluttering in people's doorways when she was the tiniest thing, and was fascinated by Will's stories. His son Will (a third generation William), had worked with Dick at the brickyard – 'and we're still speaking,' he liked to say. Young Will broke the family tradition by calling his son Richard, after my great-grandfather.

Once or twice a year, there were other visitors: Eva's sisters,

Kitty and Margaret. After some twelve years at the Industrial School, they were delivered into the world of work. I don't know if they started out as domestic servants or if they escaped that particular fate altogether, but by the 1920s they were Manchester mill workers, sharing digs and working at full pelt to satisfy their ramping looms. Neither sister married; after the childhood they'd endured, Kitty and Margaret were pleased to look after one another.

Another welcome visitor was George. George came through the war unscathed and with pips on his shoulders: his wounds were of a different order. Within a few months of hearing of Annie's marriage, he found a bride – I'm sure there were plenty of takers for a charming young man and a brave one at that, who was making the best of his disappointment. Though he no longer lived in Derbyshire, George visited Betsy and Dick when he could – and still called them Mam and Dad – and sometimes brought his wife and small daughter. Mostly, though, he came alone, a Sunday-afternoon caller, catching the train and alighting at Wheeldon Mill. Sunday was the only day available to a busy school teacher, but it was also the day Annie was there.

Seeing George now was comforting and chafing, a reminder of something whose value Annie had always understood but could not help rejecting in favour of Willie. In idle moments, walking up to the Mill on the Sundays she knew George would be visiting, she contemplated life as a teacher's wife: their quiet conversations of an evening and the poetry they'd read together. Even as Annie laughed at herself for inventing such scenes, she wondered which verses of Longfellow she'd choose. George would have liked nothing better than to return from the war to a home that was ready and waiting, whereas Willie barely seemed to notice the bedroom suite and the silver you could see your face in. Annie was beginning to wonder if she'd made a mistake in providing Willie with a ready-made home. Not knowing the striving that went into its preparation, he seemed unable to appreciate its worth.

George wrote to Annie, care of the shop; she could reply via his school. Even in the late 1920s, George was still paying court, scribbling a pencilled note on paper torn from an exercise book; the pencil both less permanent and more secretive than ink, his casual scrawl belying thoughts he'd obviously shaped beforehand. His affectionate words accompanied a medal won for some amateur sport, a game of tennis or cricket (George was made for cricket whites).

'My dear,' his note begins, 'Will you accept this?' George was sending a love token, a knight wooing his distant lady. His friendly greeting is full of warmth, but, more telling to me, is the way his letter closes: 'Ecrit, si'il vous plait.' Equally telling, is the fact my grandma kept it.

Annie always said how hard Willie worked at the bakery. This was not something he minded. He was happy to start early and work late into the night if this helped further establish the business. But though Willie was working hard, he was not always well. The malaria he developed in Palestine kept on at him and frequently returned to rough him up. Each time it struck was like a bad dose of 'flu; it took Willie days to recover. He thought a tonic might be the answer: the newspapers were full of advertisements and tales of their beneficial effects.

'A spot of Phosferine always puts us right,' said Mr Frank Gray, who had driven 3,000 miles across Africa. There was Gray and his fellow driver, in pith helmets, sitting on the bonnet of their car.

'When we were in bad patches in Africa, and were worn out and had lost heart and faith, we said: "Let's have another spot of Phosferine. It always put us right…"' Phosferine: the Greatest of all Tonics for Influenza, Debility, Weak digestion, Lassitude, Neuritis, Brain Fag, Anaemia – the list went on and on – but there, near the bottom, was the word Willie was looking for: Malaria.

You could buy a bottle of Phosferine from the chemist, but Willie was used to combining ingredients and so set about preparing his own mixture. Somewhere among the recipes for drop scones and Victoria sponges is the following: 18 grains of quinine; 3 drops of tincture of steel, 1oz phosphoric acid. Take 10 drops in water 3 times a day.

Around this time, the bakehouse moved to larger premises on Whittington Hill, though the cake shop remained where it was. Willie now had a half-hour walk to work, but he used the journey to plan how things would be when he had a share in the firm. One of the things Willie most wanted was a car. He had never shaken off the excitement of seeing his first car as an impressionable lad: he had wanted to drive for as long as he could remember. His enthusiasm had reached fever pitch in America and showed no signs of abating on his return. Though Willie spent far more time baking than making deliveries in his early years at the bakehouse, he'd defined himself as a driver on his marriage certificate. Back in 1916, the word sounded more up-to-the-minute than his regular, old-fashioned trade. Perhaps Willie also hoped that by describing himself thus, he'd have a better chance of keeping out of the trenches. (And if so, he was correct.)

Willie had fallen in love with a world in which you could make something of yourself and gain respect, a world in which everyone had a shining chance and it was fine to want things, unlike during his parsimonious upbringing in which everyone had to be stripped down to size. He had not forgotten his father chopping up Jim's new shoes. The feeling Willie had on the day Jim hired the tram was the kind of feeling he wanted: not a seat on the district council, he'd no political ambition, but a simple pride in a job well done and hats raised in greeting, and a good suit, a nice linen suit with fine detailing, and an elegant pin to fix his tie, and Annie in a silk hat and gloves. And a car, of course. Not forgetting the car.

There were now many more cars on the road. Jim drove a car, as did their brother Bernard, courtesy of a generous father-in-law. Cars were coming within reach of a much wider audience, albeit predominantly middle- and upper-class. Chesterfield's first Ford saleroom, opened in 1923, had garaging for 500 vehicles, plus a repair depot and a shop selling spares.

Mostly, Willie favoured a saloon car: a Ford, an Austin, a Riley, a Singer or perhaps a Morris Cowley. 'You Can Buy a Morris on Terms to Suit Yourself: a two-seater Morris Cowley could be yours for £40 12s 8d, plus 12 monthly payments of £10 17s 4d.' (A baker's average weekly wage, around this time, was £3 3s 5d.) Occasionally, Willie fancied something racy with a dickey seat. But a car, at any rate. Jotted beneath the ingredients for almond paste and almond tarts in his bakery book is a different kind of list altogether: 'Ford Com Wires: Green Blue Red Black'. Each time Willie scrubbed the bakery table, his dream came that little bit closer.

11

Motherless Mites

MY GRANDMA WAS BEGINNING TO REALISE THAT FIERCE DESIRE was not enough. No matter how much she and Willie longed for a baby, longing was not making it happen. They were past reassuring one another that all would come right and they would have their own child. Annie was in her late thirties now, and any desire between them long since strained when, month after month (year after year), there was no baby.

In recent years, the law had changed. The 1926 Adoption of Children Act enabled you to adopt a child with the sanction of the courts. And a baby too. Annie very much wanted a baby; she still ached to hold that warm bundle. An orphanage child was not the same as a baby you could bring up from scratch. And the Adoption Act meant the baby was yours for keeps. There was no chance of the mother reclaiming her child, as had sometimes happened in the past. There was talk in the press of 'Bought Babies' and the dangers of taking on someone else's child, but the latter held no fears for Annie. How could it? Her whole family was founded on doing that very thing.

Willie was every bit as keen as she was; he was pleased as punch at the thought of adopting a child. Annie's doctor told them about the National Children Adoption Association, based in London and highly regarded; the NCAA had been established to help people just like them. Its annual report doubled as a promotional booklet with photographs on glossy paper and details of the Association and its hostel, Tower Cressy, where young women training to be nursery nurses helped to look after the babies. They were nearly all babies in the NCAA's care; every single bed was occupied and every vacancy filled straightaway.

You only had to open the report to see the whole thing was top drawer. Chairman: Her Grace the Dowager Duchess of Abercorn; Vice-Chairman: The Lady Violet Brassey; President: HRH The Princess Alice, Countess of Athlone; Lady-this; Viscountess-that – the list of Vice-Presidents was almost overwhelming, and included Right Reverends and prime ministers' wives: Mrs Stanley Baldwin and Dame Margaret Lloyd George. Even when you turned the page, the list of Honourables kept coming and, some pages later, there was HM the Queen, dripping fox fur, photographed with the NCAA's founder, and Princess Alice, who was wearing the most extraordinary hat.

The Foreword emanated sunshine: 'Peace and happiness are the order of the day in the beautiful nursery and new sun balconies… It must be jolly to be a babe at Tower Cressy.' The hostel's nurses wore the whitest of white uniforms to hold the white-draped babies. Chubby toddlers played in a nursery whose cots had pristine canopies, lace-edged sheets and bows. There was a picture of the toddlers' bathroom – lucky toddlers – Annie and Willie made do with a zinc tub that hung from a nail when not in use. It was a real-life sunny story.

Grateful mothers had written to the NCAA expressing thanks: 'I am very glad that Baby has been adopted by such nice people. I feel sure she will have a good home. I am thankful to you for all you have done for me.' New adopters sent reassuring messages: 'Will you write and tell Michael's mother that I will do my very best for him and she need never worry about him at all...' Some adopters brought their children back to the hostel to see its Christmas tree, or returned to adopt more children. You could choose a child from a photograph or go to the hostel yourself. This one small biscuit-coloured booklet was a rich gift.

Annie's doctor assisted with their application. There was a form to fill in, photographs to send, and two referees to provide: Dr Duthie, of course, and, possibly, Jim, though not in a brotherly role, but as businessman and respected councillor. The procedure required a local associate or health visitor to assess prospective parents if they lived too far away to be interviewed by the NCAA Case Committee or one of its Branch Committees.

I picture the health visitor coming into the living room behind the cake shop and asking questions over tea and one of Willie's cakes, her eyes flickering all the while over Annie's best cloth and the shine on her silver teapot. Her glance takes in a home-made picture glinting with sweet-paper foils and observes how the nap of the velvet chaise longue has been brushed so it all stands the same way.

Before she comes to the house, Annie takes all the basins from the scullery shelves and washes them in the hottest soapy water she can stand, even the glassware on the topmost shelf, lest their visitor glance skywards. Though her stomach clenches in knots that would challenge Houdini, Annie hears herself sounding persuasively calm as she speaks of her days teaching little ones,

[L]ately in the Press adopted babies have been described as Bought Babies. This is an entirely wrong and misleading expression, so far as the work of this Association is concerned...

The transaction is in fact based on sentiment, pure and simple, in which the men play a conspicuous part. I myself have watched unseen in a private room at Tower Cressy a great, strong rancher crooning over a child whom he wished to make his own, and in the big ward I have seen men go from cot to cot yearning over the little ones, torn in their choice between this child's fine physique, that child's blue eyes, this one's smile, or that other one's fearless friendliness. And when after much discussion between husband and wife, the final decision is made, it would be difficult to say which of the two is the more happy and triumphant as they bear the child off to fill the void in their lives. On one occasion when I was present, the new parents were already settled in the taxi when the wife discovered that she had forgotten her satchel. Said the husband: 'Why bother about that when we've got our greatest treasure safe and sound?

– Beatrice Harraden, Foreword, *The National Children Adoption Association Report 1927–28*, read by Annie and Willie

and Willie, though equally nervous, does not offer to smoke until both upstairs rooms have been inspected, his cake complimented and small talk exchanged on how to make the perfect sponge.

It was one short visit and, at the end of it all – they were told to be patient; enquiries generally took a few weeks – they and their home were approved and, I assume, pronounced satisfactory: those pithy syllables that recur again and again, and are as mean as they are inadequate, but which, in this one extremely special instance, held out enormous promise for Annie and Willie.

The National Children Adoption Association (NCAA) was one of the two key adoption agencies of the day. Unlike the children's charities, Dr Barnardo's and the National Children's Home and Orphanage, which regarded themselves as adopters, with most of their charges brought up in residential care, the NCAA acted as an intermediary to bring together prospective parents and children in need of homes. Like the National Adoption Society (NAS), established on similar lines, the NCAA evolved in the changing climate of the Great War.

Its founder and director was Miss Clara Andrew, whose work with Belgian refugees and munition workers convinced her of the need for the organisation. Described at her death as 'the spiritual mother of all little children' by a somewhat gushing Viscountess Snowden, and photographed in an almost beatific pose in an NCAA report, she was a redoubtable committee member, vocal supporter of adoption and the rights of adoptive parents, and firmly behind the 1926 Act.

Adoption did not have universal support but, in the aftermath of the First World War, there was a greater willingness to debate the issues. The birth rate was declining, mothers had lost sons; informal 'adoptions' were on the increase. Moral distaste at the thought of War Babies was translating into women wanting to adopt War Orphans, the illegitimate baby segueing into the child whose father had died, a more uplifting prospect – and patriotic, to boot.

They enter our offices with the tremulous anxiety and excitement which are characteristic of motherly little girls going to a doll shop. They have some definite image before their eyes; most of them look for some of their own family traits in colour or form, and they want to see several children. With the establishment of the Hostels, it will, of course, be possible to allow adopters a wider choice than can be given now.

– Clara Andrew, founder of the National Children Adoption Association, NCAA booklet, c.1919

Of course, some war widows did struggle with children they could barely afford to raise, but the majority of children placed for adoption were illegitimate. The phrase War Orphan performed a neat elision: by airbrushing out the mother, it reduced the taint of immorality many found disturbing.

The road to legalised adoption was long and hard, tying up two committees of enquiry and involving considerable debate. (And even after the 1926 Adoption Act was passed, there were still difficulties to resolve; further legislation was needed to regulate adoption procedures.) While agreeing that there should be some legal foundation (and redress) for the large number of informal adoptions already taking place, the National Society for the Prevention of Cruelty to Children (NSPCC) was concerned for the vulnerability of children – in 1923 alone, the Society dealt with 38,027 cases, with only 922 prosecutions. The National Council for the Unmarried Mother and her Child (later, the National

Council for One Parent Families) wanted young women to take responsibility for their actions and not be offered the easy let-out adoption seemed to give. There was one point, however, on which everyone agreed: the women they dealt with should be *deserving* cases. To err once was forgivable, twice was not.

The 1926 Act laid the foundations for adoption as we know it today. The Act gave adoptive parents the same rights and responsibilities as birth parents, and adopted children the same rights as a birth child. A woman placing her child for adoption was relinquishing that child for good. This did not mean informal arrangements ceased altogether: agreements were still made among friends and families, and the Courts none the wiser, but the only binding adoptions were those verified by law. Until now, the only legal agreements were the wardships orchestrated by the Chancery Courts, usually involving complex estates, or those at the other end of the social scale, enforced by Poor Law Guardians taking children like Eva into their care.

By the time Annie and Willie learned of the NCAA, the Association was firmly ensconced in its offices at 19 Sloane Street and its 'babies hostel', Tower Cressy, in leafy Campden Hill: addresses entirely appropriate for an organisation whose lengthy list of supporters reads like an extract from *Debrett's*. By now, the NCAA had connections overseas and aspirations to make its work 'Imperial' (though it was not involved in the controversies associated with 'exporting' children at that time). A Scottish branch existed in Edinburgh and in 1933 the Queen would open a further hostel: Castlebar, in Sydenham, Kent.

The Association received Ministry of Health funding, but money also came from donations and events like the annual Three Hundred Ball at Claridge's, where the well-connected outbid one another to

Until the 1926 Act was passed, adoption continued to be an extremely loose arrangement. It was 'like choosing kittens', Mary Gordon said, of her own 'adoption' by suffragette Emmeline Pankhurst, founding member of the Women's Social and Political Union (WSPU). Mary was one of four girls taken on with Mrs Pankhurst's characteristic zeal and autocracy during the First World War. Fired by a concern for 'War Babies', Emmeline Pankhurst, then in her late fifties, established a home for the girls, each about six months old, under the care of faithful retainer, Sister Pine. Christabel Pankhurst soon adopted one of them; the four were brought up together 'off and on'.

Composer and suffragette Ethel Smyth described Mrs Pankhurst's 'underlying idea' as 'experimental. As a keen student of the Montessori and other educational systems, she wanted to see what could be achieved by bringing up four children in ideal conditions towards fitting them to play a worthy part in the new world she saw opening up to women.' Originally, Emmeline Pankhurst hoped for sponsorship from wealthy supporters but, when this was not forthcoming, was undeterred.

In 1917, WSPU funds were used to purchase and furnish Tower Cressy, a five-storey Gothic house in London's Campden Hill. The original plan was to adopt more children, though the number remained at four. Mary Gordon recalled running down the steps at Tower Cressy to kiss Mrs Pankhurst repeatedly – 'Oh, Mother darling,' – until she and her fellow adoptees achieved sufficient spontaneity to satisfy a press photographer. On another occasion, Mary was shown a gold chain that had once belonged to her birth mother, and when she enquired about this some years later, Mrs Pankhurst replied, 'Fancy you remembering that.'

continued on page 180...

take home an evening gown or mah-jong set. Prospective adopters were, for the most part, less well-to-do than NCAA supporters. Giving evidence to the Hopkinson Committee in 1920, Clara Andrew reported that 15 to 20 per cent of those applying to adopt children were upper class; 25 per cent working class, and the rest, middle class, whom she defined as 'including the professional classes, tradespeople, clerks and sergeants in the police'.

The young mothers who came to the Association for help were recommended via the usual sources – doctors, clergy, health visitors, Poor Law Guardians, welfare workers, and so on; sometimes, friends or relatives applied on a child's behalf. Mothers were required to supply 'a very complete history of the case', as well as referees, a doctor's certificate, a birth certificate and a photograph of their child. No child was admitted unless judged to be 'sound

The girls were encouraged to 'read and read' and to think for themselves, but were not cuddled or shown any affection, and were only presented to Mrs Pankhurst at four-thirty if they behaved (and even then, did not have her undivided attention); an exceedingly cool response by today's lights, but one that chimed with the experiences of many young women of Mrs Pankhurst's social class.

Like so many before them, the girls were enthralled by Emmeline Pankhurst. Mary Gordon adored her. She was 'our God. She was everything to us. Nothing mattered but Mother.' If they earned it, she promised them, they would one day carry the Pankhurst name. 'That was our great ambition.' It was not to be.

Emmeline Pankhurst was now in her sixties, and in financial difficulties. Two of the girls were sent away. Until then, they and Sister Pine had accompanied Mrs Pankhurst on lecture tours and other travels, but Sister Pine left her employ and, in Mary's words, fellow adoptees Kathleen and Joan, then aged about ten, 'came on the market' and were re-adopted.

This was not that rare. Children were re-adopted as easily as they were returned to Industrial Schools. After Mrs Pankhurst's death, Mary herself was re-adopted, having already been sent to live elsewhere. Her adoration remained undimmed, however. She described her childhood as 'marvellous'. On her thirteenth birthday, shortly before Emmeline Pankhurst died, Mary visited her for the last time. On that occasion, she was hugged and kissed, and wept over: 'She was delighted to see me again, her last chick.'

in health, or likely to become so with care and proper feeding'. (Susan Musson of the National Council for the Unmarried Mother and Child advised adopters to 'insist on the strictest medical examination' of the child in case of 'physical or mental taint.')

Between 1919 and 1928, 1,200 children passed through Tower Cressy, a large number of whom, but for NCAA intervention, would, according to its own literature, 'certainly have come on the Rates'. By 1932, the number placed in private homes reached nearly 4,000. They ranged in age from one month to five years old, although the majority placed for adoption were aged less than twelve months.

In a Voluntary Social Services handbook from the period, the NCAA was defined as placing 'destitute or orphaned or friendless or neglected children with people who are prepared to adopt them for love alone', the final phrase, with its quiet insistence on no money passing hands (though some adopters subsequently made donations) distanced adoption from the far more lurid taint of baby farming. Though the notorious cases of this practice belonged to the past, prosecutions were still taking place into the 1920s and beyond.

The children discussed by Clara Andrew's Case Committee were not necessarily 'friendless' or 'neglected' but, in the days when stigma and economic necessity combined to make it practically impossible for women to choose lone parenthood, those who became pregnant out of wedlock (and with no prospect of marriage or family support), had little choice but to surrender their child. Many unmarried mothers must have felt that nothing had changed since the eighteenth century, when desperate women paced London's streets before handing over their babies to Thomas Coram's Foundling Hospital.

Of all the tokens left by mothers at the Foundling Hospital, and now on show in London's Foundling Museum, the tiny beaded purse is, for me, the most resonant. Its silk has practically perished, but the beading is intact and steadfastly spells a woman's initials. Worldly goods may vanish, it seems to suggest, but my love for you will survive.

I don't know what message this mother would have written for her child (if she were able to do so), but, whatever her sentiments, she did not envisage that, more than 200 years later, this intensely private item would be a museum piece, under glass. The child for whom the purse was stitched with loving care never saw it.

Mothers left tokens – and there are many of them – with Thomas Coram's Foundling Hospital, to prove a connection with their child should circumstances allow them to be reunited in the future. However, few mothers were able to reclaim their infants; the tokens remained with the institution. Even when the children grew up and left the Hospital's care, they did not receive them. A minuscule ring or coral bracelet (telling reminders of how slight eighteenth-century women were) would have been something for a child to keep in later life. Instead, they suggest heartbreaking stories. Many tokens express poverty as well as love. The handmade ones, such as the flower-shaped ornament fashioned from card and decorated with a scrap of lace, are perhaps the most poignant. What loving thoughts went into the creation of that sad flower? Perhaps the crudest of all is the necklet spelling one word, 'ale', and thereby suggesting a double tale, a factor in the mother's undoing and a token left by a woman with nothing else to give.

*

In the tree-lined suburbs of North London between the wars, many detached houses had a live-in servant who served corn-beefed hash and chocolate 'shape' at luncheon before retreating from view. Jessie Mee was among their number. For all the anxiety surrounding 'the servant question' at this time, women like Jessie were employed in middle-class homes until the Second World War.

In 1929, the year she enters my family story, Jessie Mee was working as a cook, and so already had some years of service under her belt (a belt pulled tight across a neat, plain dress) by the time she came to Hazelmere Avenue. Her employer was a widow, a Mrs Sedgwick, whose husband had died two years earlier. The Sedgwicks purchased their Finchley plot in 1925, after having lived in America for some years. With its mix of professionals with young children and older couples like themselves, the Avenue made a nice spot for their retirement. Each house asserted a touch of individuality, be it stained-glass windows, mock-Tudor beams or rustic porch. This was a comfortable middle-class area.

Mrs Sedgwick's needs were unlikely to have stretched beyond a cook and a daily help, and unless she did a great deal of entertaining, Jessie's responsibilities were far less onerous than those facing many cooks. She had her own kitchen – and a modern one at that, the kind with a serving hatch, a window on to the garden and white walls, not a damp treacle-brown coloured basement – but standing in a kitchen all day was a lonely occupation all the same. The Avenue was all houses and there were just houses in the streets nearby. There was no call to run to the shops. When provisions ran low, Jessie telephoned the grocer or the butcher with Mrs Sedgwick's orders and awaited their delivery boys.

Unless you could afford to train as a cook, the usual way to learn was by starting on the bottom rung as a kitchen or scullery maid, like those poor girls in Industrial Schools, although, unlike them, young women from stable working-class backgrounds grasped some of the ropes at home. By caring for younger siblings, they learned discipline and a sense of responsibility at an early age, along with domestic chores. Even before they started paid work, many working-class girls were well on their way to becoming biddable servants.

That did not make the role any more palatable, nor the route to advancement any simpler: up to your elbows in greasy water, hands stung by washing soda and the paste of sand, salt, vinegar and flour mixed for cleaning copper-bottomed saucepans. There were mountains of vegetables to peel and, over the years and in different households, tips to pick up from different cooks – how to make an entrée, chicken in aspic, jugged hare – though with little time or opportunity to practise the recipes yourself.

At some point during her years of service, heartily sick of skivvying and desperate for better pay (a London cook could earn in the region £54 to £63 a year in 1930, more than twice as much as a kitchen maid), a young woman might be emboldened to answer an advertisement for a cook, or put her name down at a domestic agency. 'Good plain cooks' were always in demand, even those whose actual experience was shaky. Hazelmere Avenue may even have been Jessie's first post in this role; landing on the doorstep with a nervous smile, a newly thumbed copy of *Mrs Beeton* and the tin box containing her belongings.

If she looked through the kitchen window while doing the washing up, Jessie could see next-door's servant pegging out clothes and, if their time off coincided, and provided they were home by ten (buses became pumpkins after ten), they could link up and catch the latest picture at the Finchley Bohemia. A cook might have every other Sunday afternoon off, plus an afternoon and evening a week. It was hard to meet new people, with your freedom so tightly prescribed, and hard to maintain friendships too, with each job taking you to a different part of London; servants palled up when they could.

The best domestic servants were supposed to be a hidden current running through the house, making its smooth running possible in all manner of unseen ways. At worst, you were 'a menial, a nobody'. Even a cook, at the top end of the female scale, was part of that separate species, not reckoned to have thoughts or desires of her own. Unwritten rules governing boundaries and behaviour were understood by both sides; published guidance was also available. Domestic manuals included chapters on servants, mainly directed at employers, but, in *Waiting at Table: A Practical Guide*, Mrs C. S. Peel produced a whole volume of advice for the young women themselves: 'Do not speak unless necessary... Do not breathe heavily. Move quietly but quickly... Do not rattle knives and forks.' In other words: make yourself invisible. Jessie Mee could not to do that. She brought her own life and feelings into the house. In 1929, she was pregnant.

A pregnant young servant was hardly a rarity; this was the fate of many naïve young women, and domestic service, with its circumscribed hours and strict routine, is thought to have ensured that servants remained naïve longer than most. They were also desperate to get away and live their own lives instead of underpinning someone else's. There was nothing unique about Jessie's plight, but that did not make it any less real.

In 1929, a time when 'immoral conduct' usually secured instant dismissal, a woman of Jessie's age and circumstances had few options. The NCAA wrote of finding live-in work for some of the young women who came to them, in households willing to take a mother and child, but there were very few of these jobs available. Few employers wanted a woman with a child, let alone a single woman with a baby. And think of the practicalities and the questions, the constant suspicion and pursed lips. The NCAA also suggested that, 'when possible', a young woman could stay in its hostel with her child, while engaged in domestic work elsewhere, but this would obviously provide only a temporary solution and 'when possible' manages to convey how infrequent a solution this was. Some welfare hostels took on unmarried mothers, but these

You must remember that your moods do affect your child *through* you, and therefore, for its sake you must shun the ugly and depressing things of life and keep as cheery, as happy, and as light-hearted as you possibly can.

– Advice to Mothers, *Home Management*, 1934

placements usually came with a large dose of moral medicine.

A bold option would be for Jessie to buy a cheap ring and pretend to be recently widowed – but she could find no new domestic work without a good 'character' and could hardly expect Mrs Sedgwick to lie on her behalf. If she took a different kind of job altogether, she'd need someone to mind her baby, which had its own risks (the bogey of baby farming still stalking recent memory and, occasionally, the press). Hers was the age-old dilemma. With a child, she could go neither forward, nor back.

I know almost nothing of Mrs Sedgwick, but she seems to have been compassionate and broad-minded, and far more broad-minded than most. I assume her wider experience of the world accounted for that. And it's possible that, given this small household, theirs was a more companionate relationship than many. Jessie remained with Mrs Sedgwick for some months after the birth. They must have made an odd pair during the Christmas of 1929, an exceptionally cold winter, when even the River Thames froze. Outside, freezing temperatures; inside, the widow, the cook and her baby, awaiting the next year and all it would bring.

Hazelmere Avenue was the address Jessie gave when she registered her baby's birth, and she waited a very long time to do that, either because of a reluctance to commit reality to paper, or perhaps because she hoped – and, if so, how fiercely she must have hoped – that the baby's father would acknowledge their child.

I've been to the house on Hazelmere Avenue. I went there with my mum one November afternoon. It was a drear, cold day and the road itself inaccessible, a bus journey across unknown territory, following a tube ride towards the edge of the map. Jessie was long gone, of course – we weren't expecting to see her. No one answered our knock at the door. We left the Avenue with nothing.

We could have gone back another day. Why didn't we? My mum put a note through the door and the owner replied, inviting us to visit. We never did. Why ever not? What madness, we say now. And I gather that, at the time, the interior of the house was more or less the same as when Jessie lived there. It seems ludicrous, when there are so few clues, but our failure to return was not just the fact of my mum not living in London, and it being the other side of the capital from me. It is hard to convey how intensely distressing that grey day was. Years passed; the owner died and his invitation with him. I've been back there since: sunny afternoons on both occasions; light dancing on the Avenue's trees, and found the journey, now freed of those initial weighty expectations, straightforward and easy.

I've stood outside that house and willed it to give up its secrets, but bricks and mortar won't do that. I've pictured Jessie looking through the landing window while considering what to do for the best. Through its stained-glass panes she could watch the garden flush green, yellow, blue or scarlet, but whichever coloured landscape she observed, nothing altered her situation. In 1930, Jessie went to the NCAA and was interviewed by its gentle, pearl-throated inquisitors.

She would not have found the Association by herself. Mrs Sedgwick and her youngest son, a married doctor, probably made enquiries on her behalf and vouched for Jessie's good name. Mrs Sedgwick would have been at ease in this milieu (or was, at least, a woman who knew which questions to ask); her son's profession gave him some knowledge of adoption. However it came about, the result was the same. In June of that year, Jessie Mee gave up her baby.

*

I've never seen the NCAA hostel, Tower Cressy. I've seen photographs and a line drawing, but not the real thing. The building no longer exists, but, in the summer of 1930, when Annie and Willie went there, one unrepeatable afternoon, it dominated Aubrey Road. I can only imagine their feelings as they walked towards its imposing Italianate structure. Built in the 1850s for Thomas Page, creator of Westminster Bridge, this turreted Gothic building was later home to the designer Christopher Dresser and his thirteen children (thirteen born into the right social class), and was owned, for a while, by the Women's Social and Political Union (WSPU) during Emmeline Pankhurst's foray into adoption, before being gifted to the NCAA. It was a landmark in the area as well as in my grandparents' lives.

There was always an other-worldliness about Campden Hill; those magnificent houses and mysterious squares from which Turner painted sunsets. Novelist Naomi Mitchison wrote of a house she often visited (her mother-in-law's) and yet could not find when she returned to the area years later. To me, that seems at one with the landscape and the fairytale quality of Annie and Willie's experience. I know Tower Cressy was real, but it feels like something invented.

Despite its ornate and intimidating façade, everything within the 'babies hostel' was built with comfort in mind, and with institutional elements kept to a minimum. A visiting journalist writing for *Woman's Own* compared Tower Cressy to a 'huge private house, beautifully arranged and furnished, in which you see happy toddlers playing together with their toys and smaller babies chuckling at each other'. The photographs accompanying her feature show children straight out of Mabel Lucie Attwell:

1930s cherubs and toddlers with pudding-basin haircuts and big eyes. These days, they were no longer 'war orphans' but 'motherless mites'.

In sentiments equally reminiscent of that popular children's author, the journalist concluded: 'There are all sorts of babies – fair and dark, large and small – a constantly moving stream of them, for often their stay in the hostel is for only a few days, and then their adopted mother comes and takes them away, and a cot in the peaceful nursery…is filled by another motherless mite, and so the story goes on…For there are always babies who need a mummy and a home, and always women who yearn for the baby who never came.'

Annie and Willie could not believe what stood before them when they arrived at Aubrey Road. The journey itself was remarkable enough, but after street upon street of royal icing stucco, they

thought they must have stumbled upon Béla Lugosi's house. Willie took out his camera and, as if made dizzy by what he saw there, took a leaning photograph of Tower Cressy. Inside, all was courtesy, smiles and politeness, with nursery nurses in starched uniforms moving stealthily through sunny rooms.

Annie was gripping a letter the postman had brought to the cake shop; a postman turned stork, though he'd no idea what he was delivering. HRH Princess Alice, head of the NCAA Case Committee, had studied my grandparents' photographs and selected the child best suited to them. There was a baby waiting for Annie and Willie, a baby chosen specially by her royal self. Imagine.

My grandparents wanted to remember every single detail of that extraordinary day and so, when Willie stepped into the

garden, he photographed some babies asleep in wicker cots. Clara Andrew is in the picture too – throwing up her hands at his impertinence. Thank you, Willie, for your impertinence, if that's what it was. That forbidden snapshot is a tiny piece in the jigsaw of my mum's story.

When they left Tower Cressy that afternoon, Annie was clutching an eight-month-old baby wrapped in a shawl, and Willie, a set of instructions, details of the baby's feed. Until I saw that simple handwritten sheet, I had no idea a list could make your heart ache.

Part Three

12

Cora

MY MOTHER WAS BATHED IN A BLUE ENAMEL BATH THE chemist's son had outgrown, but her rattle was brand-new and at last Annie could stitch daisies on to the bodice of a dress: eight ivory-coloured threads radiating from each silk knot.

On fine days, Cora's pram stood in the old bakehouse yard, its front wheels and hood visible beyond the door leading into the cake shop. 'If you'll excuse me a moment,' Annie tells her customers, the minute Cora cries, 'I must just attend to my baby.' She has waited thirteen and a half years to say those words.

One day she was Mrs Thompson, with no children; the next she was a mother pushing a pram. There was little chance of Annie pretending to be Cora's birth mother to her near neighbours, though stranger things happened all the time. My family all knew women who introduced new babies, although their daughters had been the ones gaining weight. Mystery babies were not unusual. People shrugged their shoulders and got on with their own lives.

Everyone at the Mill was delighted and when they'd finished holding Cora aloft for the camera and posterity, and toasting her future in glasses of warm beer, Dick chucked the little duckie under her chin and Eva blew her enormous bubbles that quivered before they burst and disappeared.

On Sunday mornings, Annie pushed the pram up to Wheeldon Mill as proudly as Boadicea driving her chariot. Long after Cora was too old for her pram, the pram accompanied them, enabling Annie to wheel her back at night. It was a considerable walk for a woman with a baby, and parts of it quite deserted after ten, but that didn't trouble Annie. She passed the time by describing the stars to her daughter: Orion's Belt, the Plough, Cassiopeia.

Eva jiggled Cora on her knee and did not mind when she bit into her raspberry-coloured beads when teething. She even forgave Cora the loss of her front teeth. It was an accident, of course, the act of a baby flinging out an arm while holding a glass feeding bottle, but the bottle caught Eva squarely on the mouth and broke her teeth. 'Those two have got to come out,' the dentist said (no string and door slamming for Eva), 'so why not remove the lot of them, and save yourself trouble and expense later?'

People did that all the time; some poor devils had the cost of the extraction presented as a birthday gift. In the days before complex dentistry, replacing your own teeth with dentures was thought to be doing yourself a favour. So Eva did the sensible thing. She spent a hideous morning at the dentist and returned home with a vastly swollen face and a jaw that felt it had gone ten rounds in a boxing ring. Her own teeth were exchanged for a set of gleaming ceramic 'pots' which loomed in her mouth, overcrowding it. She persevered for a while and each set of dentures was an improvement on the last, but Eva hated the wretched things and hardly wore them.

She managed the adjustment remarkably quickly and her mouth did not turn down in a permanent sag. The oddities became the occasions Eva wore her teeth, not the days she ignored them. Though she grieved for their loss, there was nothing she could do. Teeth were one of the things Eva learned to go without.

My mum's adoption was formalised in 1931. The court officials told Annie and Willie she was the first child to be legally adopted in Chesterfield since the Adoption Act had come into force in 1927. The officials offered their warm congratulations and my grandma's answering smile burnished that January day. Annie and Willie were thrilled and proud, and all those others words used to describe new parents that don't come close to conveying the immensity of

their feelings, but pride notwithstanding, the adoption itself was not something they intended to dwell on. They were a family now and that was all that mattered. It was nobody's business but theirs.

Annie was now the mother she had always hoped to be, but mothering at thirty-seven (which was older then, than now) came as a considerable shock. In the inter-war years, childcare guru Truby King reigned supreme in instructing middle-class mothers how to care for their babies. Tower Cressy prescribed the four-hourly feeds that were fashionable then but, unlike other Truby King novitiates, Annie had no nursemaid or nanny. She also had a cake shop to run. Childcare gurus and middle-class adoption associations did not consider the practicalities of life for a working mother. In the one photograph that exists of my grandma with her young baby, she looks completely done in.

Half-day closing was perfect for catching the latest release at the

---

LIFT-THE-LATCH (BABY GAME)

Ring the Bell (gently tug the baby's forelock)
Knock at the door (gently knock on the forehead)
Lift the latch (lift the tip of the nose)
And walk in (walk fingers to the mouth)
Take a chair (jiggle the left cheek)
Sit yourself down (jiggle the right cheek)
How do you do this morning? (chuck the baby's chin)

– Game played by Eva and Annie with Cora

Lyceum or catching up with sleep – Annie and Cora, both. My mum slept through umpteen films cuddled close to Annie and, until an usherette complained, amused herself as a toddler by pounding up and down the aisle while Annie sat engrossed in the main feature.

Letting Cora run wild at the cinema was all very well, but Annie needed help while she was occupied with the cake shop, and made an arrangement with a neighbour whose sixteen-year-old daughter needed work. Cora loved Nancy or, Nanny, as she called her – not to glorify her role, but because the word was easier to pronounce. On fine days, they played together in the old bake-house yard or Nancy took Cora along Whittington Moor in her pushchair, running errands for Annie and examining the shop windows along the way: Miss Greaves' dress shop, which was thought to be a cut above; milliner Miss Crookes', where Betsy and Eva bought their hats (Betsy's a sober straw, Eva's an elaborate cloche with a snazzy brim). If Cora and Nancy called at the butcher's, he broke into song to entertain them. But a verse of 'Wheezy Anna' did not encourage Cora to eat the limp rabbits hanging by their feet, nor his pink chops and chitlings. Vans trundled past, including that for Thompson's Bakery, with Uncle Bernard at the wheel. If he saw Cora, Bernard gave a double toot, and if his wife Ida was dressing a mannequin in one of the windows of Derbyshire's outfitters across the way, she came to the door to say hello. There was a lot happening in this busy street, but there was one golden rule: 'Do not step off the pavement.'

Indoors, Cora and Nancy practised telling the time with a large cardboard clock with yellow hands. When the shortest hand reached one, Annie shut the cake shop for an hour; when the arrow approached five, Willie was due back from the bakery.

Cora's face was full of smiles for her daddy and his Box Brownie – Cora in the yard, Cora astride a toy horse; Willie did not need a special occasion to snap his daughter. He sang her 'Little Pal' – she is his pal, he tells her, the song was meant for her – and pulled her on to his lap for 'Sonny Boy'. Her birthdays were celebrated with cakes demonstrating every peak and swirl of piping Willie could produce, and perfected with a kiss of cochineal.

One of my mum's earliest memories of her grandma's shop is of sitting on the doorstep with Ethel's nephew, Georgie Stokes. They're both sucking dummies and, from time to time, Georgie slugs cold tea from a medicine bottle equipped with a teat. There is not much to see at this level except shoes, more shoes and hemlines, as customers swerve to avoid them on entering and leaving the shop. Some women stoop to say hello, but mostly she and Georgie are ignored.

Although this is the doorway through which Cora passes when she visits her grandparents and aunt, the shop itself is more or less a blur at first, a mere corridor through to the back. It is the house and the people inside who matter. Her tall grandma with her big strong hands who washes Cora's hair and won't let her venture far until it's dry, lest she catch her death; her white-haired grandad with a twinkle in his eye, who can nearly always find a marble or a toffee in his pocket and is fond of pulling everyone's leg. ('Oh you naughty man,' says Eva, smiling and rolling her eyes.) Sometimes, Dick seems no more than a big boy himself, a playmate and prankster for Cora, but at other times he gentles the horses in the publican's field and comforts Cora when she cries at the sound of mussels squealing when they're boiled in a pan for his tea. And, of course, there is Eva, her fun-loving aunt, who serves in the shop, but is always ready to entertain her niece.

On sunny Sunday afternoons Eva and Annie crown Cora with daisy chains while Dick checks the wire on the hen houses. The entrance to the wood now has elaborate steps fashioned from living tree roots, a sturdy gate and a hawthorn hedge near the path. Teddy, the current terrier, races round and round, chasing his shadow and his tail, but the hens are used to his daft antics by now and ignore him. Dick shows Cora how to look for eggs in the long grass and which particular spots the hens favour, and at the end of their treasure hunt, laughs instead of being cross when she drops the eggs into his bucket and breaks them.

Dick has saplings to tend, green shoots to protect from rabbits and a battle to wage against the bindweed that, given half a chance, would choke the hedgerows and the dog roses and honeysuckle climbing through them. While Dick smokes his afternoon pipe, Eva throws sticks for Teddy and Annie stretches out on the grass. At moments likes these, the wood is a quiet, secret place. Station Road is concealed by trees and all factory whistles and colliery hooters are silent. A cerulean sky frames the Crooked Spire in the distance. This family is home and complete; three generations woven together by their willingness to love and trust strangers.

My mum had not entirely forgotten her earlier life. She burst into tears whenever George Harding delivered milk to her grandma's shop. He did not even have time to unload his churns from the dray; Cora started crying as soon as she saw him. It was not kindly George who frightened her, but his misshapen hat that seemed to sprout tweed at odd angles. Other men round about wore flat caps, and Willie and his brothers, trilbys; no one else wore a hat like George Harding's, but the nurses at Tower Cressy had elaborate headdresses fashioned with stiff bows and my mum's distress was ascribed to her memory of these. Seven months old and suddenly alone; no familiar face or voice nearby, no matter how hard you seek it. Instead, women in peculiar hats that overwhelm their features are peering into your cot.

In the early 1930s, Billy Thompson, Jim's eldest son, joined the bakery. Baking was not Billy's passion, but he gave it a try for a couple of years and it was during this period that Willie realised his mistake. He had misunderstood his brother's plans for the firm. His hopes for the business, his name on the deeds: the whole thing was the worst possible mix-up. The partnership was intended for young Billy Thompson, Jim's son, not Billy Thompson, Jim's brother (Willie was always 'Billy' to his brothers and friends). Young Billy who cared little for the bakery and was still a child when Willie started winning bakery medals. But, of course, Jim wanted to share the business with his firstborn son. How had things become so back-to-front? How could he have been so foolish?

Willie went to work the next day and the days and months after that. For the next two or three years, he continued standing at the bakery table five and a half days a week, although scrubbing its white surface at the end of a long day no longer gave him the satisfaction of a job well done, nor did baking a wide range of bread and fancy cakes. Pummelling, kneading, pushing, turning, flouring. Kneading, pushing, lifting, turning, flouring, shoving with the heel of his hand. Four dozen rock cakes, thirty loaves, half a dozen jam sponges; four cherry Genoas, four seed cakes, one slab fruit cake, four dozen raspberry buns. All hopes of a Morris Cowley receded.

It must have been hard for my grandma, in the years before she adopted Cora, wanting a child all that time and having to answer the thoughtless questions posed by strangers who assumed all married women had children: 'I did have a baby. She died.' Annie was pleased for other women and their good fortune and, if asked, held their new babies with a smile, though tears pricked her eyes the minute she felt the soft weight in her arms. First steps, first words, first day at school – all those non-anniversaries pierced her; she lived with the burden of that grief. So perhaps it is not surprising that when my mum joined the family, she became my grandma's child: Annie's child, not Willie's. Though there were songs and cakes indoors, and photographs in the backyard, outside

their home, Cora was entirely Annie's little girl.

Willie was not allowed to do anything for Cora, nor take responsibility for her in any way, although he'd wanted to adopt a child as much as Annie. It was the best decision he ever made, he often said so. Indeed, in later years, it was one of the few things on which he and Annie agreed. But what is harder to unravel is what came first: Annie's refusal to allow Willie to look after Cora or what she termed, 'William's hopeless irresponsibility'.

On fine evenings, you'd hear Willie singing as he came along the road on his return from the bakehouse. Neighbours remarked on his good voice, which was just as well, given how often they heard it. Pay days were especially cheering: 'When you're in the money, you're a brick, brick, brick…' Willie liked to stand drinks for his friends; even friends of friends could tap Willie for a beer if he was in the right mood on pay day. 'Oh, the world is full of honey…' Sunshine beer was his favourite: a beer and a whisky chaser.

My grandma always said that Willie's drinking stemmed from his disappointment over the bakery. That was when his liking a drink became a problem for her. My mum has no memory of ever seeing her father drunk – can only recall him 'merry' on one occasion – but Annie's perspective was different. Part of her anxiety stemmed from childhood: she'd seen what drink could do. Most of it, however, was reducible to paper and base metal: the pounds shillings and pence required to look after a home and a small child.

One morning, Willie left for work but got no further than the Railway Tavern a few hundred yards down the road, waylaid by a friend or his niggling stomach. 'Just a quick one, then. Why not?' It was not the first time Willie had made a detour to the pub. Someone saw him and told Annie. Her sense of frustration and fury was so immense that she asked Nancy to mind the shop and marched up to Wheeldon Mill.

Even the half-hour walk did not calm her; she was still furious when she arrived. Time and again, Betsy and Eva had been ready with advice and Annie equally ready with her answer. 'They can all deal with the devil except them that's got him.' That usually shut them up, but, on this occasion, Willie's behaviour was so provoking, all three women decided to intervene.

Lord knows what possessed them, and how they expected Willie to react when confronted with his mother-in-law, his wife and her sister. And these women did not usually venture into pubs; the closest any of them came to stepping over the threshold was Eva fetching the family's Sunday-lunchtime jug of beer via the side door of the Great Central Hotel. However, Annie needed Betsy's help and, if trouble presented itself, Eva was not one to run away.

To think of all the women they'd pitied over the years, watching men stumble from the taproom, having handed their wages across the bar. Now Annie was among their number. It's not the same, they told themselves, not really. Whatever it was, they were determined to put a stop to it before it happened again.

They found Willie ensconced in the snug. He was sitting with his friends, the Kiplings, a local garage owner and his wife. She had a fox fur draped about her shoulders and was nursing a glass of sherry, the men had pints of beer. I would love to have seen the looks on the drinkers' faces when those three righteous women walked in.

Mrs Kipling was the first to find her voice. And whatever she said must have been pretty strong because Eva, who was lightning fast at retaliation, picked up Mrs Kipling's sherry and drenched her (and her fox). Mr Kipling sprang to his feet and in the kerfuffle that followed, landed Betsy a black eye – intended for Eva. Then the landlord intervened and ordered Betsy, Annie and Eva from the pub. (He had more sense than to bar good customers.) All three women were shown the door for brawling and, in their embarrassment and hurry to leave, tumbled down the Tavern steps.

My poor proud grandma and poor Betsy, who had such firm views on good and bad behaviour, and had so often sympathised with women about their husbands. Now she was required to stand behind her counter with her own swollen eye and fend off neighbours' glances. Some of them regarded Dick with a new note of enquiry, but their curiosity was short-lived. Plenty of women walked into a door at one time or another. My great-grandma's black eye faded, unlike the difficulties between Annie and Willie.

My mum has few memories of this period, but she remembers her grandma's black eye; she also remembers being upstairs with Annie one day while she was cleaning. The sheets were thrown back to air, the windows were wide open, when Willie came into the room holding out a bag of sweets. He offered one to Cora. This was no four-a-penny sweet, but an expensive-looking chocolate, wrapped in foil; there were only three or four in the bag. 'Where's mine?' Annie asked, half teasing, not really believing there was no sweet for her, but that was Willie's intention. Feeling uncomfortable and uncertain, the chocolate warming in her hand, Cora looked from her mammy to her daddy, then gave her sweet to Annie. Willie huffed and left the room. A few moments later, they heard the back door shut. For the first time, Cora realised her parents did not like one another very much.

13

Nobody's Sweetheart

THE CORNER SHOP SOON BECAME A PLACE OF ENTERTAINMENT
and temptation. Its blurry jars sprang into life, revealing Lemon
Sherbet, Everlasting Strips, Swizzels and Torpedoes. Though not
allowed to play there when customers were present, Cora could
take one or two sweets after hours. 'She's pinching,' Betsy would
say in a singsong, playful voice, watching her from the back room.

Cora's best friend at the Mill was Georgie Stokes' sister, Katie,
who was older than her but of an age to enjoy 'looking after' Cora;
my mum called her new doll, Katie, in her honour. Katie took
her for walks in the Meadows where they gathered limp bunches
of cornflowers, archangels and daisies, though never mother-die
(cow parsley) because of the terrible warning in its name.

Though her grandma ran a real shop, Cora played 'shop' with
Katie and Enid Spencer and, occasionally, was allowed to stand
behind the actual counter and serve her friends with sweets. Betsy
showed her how to twist the tops of paper bags to secure them and
how to take payment. If a ha'penny usually purchased four caramel
chews, my mum's special reckoning made it five.

'P'

Parsley PD 1d

Peggy Legs 2/8

Panshine 2d, 4 ½d, 8 ½d

Pencils 1d

Pen holders 1d

Pills Parkinson's 1d, 3d

Pickling Spice 1d, 3d

Loose ditto 1/6 1b

Pest Cards Bndles 1d

Parazone 1/3

Peppermint 10 ½d

Zuff Puffed Wheat & rice 7d

Perfumes Carters 6d

Quaker Puffed Wheat & Rice 7 ½d

POULTRY & CHICK FEEDS
SPRATTS
Bis Meals 1/-, 2/-
Chikko 10 ½d
1/9 Pulto 8d, ¼

– Extract from stock list, Betsy's corner shop, *c*.1930s

Rings became another irresistible temptation. Incongruous though it seems, along with scouring pads and borax, cattle powders and bags of flour, my great-grandma's shop sold rings. Alloyed rings with cheap glass stones, as good as Woolworth's finest: covetable rubies and sapphires, in Cora's eyes. 'Gran-ma …' she'd ask in that pleading voice all adults recognise, hovering before their velveteen tray.

I don't know when it dawned on Eva that no matter how many young men came calling – and there was at least one more, after the first – no one would be good enough for her. Her role had been decided by Dick and Betsy. Eva would be the daughter who stayed at home. They loved her, they fussed her, and she thought the world of them, she often said so, but she was theirs and no one else's. I'm sure this was part of their wanting a little girl from the Industrial School. Betsy wanted another daughter – she had never thought she would have just the one – but she also had an eye to the future. A young lad would be up and gone the minute he found someone he was sweet on; daughters were more biddable and could be kept at home with the slenderest emotional threads.

Eva always insisted that years passed before she considered the life she might have led. At the time, she simply accepted her situation, which was not uncommon. The years between the wars were full of women like her; one in four did not marry. The 1861 census was the first to reveal a so-called 'surplus' of women, but in the aftermath of the First World War, with women exceeding men by 1.75 million, the imbalance acquired a new pungency: all those women who could never marry the young men lying dead on Flanders Fields. Add to this calculation the nineteenth-century codes to which their mothers subscribed (for their daughters, if not for themselves) and which demanded filial Duty, Gratitude, Submission, then how could they leave home? The fiction of the period is full of young women desperate to do just that. Novel after novel hinges on their desire to break free.

Facts and fiction, however resonant, can be held at arm's length, but Eva was my much-loved great-aunt whom, I suspect, had long since learned to ignore what she could not alter. However, I wonder how often, walking round to Newbridge Lane to visit schoolfriend Carrie and play pat-a-cake with her young son, or lift-the-latch and similar baby games with infant Sunday visitors, Eva was tempted to conjure her own home-sweet-home? She was always a helpmeet of one kind or another: a single woman, daughter,

sister, aunt and great-aunt. She was loved by my mum long before she was loved by my brother and me.

At the top of the house, up the final, twisty flight of stairs, is the attic, no longer a refuge for Annie's friend Ethel or a weekday lodging for George (nor even a suite for newly-weds, Annie and Willie), but a storeroom once again, with a warm closed-in smell, especially during summertime when the confined sacks of lentils and split peas, and the sand which Betsy dampens and scatters on the floorboards before sweeping, lend a gritty dryness to the atmosphere. The sacks give a satisfying crunch whenever Cora sits on them, but it's the bicycle and the large framed photograph she and Eva come to see.

This is the bike on which Annie cycled to school years ago, and propped up in another corner is her schoolgirl portrait, long since relegated upstairs ('Oh, Mam, please. Take that down and put something else there.') The bicycle's chrome handles have dulled with age and it now has a tremulous bell, but the dress guards are still in place and the bike looks just as reliable as it does in the grainy photo of Annie standing with it. Cora is fascinated by this image of her mammy with her school cap and long, flowing hair.

The bicycle is taller than Cora, and much heavier too, and she cannot easily reach the handle bars or pedals, but kind, patient Eva, who was never too busy to play, and was a willing participant always, regardless of what your game interrupted, hoists Cora on to the seat and holds her until she tires. Eva stands for what must have felt like hours, singing to my mum as she rides: 'Oh, Flo, why do you go/ Riding alone in your motor car?/ People will say you're pec-u-li-ar/ Sing-u-lar, so you are/... There's room for two, me and you...'

'Again,' instructs Cora, and so Eva sings again, 'Oh, Flo, why do you go…' They ride for miles, travelling to unknown, mysterious places, accompanied by their special bicycle song. Pins slip from Eva's hair and drop to the ground disregarded; she needs both hands to steady Cora and the bike. While Eva sings, they gaze through the attic window, looking across the rooftops towards the hills and moorland. Cora pictures magical journeys and fairy-tale trees. Eva's thoughts are known only to herself.

Willie was still not feeling tiptop. The tonic he used to douse his malaria did not always keep it at bay. He'd lie cocooned in hot sheets slick with sweat, but icy cold the minute he tried to move. Willie's bakery book contains a recipe for a second tonic, stronger than the first, with amounts more appropriate to emergency treatment than regular use: Quinine 0.67; Diluted Sulphuric Acid 2.5; Phosphoric 54.6; Alcohol 8.1; Water to 100. In an attempt to control his discomfort, Willie seems to have dosed himself with larger and larger quantities.

Sometimes Willie was forced to go to bed as soon as he returned from the bakery. And it wasn't just the sweats: his stomach was plaguing him too, a scouring sensation he couldn't account for. Cora and Annie heard him groaning. 'He's moaning again,' Annie would say, and disappear upstairs to rub Willie's back with Sloan's Liniment. What good a jar of Sloan's Liniment could do was anybody's guess, but it seemed to ease his pain and was the best thing Annie could think to offer. Doctors cost a shilling a visit and would only insist: rest, plenty of milk, a good diet. On evenings like these, Willie was adamant: 'Don't let Cora see me like this.' She did not need to see him: his groans were bad enough. She also saw how Annie's lips tightened as she headed upstairs.

Even at this young age, Cora knew her sympathy exceeded her mother's.

Occasionally, however briefly, Annie had to get away. The grocer's shop next door had a telephone tucked at the back of a storeroom and, on those days, she asked her neighbour if she could make a call. Taking Cora with her, Annie led the way up a set of stairs that smelled of Izal and old biscuits. Cora had no idea who her mam was calling. In her world, telephones were as rare as private cars. George was a headmaster by this time, however, with a private telephone in his study. 'This is our secret, Cora,' Annie always said. 'This is just between the two of us. You understand?'

Towards the end of 1933, Willie was diagnosed with a duodenal ulcer. There would be no more elaborate loaves and fancy pastries. His days at the bakery were over. Ulcers were not so easily treatable then as they are today; major stomach operations could be life-threatening. As predicted, Willie's doctor advised a good diet, nothing acidic, plenty of rest, lots of fresh milk and – no alcohol.

His bakery days behind him, Willie joined the long list of the unemployed. By 1933, Chesterfield was as gripped by the Depression as the rest of the old industrial landscape and, although it had no place there, Willie's worsening health was absorbed by that much larger story. With so many men in need of work, his being at home wasn't much remarked upon. Clusters of men stood outside factory gates looking gaunt and strained; some, with war medals clipped to their lapels, daring anyone to challenge them as wastrels. 'The shadow of unemployment' was much debated, but talking about it came nowhere close to the actual experience. People were scratching for slack on the coal tips again; children –

and grown men – went without shoes, or felt each stone on the pavement through paper-thin soles. Some men, ashamed of their situation, disappeared after breakfast to reappear at night with a story they'd concocted about their day. Willie felt it important to make a distinction: there was a difference between being off sick and being unemployed.

Then, as now, there was an appetite for personal stories of difficulty or endurance and, thanks to greater numbers owning cameras, an increasing demand for photographs of the general public. 'Guineas for kiddies' snapshots. Send Yours Now,' *Woman's Life* pleaded on its front cover. Pictures appeared week after week, none of them, in Annie's estimation, anywhere near as lovely as her daughter. Local newspapers printed readers' snaps too; Annie looked out a picture of Cora. Though it seems out of character for her to advertise their distress, I assume she wanted to salvage something from their situation, especially with Christmas drawing near. The photograph was accepted, printed, and paid for. Its caption read: 'Daddy is out of Work, but Cora believes in Santa.' Willie was furious.

14

Afternoon Visiting

THE STAPLE GOODS SOLD BY THE CORNER SHOP DID NOT change that much, though, by the early 1930s, their numbers had been swelled by modern living. Almo, Compo, Glaxo, Kelso, Mazo, Rinso, Omo, Puro…the number of products ending in 'o' far exceeded any that could be sung by a barbers' quartet. Even the manufacturers of animal feed joined in with the baser notes of Chikko. This formula permeated everyday speech: my mum thought Annie's steam puddings were cracko.

Donald Duck lollies provided a ha'penny lick; Vita-Weat, Ryvita and Energen were sold alongside the usual loaves of bread, while the begoggled chauffeurs decorating tins of Chocolate Assortment had long been replaced by slim young women with flyaway scarves and a casual wave for the pedestrians they were zooming away from.

Station Road acquired its own fish and chip shop: Arthur and Elsie Scott were doing good business in a small hut opposite the wood; Friday nights now sang with salt and vinegar. If Mrs Rudge, the current greengrocer, had fewer customers than Betsy, some

Mrs D of Derby is 35 years old and has five children (all boys) and lives in a small Corporation house. Her husband is an unemployed labourer and her housekeeping is £2 1s 0d of which she gives the following particulars of expenditure:

Rent 12 6

Gas and Electric Light (6d each) 1 0

Clothing Club 3 0

Boot Club 1 0

Coal, 2cwt 3 0

Milk 2 9 ½

Bread 3 3 ½

Insurance 1 6

2 lbs margarine @ 4d 0 8

½ lb butter @ 1/- 6d

6lbs sugar 1 3

½ lb tea 0 9

¼ lb cocoa 0 4

½ lb lard 0 3

½ lb cheese 0 3

1 doz eggs 1 6

1 lb bacon 0 11

1 bag self-raising flour 0 5

1 lb loose peas 0 4

2 boxes matches 0 2

1 lb soap 0 5

1 packet wash powder 0 2

1 packet starch 0 1

1 lb soda 0 1

1 packet salt 0 1

¼ lb cooked ham @ 1/10 0 5 ½

Old potatoes 0 6

1 lb New potatoes 0 3

1 lb onions 0 2

Radishes, spring onions and

  lettuce 0 6

Cauliflower 0 2

Oranges 0 3

Piece of meat (beef) @ 1/3 1 3

Breast of mutton @ 8d 0 4

½ lb corn beef 0 3

Piece of codfish 0 5 ½

Sweets for kiddies 0 2

Total £2 1s 0d

– From Margery Spring Rice, *Working-Class Wives*, 1939, a detailed portrait of working-class life in the 1930s that 'stripped off the veil of indifference which concealed the hardship of millions of women'

said it was because her fruit was hard as nag nails, others thought her high heels and dyed hair were a factor. 'It wouldn't do for us all to look the same,' said Betsy in her pacifying way, while privately observing how quickly fresh fruit and vegetables were relegated in budgets already pared down to their basics. 'House' shops came and went – people setting up shop in their front room, selling chocolate, cigarettes and tinned goods for a matter of months, or longer if they made a go of it; Fiddler's shop, higher up Station Road, served customers in the next stretch of houses. There were new publicans too, Mr and Mrs Simms, who, like the publicans before them, befriended Dick and Betsy, retailers sticking together.

Some things remained the same. The butcher's pressed meats still shaded from pink to pale grey, ha'penny ducks continued to seep dark brown gravy. Gas mantles were still on sale. For the first few years of my mum's life, her height was measured by comparing the distance between the top of her head and the bottom of the gas light when she stood on her grandma's table. Roach powder remained as essential as ever – for Betsy as well as her customers. One night a week, before going up to bed, she sprinkled the hearth, and came down to find a mound of black-clocks the next day. Lads still congregated outside the corner shop, still dragged on a shared Woodbine, though, these days, their cigarette smoke curled around talk of TT races and the town's skating rink.

Eva took the plunge and shingled her hair, allowing its newly shorn ends an irrepressible bounce. She returned from the hair-dresser with her rope of hair weighting the bottom of a pillowcase like some slumbering creature. No more elaborate ornaments and combs; the days of scattering pins were behind her. Eva looked attractive with short hair and wondered why she had left it so long. She took herself to Arthur's Studio and sat for a celebratory photograph.

These days, Eva often read the newspaper aloud. Dick read slowly, making out words in a laboured way, but Betsy was wholly reliant on Eva. For local news, they preferred the *Yorkshire Telegraph & Star* to the *Derbyshire Times*, and caught up with national misdoings and scoundrels via the *News of the World*. Eva marked titbits to amuse Annie and saved the Gloops cartoon, the weekly story of a lisping cat, and his antics with Aunt Emma, a typically hatchet-faced 'spinster', for Cora. For six coupons posted to the *Star*, Cora could join the Gloops Club. ('All Gloops members are enrolled on equal terms, whether sons of the Prime Minister or daughters of the Sweep.') The next time she visited the corner shop, a badge, a special password and a set of rules awaited her. 'Gloops' members should always try to be happy by Thmiling! Thmiling!! Thmiling!!'

As a treat, Cora and Katie Stokes were taken to Saturday-morning cinema, where they learned to thumb their noses like George Formby, and on trips to the seaside. (Usually, Eva or Betsy accompanied Annie and Cora on days out: one or the other, rarely both, thanks to the tyranny of the shop. Dick always stayed behind. To his mind, sandcastles and sticks of rock were female pleasures, and the walk would have been difficult for him.) Katie did not have a suitable frock and so Annie made one for her, with a pair of matching knickers so she could paddle in the sea. A day on Blackpool sands, a packet of warm egg sandwiches and a bottle of lemonade that was never quite as fizzy when they came to drink it as when they took it from the shop window.

Most of the time, Cora and her friends played on the rough ground between the corner shop and the pub, as had Annie and Eva before her. Trips to other people's houses were infrequent, but sometimes she called for Katie, whose family fascinated her. Katie's mother, Edna, was one of the girls who used to sluice her brothers' backs when they returned from the pit; Katie's father, Clem, had not worked since his return from the war. His was a desperate existence: long years spent propping up his smashed jaw. This thin, gaunt man rarely left his fireside chair. Though he always smiled and said hello to Cora, he rarely said anything more. Clem had plenty to be silent about.

Like many poorer householders in the 1930s, Edna and Clem could not afford to furnish both downstairs rooms; their front room contained a bicycle and little else. As with all the houses at Wheeldon Mill, their kitchen was the hub of the home. To accommodate the whole family, plus their lodger, Edna's brother, Charles, required some engineering. The family ate in shifts, there being too few chairs for everyone to sit down at once.

Doughty Edna was a sturdy woman and a loving mother with a big lap, like Annie's. Cora often found her cuddling Georgie, who, even at the age of six, refused to be parted from his titty bottle of cold tea, but sat on their back step with his comforter. Katie's eldest brothers worked down the pit; her middle brother, Punka – a name acquired when he was small and always up to his eyes in dirt (and mischief) – was still at school.

Edna's brother was called Charles to his face, but was known as Charlie, and would probably have been described as a 'mucky toff'. Though his weekday garb consisted of work trousers, shirt and braces, weekend evenings transformed him. When Charles went out – and only ever into Chesterfield town centre, he did not frequent the Great Central Hotel – he put on a new personality, together with his Saturday togs. This would-be dandy dressed with enormous care in a dark suit, black overcoat with an astrakhan strip, and a starched shirt and butterfly collar. His charcoal-grey gloves buttoned at the wrist; he wore spats and a grey homburg; his sharp moustache harked back to his Edwardian youth. On Saturday evenings, Charles could be seen striding down Station Road, swinging a black cane before him. Though his sister spoke in a Derbyshire brogue, his accent was slightly clipped. He wanted to make something of himself.

Whatever his weekend life and the dreams he was waiting on, Charles paid for them during the week. Reduced once more to shirtsleeves and braces, he lived on two ounces of polony, a cheap meat paste bought from my great-grandma's shop and spread as thinly as possible on to slices of bread. By the fourth or fifth day, it would be greening.

No matter what hour my mum called for Katie, or invited Georgie to come and make mud pies, the light in their house seemed dingy. Late afternoon visits were especially gloomy. I suspect that, short of the sixpence needed for the meter, Edna held on for as long as she possibly could. By contrast, whenever the living room behind the cake shop was plunged into darkness, Annie found her purse straightaway. 'Where was Moses when the lights went out?' was her immediate bright refrain for the moment it took to find the coin.

Equally fascinating for Cora were visits to her Uncle Jim. The 1930s were good for Jim Thompson, as for many others in work. His vans still drove along Whittington Moor, advertising Thompson's 'Gold Medal' Bakery ('Hygienic', with its Edwardian overtones, having fallen by the wayside). The business was flourishing, as was Jim's political career. By now, he was an Independent councillor, extremely active in local politics.

Had Willie stayed well, he would have continued working for Jim. (Provided the brothers remained on good terms. They did fall out on occasion, though neither remembered why; it was not connected with the mix-up over the bakery. 'I wouldn't cross the road to speak to him,' Willie insisted, though the argument was mended soon enough.) Jim and Bernard were still regular visitors to the cake-shop house, together with their wives, Edith and Ida, wafting Yardley's Lavender and Parma Violets into the back room, and pulling gifts for Cora from within their big fur coats.

Return visits to Uncle Jim and Auntie Edith were like stepping into a different world. A maid in a white cap, black dress and frilly apron opened the stained-glass door and showed them into the hallway. (Had Jessie Mee greeted Mrs Sedgwick's guests, I wonder?)

Hallways themselves were unknown to Cora: in all the other houses she knew, you stepped straight into the living room, having come to the back door, not the front. There were numerous rooms off the hallway, but Annie and Cora were shown into a panelled one which, on the occasions they visited, seemed to be scented with roses. This large sunny room must have witnessed some genteel parties, with ladies swishing past one another in taffeta silk. During my mum's visits, it offered afternoon tea, scones, jam tarts and sponge cake (from Uncle Jim's bakery, where else?), and sugar cubes you grasped with silver tongs. Cora loved this grander world and had no feeling of being a poor relation; Annie loved to visit too, but though Annie was fond of Jim and admired him, the contrast between his life and Willie's was looking increasingly stark. No one was more conscious of that than Willie.

Without money, it was impossible to maintain self-respect. There was Jim with his business, his seventeenth-century house, his maid and chauffeur-driven car; even his baby brother Bernard had a maid as well as a car. What could you do without money?

The cigarette case Annie bought him went first, then the cufflinks with their little ruby specks. Gold was an easy currency. Not that Willie was paid over-much. He did not slink past a pawn-broker's window, too ashamed to show he'd been there. Willie sold his jewellery outright and had real money to show for it. If he tapped his trouser pocket, the coins answered with a satisfying clink. He celebrated with a sunshine beer.

Next, it was his tiepin with the garnet in the centre. Eventually, he sold Annie's jewellery too. (If only he had pawned that – at least she'd have had the chance to redeem it.) Things disappeared so discreetly my grandma didn't notice straightaway. She did not think to look for her little lapel brooch until she wanted something to pin on her jacket. She didn't make a habit of checking her jewellery box: a rather handsome box, a deep plum velvet, in a silver filigree case. That went too, in the end. One day, there was a space on the dressing table where the box once stood. As Willie's disappointment and ill-health raced to outdo one another, his magpie ways accelerated. Years later, you might mention a particular style of jewellery and my grandma would say, 'Mmm. I had one of those. But it went.'

Betsy would not normally venture an opinion on the subject but, if asked, she said Willie was a fool to himself. Annie's friend Ethel was more forthright: 'Willie Thompson was never any bloody good.' She was still putting up her fists to defend Annie. On the other hand, Eva liked Willie and thought her sister too tough on him, which says something about Eva's generous nature as well as my grandparents' relationship. There was a thread of steel within Annie, but by pocketing her jewellery, Willie also pocketed her love and trust.

She had made her bed and would have to lie in it. You heard that phrase all the time, a blunt verdict belonging to the days when the stigma of divorce bound couples together and forced them to muddle through. Whatever their feelings, Annie and Willie were both mild-mannered; they did not shout at one another and rarely exchanged harsh words, and Willie's stories could still amuse her. He still had his blue eyes and corn-coloured hair, but the man who stood before her was a poor imitation of the one Annie loved. Living with Willie now involved learning to live with disillusion.

For the first few years of her life, my mum was photographed on her birthday. Not one of Willie's casual snaps, but a proper studio portrait: Cora in a fur-lined hat, with posy; Cora with enormous upright teddy bear and cake; Cora with brown-bear-on-wheels and cake. Willie baked the first two, but was too ill to bake the cake for her third birthday. To add insult to injury, young Billy Thompson made it instead. ('Look at that. Why ever put a row of piping there?')

After my mum's fourth birthday, the annual portraits stopped: money was tight and there'd be school photographs soon enough. The final birthday picture shows Cora sitting on the arm of her mam's chair (a studio chair, a prop). It's a beautiful photograph, though Annie is a middle-aged matron by now, nothing like the blithe young woman who married Willie. Knowing what I do, this picture shows me something more than a loving portrait of a mother and daughter. It is also a reflection of how things stood between Annie and Willie by the end of that year.

15

Back to the Racecourse

IN 1934, ANNIE, WILLIE AND CORA MOVED TO A COUNCIL
house on Racecourse Road. Chesterfield's racecourse was no more,
its last race having run ten years earlier. Built on part of the original circuit, Racecourse Road was one of two surviving markers
of a once distinguished sporting past. Long disestablished by the
turf authorities, Race Days had eventually descended into farce,
with bookies almost as numerous as race-goers and some races
supposedly delayed until their runners could be unhitched from
coal carts. The associated pleasure fair or Feast was still going
strong, however, and attracting substantial crowds. Part of the
land was now a permanent recreation ground which, it was hoped,
would prove more useful to the town than the jaded racecourse.
Other hopes expressed were tongue-in-cheek. 'Now the races are
done with,' one official remarked, 'the morals of the people of
Chesterfield will so improve that we shall be able to do without
policemen or parsons.'

You could follow the curve of the original circuit up to and
beyond my mum's front door and picture yourself six furlongs

In the modern house the decoration of the kitchen calls for as much care and attention as does any other room in the house. Light cheerful walls and woodwork should be the rule here, as well as in the rest of the house. Here are some suggestions:

In a north or east kitchen:

Ceiling: Pale primrose washable paint

Walls: Washable primrose paint

Woodwork: Leaf green (glossy)

Linoleum: Green and white large checks

Curtains: Green American cloth

Chairs: To match the woodwork

In a south or west kitchen:

Ceiling, Walls: Honey-buff washable paint

Woodwork: Same colour as walls

Linoleum: Blue and white large checks

Curtains: Blue American cloth

Chairs: Painted blue

In these days of enamelled stoves (which are easily cleaned with a damp cloth) and independent anthracite-burning stoves, these light colours will not become dirty any sooner than darker colours would, and added to this the walls are washable. Housework is much more easily carried on in bright surroundings than in the old-fashioned gloomy ones.

– 'House Decoration: The Kitchen', *House Management*, 1934

beyond the starting flag, with the Grandstand and finishing post up ahead. And, like many of the races run here in the past, the move to Racecourse Road had a lot riding on it. This was Annie and Willie's first independent home; their home, not Jim's, their name on the council rent book. The road also returned the family to its own starting point, where my great-grandfather was brought to the town.

Annie and Willie were not the first to occupy their semi, but the house was almost new and had a lavatory which, although outside, was enclosed within a porch and so was practically as good as an indoor one. Even more desirable was the bathroom, with hot and cold running water and a fixed bath, an unknown luxury until now. Annie bought herself a long-handled sponge with which to soap her back and another to dab herself with powder. Reclining in the water for the very first time, she felt like Theda Bara in the films.

My grandma sewed new curtains for the windows and, on his good days, Willie worked on an aviary that spanned the bottom of the garden, abutting the back wall. He was a competent joiner, one of the few things for which he thanked his father, who'd had Willie handing him tools as a small boy. Fellow members of the Caged Bird Society came to cast an eye over his handiwork and agreed they could not fault it: Willie had done a fine job. Next, he built a gate and solid fencing to separate their house from the next pair: a man needed his own back gate.

When he was feeling well and optimistic, Willie still whistled or sang his favourite songs: 'After the Ball', 'The Big Sunflower', 'Roses in Picardy', the same sentimental numbers as before. He sang as he slapped paint on the kitchen walls and as he dug new flower beds for the garden (front and back) and planted the pinks

and night-scented stocks Annie liked, and when Willie had finished these jobs, he decorated his tin hat with a ring of forget-me-nots and slung it on the back of the coalhouse door.

Good days were a million miles from bad ones. When the wrenching in his gut was quieter, Willie felt rejuvenated. It was only a short reprieve, he knew that, but its brevity demanded exuberance. He and Cora wound up the gramophone and danced to his '78s. Willie steered her round the living room, performed a mock foxtrot slide towards the chaise longue before dipping and swinging her back towards the bureau. Annie heard them laughing while she was preparing tea. She heard him inventing rhymes and telling Cora she's the best, and teasing Cora and generally acting the goat, but it was a different Willie who opened the kitchen door to Annie.

Willie was proud of their new home and brought his brother Godfrey and sister Gertie to see it, but it was eleven o'clock at night and, until their visitors disturbed them, Annie and Cora were asleep – Cora had a large cot in her parents' room. Laughter and enthusiastic greetings woke them, rising up the stairs and then coming into the bedroom.

'Oh, Annie, what a lovely picture, Annie (a Victorian print 'My First Tooth'). And here's Cora, isn't she a darling? Come on, Annie, get up and join us. Willie's showing us the house.' Gertie leaned over Cora's cot, wafting an unknown scent as well as her usual Attar of Roses. Godfrey followed her into the room. They both made a fuss of Cora, as they always did, and she was pleased to see them, if startled to be woken in that way, but Annie was white with indignation: fancy, waking a sleeping woman and a small child. Instantly, all gaiety subsided. The revellers scuttled off downstairs and left the house.

The new house was barely a mile from the old one and my grandparents still relied on Whittington Moor for its shops, but this was a different neighbourhood nonetheless, with neighbours who were also new to the area. Here, Annie and Willie were a couple with their young daughter. No one knew of Cora's adoption and that was how they wanted things to stay. And, better all round that Cora knew nothing about it either.

The move coincided with my mum starting school. Annie issued first-day instructions: 'Speak to everyone, be friendly with every-one, but don't put your head next to theirs.' School was the local Infants' School on nearby Edmund Street, one of the single-storey schools built between the wars and designed to maximise the health-giving properties of sunlight. One external wall was mostly glass and multiple windows allowed the sun's rays to penetrate each classroom. As an additional aid to healthy bones, Cora (like many in Chesterfield) wore a flower-shaped 'Zodo' locket around her neck. Patented by Dr J. A. Goodfellow of the town's Oldfield Pottery, the Zodo iodine vapour dispenser released 'the concentrated essence of sea breezes'.

My mum hung her coat beneath a picture of a crescent moon; a crescent moon safeguarded her toothbrush. Teeth-cleaning was a daily ritual, following lunch, after which the children rested on green canvas beds before gathering around Miss Coombes to hear the latest tale from *Sunny Stories*.

In complete contrast with this kindly, forward-looking vision was Miss Harding, the headmistress. A terrifying throwback to earlier times, Miss Harding screamed and raged and threatened, thwacking all transgressors with a baton; left-handers hadn't a hope of remaining left-handed. On Empire Day, her pupils were marched around the flag in double quick time and were regularly lined up for inspection. Dirty clothes or faces were unacceptable; the fine point of her baton twitched at the sight of unwashed hands.

Few in the district had much money, but some pupils lived in an area known as West End which, in the hierarchy of who-had-least, came slightly lower in the pecking order than Racecourse Road. Some of the girls' frocks had been worn through so many seasons that their daffodil yellows had faded to a milky primrose and their scarlets were verging on pink; some hems had been let down so many times they were starting to resemble concertinas. One afternoon, Miss Harding singled out one of the smartest pupils and paraded her before the whole school. *This* was how everyone should dress, she insisted, indicating the girl's smart Scotch kilt and jumper. *This* was correct wear for school. Even her youngest pupils were embarrassed on their headmistress's behalf. They all knew about lean times. How come the news had passed her by? But no one dared to contradict Miss Harding. Some of her pupils whispered dark words about the county asylum; others hoped that prophecy would be fulfilled.

My mum was luckier than many of her classmates. Annie's knack with clothes meant she could rustle up a frock from the skimpiest amount of material in the way a knowledgeable cook turns the barest ingredients into a delicious meal. She had learned all the basics, the cutting out, overlocking, darting, and so forth, on her tailoring course, but features were her special thing. Prevailing fashions inspired Annie to set a row of chevrons above a pocket or add a modish panel to an otherwise plain dress. She knew what wonders could be achieved by the judicious application of a vertical row of ornamental buttons in ascending or descending sizes at shoulder height, or by the addition of a fabric bow. Annie pored over the patterns in newspapers and *Woman's Weekly*, but whatever she was making, added decorative touches of her own. Though her slim figure was a thing of the past, she still favoured 'dressy' clothes. With a pinch of ingenuity and a card of buttons, Annie demonstrated her flair.

Equal amounts of thought went into the making of Cora's clothes. My mum developed her own beady eye for details spotted in films or magazines – buttons shaped like stars or animals, two pockets instead of one to decorate a skirt or dress. Annie made whatever adjustments she requested. She made all but one or two of Cora's dresses. The exceptions came via Mrs Hunt, whose daughter attended the same dance class. Three or four of Mary's frocks were handed down when she outgrew them. These were shop-bought clothes of sound quality – the first my mum ever wore, and the only ones for a good few years. One had short puffed sleeves with a Peter Pan collar and an elasticated waist, but the very best of all was a navy blue dress with white polka dots, a patent belt and a flared skirt that swung when you moved, like a dancer's.

My grandma made nearly all my childhood clothes too, jumpers and cardigans as well as dresses, but she surpassed herself with my dolls. There were none better dressed in the whole of England. One Christmas morning, I woke to find them all (some half a dozen) posing in new outfits. My mum had stealthily removed them, one by one, for Annie to take their measurements without my noticing. A tall thin doll with pointy toes was dressed for the ball in a crimson gown with a full net skirt – layers of net, not just the one – and a tiny blue corsage, the corsage the telling detail. My favourite wore a winter coat in pillar-box red corduroy with a real fur collar and matching Cossack hat; and on the year Annie and Eva took my brother and me to Scarborough (gold doubloons in Peasholm Park and false ink and whoopee cushions from the seafront joke shop), the doll who accompanied us had a holiday outfit, just as I did.

I don't know if the council-house move had anything to do with it, but around this time, Jim sold the cake shop. Annie had to find new employment and signed up as an agent for the Provident Clothing Company to canvas customers buying clothes on Hire Purchase. HP (or the 'never-never') was another sign of the times: 'Choose the "Simone" afternoon frock in suede georgette with bolero jacket front, or the "Royce" raglan-sleeved winter coat, and pay by instalment.'

Collecting Provident with Annie became one of the weekend routines of my mum's childhood (and was, incidentally, another of the things that excluded Willie, not that he would have expected to accompany Annie while she was working, but it joined the lengthy list of things that shut him out).

First thing Saturday morning, Cora and Annie walked the length of Whittington Moor, along Stonegravels and up to the Highfield Estate, a development on higher ground whose mix of council and private housing offered a different perspective in every sense. Built in the late 1920s, on land formerly part of the Highfield Hall estate (another landowner fallen on hard times), this was a desirable area, albeit a very different kind of estate from the original one. Going from door to door, opening and closing sunbeam gates, passing borders of Michaelmas daises and hydrangeas, Cora understood that she and her mam were the poor ones, until Annie reassured her: 'We're just as good as they are.'

Though Cora accompanied her on Saturday mornings, Friday evenings and Mondays were also collecting days for Annie. (Her washday was Tuesday for this reason.) As long as she presented her books to the Provident office each Wednesday, she could choose her own hours, but Annie had to canvass her customers – '*vigorously and systematically*', according to her Provident handbook – when they had money. It did not take long for her to assess who could be trusted to pay on Mondays and who she had to catch on payday. Those with a smarter address could be just as nifty at avoiding payment as poorer customers. And many pleas were genuine – unexpected illness and the need to pay a doctor could easily swallow the shillings put aside towards a new frock.

All orders had to tally with the ticks and crosses in Annie's Provident book. Annotating this while chatting to a customer, it was easy to put a mark in the wrong column. Over the years, Annie and Cora spent many Tuesday evenings checking and rechecking her figures, trying to make them come right for the next day.

The Wednesday morning ritual hardly varied. The Provident office was crammed with collectors – men, mostly – standing in line, gradually shuffling forward, waiting to be grumbled at and generally harangued by their manager, Mr Smith, whose general irritability was sharpened by any failure to produce new customers. ('*Enter the names and number of houses of those who are likely or have promised to take shares… Invite weekly the members of your agency to recommend to you other likely members… Punctuality and regularity… will soon beget for you their confidence and support.*') No mention of the door shut in your face, or the message via a child: 'My mother says to tell you she's not in.'

But Annie had to tolerate Smithy only once a week. The rest of the time was hers: out in the fresh air, independent. She could not imagine another job that would give her so much flexibility and enable Cora to accompany her on Saturday mornings. It was pleasant enough work in summer and on any other fine day, and Annie's friendly, reliable clients greatly outnumbered cussed ones. It also gave her a chance to glimpse inside other people's houses and see the three-piece-suite in green moquette, the new fawn-tiled fireplace. Long-standing customers enjoyed the company – 'Mrs Thompson's here, put the kettle on' – the walk itself was good exercise, two or three miles each time, and sometimes taking her as far as the other side of Chesterfield; and enabled Annie to pursue her own thoughts while earning money. Money that was hers for the housekeeping, not Willie's to squander.

If some questioned the fact that my grandma worked while men were desperate for employment, she had a ready answer in her child and sick husband. Annie was the breadwinner of the family, even if as far as most people were concerned, she was just another woman carrying a shopping bag. Few gave her a second glance. By the time my mum reached secondary school, however, and met girls whose fathers had higher incomes, her new friends were amazed to discover she had a mother who went out to work.

Saturday-morning Provident preceded Cora's lesson at Joan Mason's School of Dancing, a slice of pleasure for Annie as much as Cora. Joan Mason introduced a rare note of sophistication to provincial Chesterfield. A teacher with all the poise an aspirant dancer (and her mother) could wish for, she had the manner and looks to match. Miss Mason strode through her classes in Oxford bags (perfect for executing time-steps), painted her nails scarlet and spoke through peek-a-boo lips. She wore short, tight-fitting blouses above her trousers and had hair set in undulating waves; her eyebrows arched in perfect Art Deco curves. She was so impeccably 1930s she might have stepped out of a Busby Berkeley number or Noel Streatfeild's *Ballet Shoes*. No one else in Chesterfield looked or dressed like Joan Mason. Miss Mason literally turned heads.

General classes took place at Jimmy's (St James' Hall), a draughty venue whose wooden floor held its fair share of splinters for the unsuspecting dancer, but private lessons were held at the three-storey home Joan Mason shared with her parents and sister. The practice room was on the second floor, enabling Cora to walk past the partially open door of Miss Mason's bedroom. It was the perfect period boudoir, with ruched curtains in pink georgette

> It seems a great pity that so many people should have been prevented by the fog from being present at the Dance Recital and Entertainment by pupils and students of the Joan R. Mason School of Dancing, held at Bradbury Hall on Wednesday. They certainly missed one of the finest spectacles of amateur juvenile dancing seen in Chesterfield. The proceeds were for the *Derbyshire Times* Christmas Fund.
>
> The juveniles were supported by Miss Mason who gave 'My Valentine', 'A Breath of Musical Comedy' and 'The Fleet's in Port Again'. Miss Muriel Cooke and Mr A. Hardy gave solos, and sang together in duets. Miss Cooke's 'My Hero', from *The Chocolate Soldier*, was exceptionally well received.
>
> All the juveniles… entered into the zest of the dancing. Olive Bates excelled herself in solo numbers with her great versatility, and Mary Hunt performed well in her acrobatic number. The programme lasted a full three hours, and was watched by about 300 people… The finale was very spectacular.
>
> – *Derbyshire Times*, December 1936

setting off an oval dressing table positively glinting with bottles and trinkets. Unfortunately, these could not be seen in any detail as Cora was only passing by and Must Not Stare.

My mum was the first pupil Miss Mason entered for a ballet exam, and her teacher was understandably nervous about how her student would perform. When the results arrived – 'Oh, darling, you've got Honours,' – Joan, her sister Phyllis and their mother

(mother and sister *always* watched the class), gathered Cora in a mêlée of scent and lipstick. Mother and sister were almost as exotic as Joan. Phyllis wore her red hair sculpted in an Eton crop and dressed in a smart tweed suit, with a cigarette showing off her perfect nail polish. Her figure was as square as Joan's was slim; Mrs Mason's came somewhere in-between; her tailored suits were generally set off by a little cocktail hat and, occasionally, a bushy fox fur. Cora's success seemed far less significant than their effusive three-cornered embrace. Public displays of affection were rare.

Annie would have loved to linger after my mum's Saturday-morning class and continue talking with the other mums, but she could not defer the worst moment of her week any longer – worse even than her inquisition by Smithy. Annie's enjoyment of the dance class was all the keener for what came next. On Saturday lunchtimes, my grandma collected the Means Test, the money paid to families on the dole.

This was a moment she detested. Nothing could make this encounter acceptable to her. The walk into town enabled Annie to prepare for the ordeal but, even so, she had to set her face and straighten her back before she could open the office door. Annie's discomfort was palpable. 'You shouldn't be doing this,' the kindly young clerk told her, making his own assessment of my grandma's status, mentally adding her to the list of 'respectable' have-nots. 'Come back at five to twelve when everyone's gone.'

It was a relief to reach the corner shop, and freedom. Following the move to Racecourse Road, Annie and Cora spent the rest of Saturday as well as Sundays at Wheeldon Mill. They returned home overnight, but were very much a weekend fixture.

Cakes were still delivered to the corner shop on Saturday

mornings, but, by the 1930s, Saturdays also belonged to Connie and Pearl: laughing, tripping up the step, still giddy from the previous night's adventures. 'You should have seen him, Mrs Nash, thought himself cock o'midden,' describing some lounge lizard haunting the edge of the dance floor, tidying his hair with a bit of comb. Then, 'Ooh, they're nice,' Connie pointing to the latest selection of rings at the far end of the counter, selecting a topaz from its velveteen tray, lifting it to the light and on to her wedding finger. 'What do you reckon, Mrs Nash?', then twirling in a trill of giggles and private smiles.

Connie and Pearl were near neighbours and inseparable friends. 'Town topping' was their Friday-night quest, Chesterfield their destination: a rub down with a hot flannel to remove their week-day grime before heading into town for the evening; Connie walking with exaggerated care so as not to spoil the shoes it had taken six weeks to pay for, Pearl dressed in her weekend finery; letting young men buy them drinks and escaping before payment of any kind could be exacted; excited by the good-natured banter and the sense that the evening was theirs.

'I'll have a lemonade, if you're asking.' Then, half a dozen turns around the dance floor. '"I think I've found my feet now," he tells me. "Can't think how you lost them," I said. "They've been squash-ing mine the past half hour."' Another burst of giggles from Connie. Almost as much fun as their weekly adventures was the chance to relate them to Betsy and Eva the next day.

It was a pair of Connie's cast-off shoes that my mum clomped around in when she played dressing-up at her grandma's. Brown shoes, with high, solid heels and eyelets threaded with ribbon. She hadn't seen any shoes like these before, with laces that were pure ornamentation, and intended to have a pair when she grew up.

Eva was an even more intriguing source of grown-up delights. Sometimes, when playing 'ladies', Cora was allowed to borrow a handbag from the bottom of Eva's wardrobe. The room Eva shared with Betsy was a feast for curious small fingers. China figurines struck sentimental poses, blue-glass dishes displayed the brooches her grandma liked to wear at her throat; tall dappled vases flashed gold lustre, and everything was reflected twice over in the enormous mirrors Dick had bought. Three hatstands on a small chest of drawers looked exactly like the ones on Swallow's counter, though Betsy's hats belonged to a different era than those on sale in town. Even well into the 1930s, Betsy dressed like the Victorian she was.

Eva's dressing table and wardrobe brought the room up to date. One of my mum's greatest treats (and mine too, years later) was looking for 'surprises' within Eva's drawers: a parlour suite made from beaded conkers, the kind of toy you looked at on wet days but were not allowed to play with, or a tiny leather purse any doll would love, but which was actually Eva's first purse. The best objects held the promise of adult life: geometric shapes dangling on a ribbon of watered silk; emerald green brilliants in the brooch Eva pinned on her best coat; a jazzy tin of Cuticura talc; soft fur gauntlets Cora was allowed to stroke; and a midnight-blue bottle whose silver stopper released a mysterious scent.

Betsy's things were rarely so inviting but, if she asked very nicely, Cora could lift the lid on the box beneath her grandma's side of the bed and take out her Gipsy Queen shoes.

Early Saturday evenings at the corner shop could be exciting: Connie and Pearl heading off in their glad rags; Charles Parks checking his gloves and cuffs while awaiting change for a couple of cheap cigars. Another regular, if less welcome visitor, was Dabber Blair, a scruffy-looking chap who lived on Pottery Lane and was rarely seen without his handcart. The thought of Dabber frightened my mum; he had a reputation for being light-fingered (hence the nickname). 'Eva, there's Dabber,' Betsy would call, if she happened to see him through the sweet window when Eva was in the back with Cora and Annie. This was Eva's cue to jump up and join her mam, if not exactly arms-folded, on guard, then watchful nonetheless. With two women facing him across the counter, Dabber was less likely to try and filch something from the shelves – I don't know that he ever tried, but his reputation preceded him.

'Hello, Dabber. Now, what do you want?' (two Woodbines was his usual request), Betsy adopting her tried and tested way of dealing with potentially awkward customers, by combining a greeting with a command – her tone friendly, always, while making it clear she'd stand no nonsense.

Saturday nights were also for sing-songs. As soon as the tea things were cleared away, Eva settled herself at the piano, tossed her head (albeit to less effect now that her hair was shorter) and looked over her left shoulder to cue in the songsters. Mr Britt regularly joined them for a chorus or two and a tinkling of the keys before disappearing with Dick to the pub.

Nearly all the family tunes were from bygone days – there were no contemporary songs, nor any from the recent past: no ragtime jazz or Al Bowley. Eva favoured First World War numbers or music-hall tunes with rousing choruses, like those that came courtesy of the *News of the World*, and which enabled her to add trills as abundant as any she could produce with her pen. Pressing down hard on the pedals and keys, Eva flexed her fingers and her voice: 'Do You See That Boy How He Winks His Eye...' Betsy's tastes were similar. She still preferred Variety to anything contemporary; an evening's cinema was nowhere near as reassuring. (Cinema gave too faithful a rendition of the world. 'It's not real, is it, Eva?' she'd ask.) Annie joined in with all the songs, but made no special requests, though she and Willie had once contributed a whole list of favourite tunes. Those days were gone. No point in raking them up again.

The crowning moment of the evening awaited Dick's return from the pub. After thrashing his neighbours at dominoes – he was known locally as the Domino King – and with the benefit of two or three pints inside him, Dick sang for each of them in turn: 'My Old Dutch' for Betsy, 'Annie Laurie' for Annie, and 'When Irish Eyes are Smiling', in recognition of Eva's heritage. He'd sung these songs for donkey's years; no Saturday was complete without them. There was no particular tune for Cora, but she was included in the general embrace.

The best sing-songs were at Christmas, when Annie and Cora stayed overnight, Annie squeezing into bed with Betsy and Eva (all three in the same sty), and Cora sleeping in a put-me-up beside them. There was nothing very elaborate about their Christmas preparations – a few coloured trimmings and a small tree – but the house looked festive nonetheless. Everyone had a present, however small, and there were always three or four for Cora: a doll's tea set boxed in cellophane, a Shirley Temple doll with cut-out clothes and books, always books, including one or two from George, though Cora was instructed not to tell Willie. If her dad asked, the books were from Annie's cousin, Uncle Walter (though Annie hardly saw that Walter from one year round to the next). The name was convenient and, after all, not such a large fib: Walter was also George's name; he was always Uncle Walter to Cora.

Before going to bed on Christmas Eve, Cora hung her stocking (one of Dick's) beside the kitchen range and, to keep hers company, her grandfather pinned up its partner. The following morning, Dick made a big to-do of guessing what his stocking held, before drawing out – good heavens! – a potato.

As New Year's Eve approached, some of the local lads came knocking on the door: 'Here we come a-wassailing among the leaves so green,/ Here we come a-wandering/ So fair to be seen…'

With hardly an overcoat between them, no matter how sharp the wind, they crowded into the back room as soon as they finished singing, big lads suddenly self-conscious, twisting their caps between numb fingers while Betsy found her purse. On New Year's Day itself, they reappeared with anyone they could gather ('We'er goin Tuppin, a'tha comin?') to perform the Derby Tup outside the Great Central Hotel, with their neighbours a ready-made audience. The boldest lads stood in front, leading the verse and the actions, the others joined in at the chorus, and especially for the rousing finale, before coming forward, cap in hand.

Willie was not part of these jollities. Sometimes he visited friends, or was invited in by a neighbour. If not, he spent Christmas alone.

16

Oh Romany, I See the Campfires Burning

BY THE TIME MY MUM JOINED THE FAMILY, THE WHEELDON Mill Plantation was such a strong feature of my great-grandfather's life it was hard to consider him without it. Absorbed by its seasonal timetable and daily routine, Dick blended with the landscape as naturally as the steps fashioned at its entrance. The rhythm of the wood dictated his days: up early to feed and let out his chickens, cast corn, secure their huts and runs; cut hazel switches, plant and protect new saplings. There was always a job to be done: some sawing and repairing, the grass to keep down or a hedgerow to trim. Dick returned home in the middle of the day, and then back to the wood until teatime, and again to fasten the hens for the night.

The accident that propelled him to rent the wood finally enabled my great-grandfather to buy it. Eventually, Dick received compensation and used the £200 to purchase the land outright. On Christmas Eve, 1934, the four acres, three roods and seventeen perches became his. It was the best Christmas gift Dick could envisage. After his family, the wood was his greatest treasure.

My great-grandfather was nearing seventy when my mum was adopted; her memories are of an elderly man. In addition to the cumbersome walk caused by his raised shoe, Dick was becomingly increasingly deaf. At home, this made conversation difficult; in the wood, his loss of hearing did not matter. This four-acre spot was his kingdom.

No one outside the family came to the wood without an invitation, and very few people received one even then, but three of Dick's neighbours visited him there: Mr Britt, Mr Radcliffe and Mr Woolley. Elderly musketeers, these companions in old age liked to debate the changing world over an afternoon pipe full of Twist. But, as often as not, Dick was alone there; restored to beginnings he could only dimly remember, or of which he had no memory at all.

The little that is known of my great-grandfather's origins lends itself to romantic elaboration, especially the possibility that he was Romany, a piece of family lore strengthened by the arrival of a gypsy family at Wheeldon Mill. The summer the gypsies came was the hottest for some years. The shop door seemed to be

permanently propped open; Betsy kept a fan behind the counter so that she and Eva could cool themselves where they stood. The pressed meats sweated in the meat safe; even the wrapped sweets in the shady window began to melt, though no one wanted chocolate in that weather. Fly papers suspended from the ceiling recorded multiple deaths with a constant buzz. Towards the end of the week, the middens, awaiting their visit from the night-soil wagon, stank to high heaven (as did the rag-and-bone yard on Lockoford Lane, if you were unlucky enough to be down wind of it). Children dammed the river, scrawled letters in the rough ground in front of the shop, or played half-hearted games of marbles, hardly bothering to squabble over who'd won. This lethargy carried over into the evenings. Cora listened for the cry, 'Paling, Paling,' and the repeated tinkling of a bell, as Mr Paling, ice-cream seller, drove over the canal bridge.

The arrival of the gypsies seemed part of the unreality of that summer. One weekend, the publican's field was empty, the next, it contained two gypsy wagons, proper old-fashioned vardos, with canvas stretched over their circular frames and puthers of smoke rising from tin chimneys. Two horses grazed nearby, while a dark patch on the ground showed the remains of a recent fire. It was a proper gypsy encampment. Dick knew all about it. Mr Simms had given them permission to camp in his field.

My mum knew gypsies from her storybooks and songs. She also knew Gypsy Smith, an ancient Romany who called at the corner shop for the bacon bits and cheese parings Betsy and Eva would otherwise have thrown away, and for tobacco shavings which she tamped into a long clay pipe. On Gypsy Smith's death, Romanies cames from miles around to attend her funeral.

Romany camps and lone wagons were still relatively common

sights during Cora's childhood. She grew up with a fascination for gypsy ways. In part, this came from her grandparents, Dick and Betsy, but also from the people she met.

Over the coming months, Cora saw the gypsy family most weekends. Its matriarch, an elderly Romany my mum knew as 'Grandma', dressed in black from head to foot. Her lined face suggested a thousand stories which she seemed to be recalling while sitting on the topmost step of the farthest wagon, looking out towards Bluebank Wood. The younger woman was so slim and fragile-looking you would think a gust of wind would knock her down, but even in the harshest weather (the family stayed until the following spring), she knelt outside to bathe her little boy; up to her elbows in soapy water, bare arms exposed to the cold. Her son had a nursery-rhyme name, Johnny Shafto, which suited his rosy cheeks and thick, dark hair. Finally, there was Bud, 'Uncle Bud' to Cora, a tall, imposing man with a weathered face. Bud's hair shone like the darkest jet: hedgehog oil was the secret, he told Cora. Whenever he found a dead hedgehog at the roadside, he brought the animal home and baked it on the fire, before draining the carcass of its oil. Far better than any shop-bought potion, Bud assured her, showing Cora his current jar.

The family said hello if she passed them in Station Road, but mostly kept themselves to themselves. Years of suspicion had made them wary, no doubt, though no hostility was expressed within my mum's hearing. The Great Central Hotel supplied the family with water, which Bud and the younger woman carried to the field in heavy flagons. Betsy and Eva saved the remnants of pressed meat, heels of cheese and similar trimmings they had once donated to Gypsy Smith. The family also ate rook pies, courtesy of Dick's wood.

Bud was the exception to my great-grandfather's rule. In all the years he owned the land, Bud was only person outside the family whom Dick allowed to enter the wood by himself, and the only man he gave permission to shoot there. He always spoke of Bud and his family with immense respect and concern for their welfare. I hardly need to invent gypsy origins for Dick: he contributed to the mythology himself.

The gypsies returned the following year and, towards the end of their stay, invited my family to visit their wagons. Betsy and Cora went first, and then Dick and Eva, so there would always be someone minding the shop. (Annie was Providenting, as usual.) Conscious of the honour bestowed upon them, they walked very carefully up the steps. Inside, all was polished brasses, patterned rugs, cushions and soft chairs (the softness of the chairs a particularly memorable feature, compared with Betsy's horsehair sofa). To my mum's delight, their wagons were every bit as colourful and comfortable as anything described in *Mr Galliano's Circus*.

A further occasion to see gypsies – or the promise of them, at least – was the annual Feast on Stand Road. This was an early-evening excursion for Eva and Cora; Annie disliked fairgrounds and Willie preferred to visit after the pub. (Pub or no, he was a crack shot with a wooden ball and nearly always brought home a coconut.)

If Cora hovered near the edge of the fair, tiptoeing as close to the caravans as she dare – hardly close at all, though it felt dangerously close to her – she might, just might, spot a gypsy. The half-light rarely revealed anyone, but there was never anything disappointing about the Feast. A bombardment of noise and excitement, swingboats flashing colour out of darkness, raucous voices adding to and clashing with the hum of generators and the medley of fairground tunes. Penny rides and penny fortunes, merry-go-rounds and helter-skelters, a whirl of noise and gaudy paintwork, the smell of sweat jostling with that of spun sugar, frying onions and sixpenny scent.

Some Feasts had sideshows; one year, a flea circus, a pitiful attraction in which fleas the size of house flies navigated miniature bridges and other obstacles placed in their path, and walked round and round an oversize table. Larger crowds (no less curious than their nineteenth-century cohorts) queued to see the Freak Show, approached via a walkway raised like a gangplank, but with handrails. Two pelicans, snapping sentries, stood either side of the entrance; one sharp beak clipped my mum when she and Eva reached the tent. A further rope penned them, forcing all spectators along a narrow path designed to channel their excitement for what lay ahead. A waif-like girl with a delicate face and long fair hair sat waiting in a white muslin gown with a blue sash. Her sleeveless dress revealed that she had tiny hands and fingers, but no arms; a tiny silver wristwatch emphasised the delicacy of her tiny wrist. The crowd slowed down to stare, examining her on all sides and from all angles, before disappearing into the night to get their money's worth on something else. The poor girl remained there, roped off, marooned in the middle of the tent.

Popular children's hairstyles of the day were the pudding-basin haircut or the bob with a side parting, and strands of hair caught up in a slide or bow (the bow half-mast come playtime). My grandma favoured neither style for Cora. She took her lead from Royalty.

You could follow the lives of the Princesses Elizabeth and Margaret Rose in newspapers and women's magazines. The first royals to truly grow up in the eye of the press, they were snapped whenever possible and fed to an eager public whose fascination with the little royals (and girls too, how charming) meant their lives, clothing and hairstyles were well documented. *Modern Home* promised 'Princess Elizabeth's Life Story'; *Home Chat* invited you to save coupons for a child's cut-out frock 'like Princess Elizabeth wears'.

The Princesses Elizabeth and Margaret Rose wore their hair slightly longer than the fashion and it curled in natural waves. My mum wore her hair slightly longer too, and she had curls, soft ringlets, although hers had to be created overnight. No matter how tired she and Annie were, Cora's hair was dampened and twisted on to the cotton rags she slept in to produce loose ringlets the next day. Cora enjoyed the effect as much as Annie. She also wore her hair in a fringe, a style favoured by some of the toffs, and which was, I suppose, entirely appropriate for a child chosen by Princess Alice.

My grandma's generation was steeped in pageantry and flag-waving. Born in an age of deference, Annie was drilled in the Kings and Queens of England, and taught them in her turn (a parting gift from one grateful school was a history of the monarchy, bound in suede – purple suede, of course). Royalty always fascinated her. Deference informed my mum's childhood too. Her infant years were chequered with school holidays for royal occasions. School closed for royal weddings (and George V's funeral); pupils regularly saluted the flag. A whole week's timetable was given over to the 1935 Silver Jubilee, with a day off for the actual event. Annie and Eva both ordered Jubilee picture books (one between two households wouldn't do).

Buoyed up by this general enthusiasm, Willie bought a Silver

Jubilee flag, not a little tu'penny-ha'penny flag to wave in a deferential gesture, but a large Union Jack which he hoisted outside the landing window. If he thought to curry favour with Annie, it was another poorly judged scheme. Annie had better uses for a shilling and no desire to make a show of the house.

OUR KING, A SHINING EXAMPLE OF FITNESS

There can be no need to draw to your attention to one feature which stands out from the remarkable pictures of the King with the soldiers of the Empire which appear in to-day's issue, for it will be obvious to every reader. The King, as revealed by these pictures, is clearly not only of fine, soldier-like bearing, but of excellent physique.

'He looks like a Test cricketer just back from Australia,' we heard someone in the crowd the other day say of His Majesty. It was not an idle compliment, it was the truth…

…The King is indeed filled with that kind of energy and enthusiasm which can only come with robust health and a good constitution. He has come to the Throne at a time when 'keep fit' is a slogan, when a determined effort is being made to improve the physique of everybody, men and women as well as children, so that they may the better take their share of the tasks that lie ahead. And in his own person he is a shining example to us all.

– From a leader, Annie's *Daily Sketch*, 15 May 1937

Even more elaborate celebrations were planned when, in 1937, the Duke of York ascended the throne. The Coronation medal Cora received at school was as nothing compared with the cut-out Coronation game Annie bought her, complete with crown and sceptre, liveried footmen, carriage and courtiers, not to mention tiny cardboard princesses. It was all such a relief after Edward (another topic for Sunday afternoon debate: the family loved Edward because he talked to the Derbyshire miners and was a

The Family that holds the love of all the peoples of the Empire

friend of the common man, but – that woman! While Annie and
Eva discussed the Abdication, Cora drew a picture of a figure with
corrugated hair and wrote underneath it: The Woman He Loved.)

Chesterfield fêted the new king and queen with bunting,
banners and streamers. Flags flew from the roof of Eyre & Son's;
Woodhead's Grocer and Café (which could always be relied on
for decorum) favoured window boxes with red rhododendrons,
blue hydrangeas and marguerites. Eva's *Coronation Souvenir Book*,
with its bright gold boards and colour images (plus a surprisingly
cordial press for Wallis Simpson), was far superior to her Silver
Jubilee volume. The *Daily Sketch* promised Annie the Best Royal
Pictures Ever (one penny).

But it rained like the devil on Saturday, 12 May. By lunchtime,
Chesterfield's High Street was a vision of soggy bunting and droop-
ing flags. The town's main celebrations were deferred for a week,
but numerous children's teas went ahead, including the one Cora
attended at Wheeldon Mill, a squall of sticky buns and weak
orange squash in the hangar owned by local businessman Joe Pass.

All manner of children's treats took place during my mum's childhood; countless buns were consumed at trestle tables and sack
races run, with a colliery band oomphing in the background, but
the most memorable, as far as Cora was concerned, was organised
by the *Derbyshire Times*.

On alternate years, the *Derbyshire Times* provided a Christmas
Treat for the children of Chesterfield's unemployed, and made an
appeal for donations. Benefactors' names were printed in the paper;
in 1936, the proprietors kicked things off with £10. All surplus
money supported a fund which, since its inception, had provided
nearly 10,000 pairs of boots for the borough's poor and destitute

children. While weighing up their charitable instincts at the break-fast table, readers could turn the page and observe those with far deeper pockets than themselves: the Marquess of Tweeddale, the Viscountess Massereene and others of their party, photographed shooting in Derbyshire's Alfreton Park.

The 'ladies of Chesterfield' dressed more than 800 dolls for that year's Treat, which were put on general display before being distributed. The 2,300 children invited to the event (which included the children of widows) necessitated parties on two consecutive afternoons.

My mum was entertained by Punch and Judy, conjuring tricks and knockabout clowns. There were sweets as well as cakes for tea; a tinsel headdress for each girl and paper caps for the boys, but the whole thing was quite overwhelming. A thousand-plus children enjoying themselves in a cavernous hall make a terrific din. Cora's chief memory was of the community singing and of the helper pointing out each phrase on a vast scroll of paper, pantomime style. Though she did not know 'It's a Sin to Tell a Lie' (someone's idea of combining a moral lesson with a party song?) when she arrived at the Treat, she was word-perfect by the time she left. My mum was one of the girls who received a doll (other gifts included pencil cases, books and tea sets), a pretty blonde doll in pale pink net. She swapped her for a dark-haired doll in a silver lamé jacket, which at least looked a bit more like her.

Cora must have mentioned the Boot Fund Treat at school because her Junior School headmistress, Miss Holden (who was nothing like the Infants' tyrant) took Annie aside and advised her that this was not a suitable event for her daughter, and on no account should she attend another one. My mum was immensely relieved to be spared further regimented entertainment.

For some of the girls attending the *Derbyshire Times* Treat, a doll was their only Christmas gift – as in the 1900s, poor children still looked to charity for dolls. Not so, my mum. Her circumstances were a mishmash of the times: weekly cinema-going versus the Means Test, brand-new toys versus an invitation to attend the Boot Fund Treat. Cora danced at a concert intended to raise funds for the Treat she later attended (Joan Mason's School of Dancing put on the show). She was entertainer and recipient both.

The Boot Fund Treat and Means Test bore the stamp of official-dom but, for Annie and Cora, these seemed like the aberrations in their life. Family treats were provided by Betsy and Eva whose own needs were relatively few, and, if Annie had money to spare, it was spent on Cora. There were comics to read – from *Chick's Own* to *Comic Cuts* and the *Beano* – as well as Christmas books, and piano lessons along with dancing classes (Eva paid the 1/6 for Miss Alice Brocklehurst to teach Cora on her baby grand). Falling on harder times did not mean the neglect of former values. And Annie's ability to run up a dress or make one over meant that clothes could always be provided. In fact, at a time when even girls whose parents were reasonably well-off had relatively few clothes, my mum had quite a number. (I know this because, a few years later, she made a list.)

None of this would have been possible without the generosity of Betsy, Dick and Eva; and Annie, too, when she had the shillings – but their larger generosity was of spirit. Instead of the prevail-ing attitude, 'You'll have what you're given,' there was choice, a concept making waves in the adult world by this time, but which was far slower to percolate down through childhood. My mum chose the pattern and colour of the jumpers Eva knitted for her birthdays, and the buttons and any detailing Annie put on her clothes. 'If I've got it, you can have it,' was their view. It was still present in my childhood too with Annie and Eva. And although it manifested itself in material ways, this generosity was really all about nurturing and encouragement. In all kinds of ways, small as well as large, my mum knew how much she was loved.

One of Willie's less contentious schemes was his acquisition of an ornamental clock. A cast-iron clock with a small ceramic face, it depicted a country boy in a soft hat, open shirt and knee breeches, striding with his hunting horn, his faithful hound bounding on ahead. Green grass, willowy trees, fine flowers, birds flying above in an eighteenth-century rural idyll; the grass all the greener when Willie took up oil painting and added his own small dabs of paint. The clock was said to be a copy of one owned by local industrialist Charles Paxton Markham, owner of the Staveley Coal & Iron Company, magistrate, thrice Mayor, and reader of the Riot Act. This 'man of plain words', who 'liked plain speaking,' as the *Derbyshire Times* reported at his death, was something of a local celebrity, and was often referred to as 'Charlie'.

There are many stories about Charlie Markham: of how he drove his car – a yellow Rolls-Royce – into the closed gates of his home, Ringwood Hall, when his (second) wife refused to get out to open them; and of how he bought his mistress a fur coat, on condition – so the story circulated within Chesterfield's public houses – that she wear nothing beneath it. (Though how the taprooms knew what Charles Markham told his mistress is anybody's guess.) This great industrialist asked that, when he died, 'the fumes and smoke of the Devonshire Works would blow over his remains'. As in life, so in death, Charles Paxton Markham got his wish. When he died in 1926, he was buried in Staveley

Cemetery, a few miles from my great-grandma's shop. His clock outlived him. Willie's replica stood on the hearth in the second bedroom for many years, contributing its own small detail to the Markham legend. A drinking pal of Willie's had supposedly copied the original for himself. 'Would you do one for me?' Willie asked. '*I* won't tell, if you don't.' (And nor did he.)

One dark night, when Annie and Cora returned to Racecourse Road after an evening dance class, it was obvious someone had been in the living room. The house was silent but the table and chairs had been moved and, when they called upstairs, no answer came from Willie. They were only just starting to absorb this when Mrs Blake, their neighbour, shouted through the door and came into the house without knocking. Willie had been taken to hospital and the furniture moved by the men who stretchered him away. He had groped his way downstairs and knocked on the party wall to alert their adjoining neighbour to run to the pub and phone for an ambulance. Willie was diagnosed with a perforated duodenal ulcer.

The hospital was a vile place with miles of dark-green walls and intimidating smells. It took several minutes for Annie and Cora to reach Willie's ward via identical duplicating corridors. Two rows of men with putty-coloured faces and crumpled pyjamas looked up when they entered the room.

They heard Willie before they saw him; caught his unmistakeable laughter, saw smiling faces in the adjacent beds. He was entertaining his fellow captives with a funny story. They were in need of humour there: all conversation was interrupted by men coughing and hacking into sputum dishes. Nurses patrolling the ward handed out fresh ones as if distributing sweets.

My mum danced around the table when Willie came home, and told him everything that had happened to her that day, conjuring up and embellishing all the minutiae of school to entertain him. Even as she was doing this, Cora knew that her excitement, though every bit of it was real, was also a performance designed to show Willie how much she had missed him and how pleased she was he was home.

A fire was lit in the second bedroom, where Willie slept by then. (Cora had been promoted from her large cot to share a bed with Annie. 'It's better for him here,' Annie explained, when the move took place, 'and will ensure your dad gets sufficient rest.') It was winter and the firelight in the room was reflected in the handles on the chest of drawers, and snickers of flame were repeated in the wardrobe mirror. A bedroom fire was a rarity; its reddening glow was transforming.

Willie's brother Godfrey and his sister Gertie came to visit, bringing laughter and talk into the room, as always. For once, Willie is the centre of attention. Warmth, laughter, firelight dancing on dark wood: everything is going to be all right now, Cora is certain.

The far end of the living room, made narrow by the stairwell on the other side of the wall, was given over almost entirely to my mum. The space beneath the front window sill, crammed with Annie's Busy Lizzies and pelargoniums (I only have to rub a lemon-scented leaf and I'm back at my grandma's house), made a discrete play area. A chair and a small table at the opposite side of the room made a snug corner for Annie; Willie sprawled on the sofa to read *John Bull* and *Picture Post*.

When she was small, Cora could sit in her mam's big lap, sinking further and further into her skirt, while she heard all about Diddums and similar characters. Lovely Annie, gentle and kind (except when it came to Willie), knew how to entertain a child. She and my mum read *Now We Are Six* and recited its verses together; Cora coloured in Ernest H. Shepard's illustrations (and those she left blank, I coloured later, when it became my turn). But my grandma was a schoolmistress too; there was always a hint of the schoolma'am about Annie. 'Have you been a good girl, Jane?' she would ask, borrowing from A. A. Milne a question that was never only playful.

When she was able to read by herself, Cora worked her way through Enid Blyton's books as they were published, *The Wind in*

DOES DETECTIVE FICTION LOWER OUR ETHICAL STANDARDS?

Do we read [detective novels] because they fulfil our ideas of life and morals? Or are they built up as they are to suit our prevalent conceptions? Are we for them, or are they for us?

I do not know... One conclusion has fashioned itself in my mind and it is this: the mass of detective novels are pitched on so low a plane of morality that they are an insidious danger to the national morals... All this crime fiction is infinitely more vitiating than the so-called pornographic literature because the latter frankly sets out to be naughty...

– Helen Normanton, pioneering lawyer and columnist, *Good Housekeeping*, July 1931

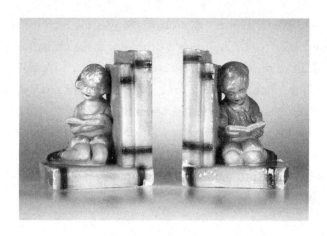

the Willows, *Anne of Green Gables*, *Little Women*, *The Adventures of Huckleberry Finn* and *Tom Sawyer*. She also read *Daddy-Long-Legs* – Annie and Willie loved Mary Pickford in the film and bought this orphan's story for my mum, who delighted in its pages without knowing she had mysteries in her own childhood too. When Chesterfield's New Children's Library opened in 1936, Cora was one of its 5,000 members. She produced labels for each shelf of Annie's bureau, their subjects enunciated as clearly as in any proper library – Drama, History, Shakespeare... Apart from her Uncle Jim's house, theirs was the only one Cora knew with books and a bookcase on view.

Further along from *Westward Ho!* and *Vanity Fair* stood Edgar Allan Poe and Edgar Wallace. Annie liked Horror but her secret vice was Crime. She no longer had time to read novels, but satisfied her longing with *Detective Weekly*. Sinister figures loomed large and terrifyingly on its front cover; Cora turned over the magazine so she could not see the nightmarish silhouettes making intimidating gestures by lamplight.

Annie's all-time favourite was Sexton Blake, the 'Crime Expert of World-Wide Repute'. Sexton Blake was everywhere. ('I am Sexton Blake,' one Chesterfield drunkard insisted, before being hauled off to the cells.) On the evenings Willie disappeared for a pint at the Victoria Club, Annie settled into her chair with the latest exploits of the famous detective and his loyal side-kick, Tinker. Page-turning-page of suspense, with only the occasional illustration to relieve the tension until, 'The wooden door flew open, and standing on the threshold was the figure of Sexton Blake.' By the time she reached the denouement, Willie was due home.

Far more intriguing (and with no immediate and satisfying conclusion) was the visit from the mystery lady who came to Racecourse Road. My mum was six years old when Annie appeared in her classroom and asked if she could remove her daughter. This was memorable in itself – teachers (and Annie) were sticklers for school rules: no one left the classroom before the afternoon bell. And this was no swan-like Annie either. She lacked her usual poise and seemed hot and flustered, as if she'd run the four hundred yards to the school.

'Someone very special has come to see you,' she told Cora, hurrying her into her coat, 'a lady in a chauffeur-driven car.' Cars were still rarities in Racecourse Road, let alone cars with chauffeurs. But as Cora and Annie rounded the curve and the house came into view, there was no car ahead of them. 'He must have left the lady in the house,' Annie said. Yet, when they reached the house, there was no lady there either.

The cupboard where my mum kept her books and toys was open, with all its contents revealed as if on a stage. Her child-size desk and chair stood beside the open cupboard doors and her doll's house beside them. 'I showed her your things,' Annie said, 'and your photographs.' All the photographs on the piano were of Cora. 'And she wanted to see you. But, obviously, the lady couldn't wait.'

The lady was wearing a mid-calf navy-blue costume (ladies wore 'costumes' in those days), with a matching hat and, possibly, a short veil – at least, that's how I see her, though I've actually no idea what she wore. My grandma did not describe or explain her, and my mum was too young to ask many questions. Some time later, Cora asked Mrs Blake if she had seen the lady, but she had not, nor the car, and no other neighbour mentioned seeing a vehicle. Which was just as well. The sight of a smart woman stepping from a chauffeur-driven car could have licked like a flame round Racecourse Road, though that thought probably did not occur to their well-heeled visitor, who disappeared as quickly as she had arrived, leaving a mystery behind her.

17

Woolworth's Gems and Saturday Treats

Dorothy and Eileen were a bit older than my mum but adapted to her games with good grace, making bottles of rose-petal scent that reeked after one day and had to be poured down the sink. Occasionally, they were joined by Margaret, who was older still and rather superior. One day, she mentioned church. She was Church of England. What were they? Eileen went to the Catholic church; Dorothy attended Chapel. And Cora?

'I go to Woolworth's,' she said.

Woolworth's belonged to Eva's days off and was part of a larger excursion into town via the Great Central Railway, one of the few times my mum caught the train from Wheeldon Mill: a three-penny ticket and a Nestlé's chocolate bar expelled from the machine on the station platform. Eva and Cora travelled into Chesterfield throughout the year, but their winter trips were the most memorable because of the return journey: clouds of steam billowing against the dark night sky and the gaslights winking as they stepped from their compartment into the grip of cold air.

Trips into town required a special effort: a brown leather clutch bag, gloves and cloche hat for Eva; a brown velvet handbag for Cora, with an appliquéd Minnie Mouse on the flap. If Eva took out her compact to check her face for smuts from the train, my mum consulted her Mickey Mouse mirror.

There were always several things saved up for their next expedition: a pair of T-bar sandals for Cora; stockings or talc for Eva and Annie, purchased from Swallow's or John Turner's, with their hushed and carpeted interiors and canisters of loose change whizzing along overhead pipes. Woodhead's grocer had its own particular fragrance of loose tea, and a recently refurbished café upstairs. No longer turn-of-the-century Oriental, it was now thoroughly up-to-date with dark wooden panels and chrome-edged swing doors finished in pistachio green. Eyres' was equally modish, selling muffineers and match-holders by Clarice Cliff.

Woolworth's cornucopia of tat came near the end of their itinerary and regularly supplied sixpenny treats: a toy watch with an elasticated strap or a sparkling ring. Some Woolworth's gems shone even brighter than those sold by the corner shop.

Chesterfield market was their final stopping point, its stalls bustling late into the evening, the whole market aglow with a

greenish hue from naphtha lights pinned to canvas awnings. The market was a reliable source for buttons and knitting wool, with baskets you could rummage through for lengths of decorative braid. A man in a striped blazer supplied sheet music: 'Daddy Wouldn't Buy me a Bow Wow,' if Eva was choosing; something from *Snow White and the Seven Dwarfs*, if the decision was Cora's. Last stop of all was the stall where Eva bought a cup of mushy peas. Cup and spoon were passed between them, sixpenny winter warmth.

Afternoons with Eva generally involved a degree of adventure, however small; she could make the most ordinary walk seem exciting. If there was something unexpected to discover in a hedgerow, she found it: a discarded toy or a hair ribbon fluttering from a twig. Eva walked fast, but her walks could be quite slow because of the number of people she knew. And there was afternoon visiting with Eva, and, of course, seasonal galas.

My mum had a prestigious role at galas, accompanying Eva selling sweets, still the same usherette's tray; still sprinting and egg-and-spoon races and, one year, a much-anticipated motorcycle demonstration. Half a dozen men wearing leather helmets with narrow chin straps and enormous leather gauntlets lined up their metal steeds to perform daring feats, revving up their bikes on to planks laid across a series of oil drums, and leaping from one to the next. They executed bold skids, before coming to a halt with one foot on the ground, swerving only feet away from their audience. Back at the corner shop, Cora's tin motorcyclist leaps from the sugar bowl to the milk jug to show Betsy what she's missed.

There was nearly always a greasy pole and a rowdy tug of war, which presented no difficulties to those who battled subterraneously with enormous tubs of coal but was harder work for the

Sheepbridge clerks. To get a better purchase before grasping the rope the colliers spat on their hands. 'There's no need for you to copy that,' Betsy tells my mum when she mentions this particular manoeuvre.

Dick winks at Cora. There is a kind of pact between them. It's as if Betsy is in charge of them both. Being deaf means that, if Dick's chair is in the way, or he fails to respond, Betsy gives him a shove. 'Am I 'im?' he asks Cora. 'You are, Grandad,' she answers solemnly. 'Oh, you are a man,' Eva chips in, laughing at them both.

The grandfather who was happy to be called Dickie Dutton by Cora while she combed his white hair, and who, having no idea of his actual birthday, agreed to celebrate it on 1 April, had a side to him the family never saw, which was reflected in his member-ship of the Buffs. In the early 1930s, Dick was raised to the Buffaloes' Roll of Honour and photographed in the full rig – medals, braided cuffs, embroidered apron. The man in that picture is a revelation to me. He looks nothing like the genial father and grandfather who never raised his voice or fist. Those stern features turn him into someone else entirely: a character he put on, along with his Tuesday regalia. Dick was reasonably satisfied with the result and thought the picture a fair likeness, but his daughters felt he had tried too hard and overdone the formality. Whenever Annie or Eva came across it, they said the same thing: 'I don't know what my dad was doing, pulling a face like that.'

America, France, Africa, Spain, Italy, Egypt, India, Persia, Turkey, Palestine…Cora produced a list of Countries My Dad has Visited. Nineteen in all, but she wanted a round twenty: 'Oh, alright then,' Willie said, 'Put Alsace-Lorraine, that little place the French and Germans are always squabbling about.' He taught her American

currency (that went into her notebook too), the source of the Tigris and Euphrates, and how to spell Mesopotamia. She was proud of her dad's achievements and when she got a new notebook, listed the countries all over again.

Notebooks came in handy while adults talked. After the Saturday tea things had been cleared away, there was invariably an hour or so of talk. While Annie and Eva discussed the events of the week, Cora occupied herself by writing or drawing. Being an only child meant that if she crayoned quietly, adults tended to overlook her presence when they were engrossed in conversation. Some of the topics they discussed were already known to Cora – the Mill kids had told her of the eighteen-year-old who shot himself in the stable beside the gypsy field and of the boy her age who drowned in the River Rother – other events made an impression because of their effect on Annie and Eva.

Today, a marble angel guards the graves of Rhoda Bradford and her young children. At the time, their disappearance made local headlines: 'Have You Seen Them?' Even Scotland Yard became involved. Annie and Eva didn't think much of Rhoda's husband, but they liked her and the children and were appalled to hear they'd disappeared. Their last known sighting was at a sweet shop where Rhoda bought sweets to pacify the children who were fractious and crying. 'Come on, ducks,' she said. 'Let's go home.' These were the last words she was heard to say before the three of them stepped out into the fog.

Their bodies were not found straightaway, nor were they together when the river finally gave them up. Another death preceded theirs: eleven months earlier, Rhoda's eldest daughter had been 'called home', aged six. Rhoda had visited the grave on that last afternoon. Some anniversaries are too hard to face; some griefs cannot be mended.

'He'll be alright till t'bobby sees him,' was a common enough phrase used of husbands as well as sons who seemed to be up to no good and wouldn't 'be said'. Lads still made their plans within Betsy's hearing, but when she heard mention of a rope and of a window that was generally left open, and listened to voices rising and falling in whispered exclamations, she was uncertain what to do for the best. She needed her neighbours' trust, but she could not bear to hear these young lads plotting something as foolish as a robbery (and what would Mrs Pollard say if her young Arnold was sent away?).

The local bobby still called at the house for his mid-evening cuppa and so, despite her reservations, Betsy reported what she'd heard. A quiet word from the constable foiled the would-be robbery and the plotters even laughed when Betsy told them of her intervention in their scheme. It seems extraordinary that they could joke about it together, but perhaps their plot was 'too daft to laugh at', as my great-grandma used to say, and she wanted to shake these youngsters into some common sense or at least deter them from plotting within her hearing.

On one occasion, Betsy consulted the bobby on her own behalf. Although afternoon strollers regularly used the shop at weekends, it was rare for a stranger to call midweek, and in all the time my great-grandma ran the corner shop, only one customer was in any way threatening. A middle-aged man came into the shop when she was there by herself; a bedraggled-looking chap, though no more scruffy than some of her customers. It was not his clothing that aroused Betsy's suspicions, but the fact that he did not seem to know what he wanted and appeared to be eyeing up the stock and her with it. The stranger had made a mistake with my great-grandma who, though in her seventies by now, was far from fragile and could still manoeuvre the vinegar barrel and sacks of corn when need be. Betsy had his measure straightaway. He had not reckoned on Teddy either, whose crescendoing snarl seemed to come from nowhere.

'I'd leave now if I were you,' Betsy said, summoning her most authoritative voice, 'or this dog will have you, and I'm going to tell the police.' She half turned as if to open the house door. There was no phone in the building, but the stranger couldn't know that. And, like most people who encountered my great-grandma, the man did exactly as he was told.

Detectives sometimes swelled the Saturday evening numbers, knocking on the house door to ask if they could watch the comings and goings at the Great Central Hotel. They could stand un-observed in the shop's dark interior and keep an eye out for those they wanted to question about poaching or some other dodgy deal. Pub-watching provided family entertainment too. Betsy, Annie and Eva regularly peered through the gloom at tipping-out time. Friday and Saturday nights were invariably occasions when arms-around-the-shoulder, good-natured camaraderie could flare into anger in an instant. Some pantomime swings were taken by brawlers too drunk to land a punch, but there were serious fist fights too, with men squaring up to an opponent. Annie and Eva were used to sights like these; street fights had been part of their childhoods, and, although neither had any desire to be closer to the scene, they thought nothing of positioning themselves for the best view – in front of the counter, slightly to the left side of the sweet window.

For three or four weeks, they watched Bobby Taylor challenge whoever was willing to take him on. This short, stocky man flared up in his cups; at other times, no one took much notice of him. Perhaps that was part of his problem, though I suspect that, like his brother Albie, Bobby was a tin god at home. For weeks, he challenged anyone who crossed him and took a swing at those fool enough to intervene. He was never staggering drunk – and there were many who said no man was drunk unless he was staggering – but he made a nuisance of himself all the same. After several weeks of this aggravation, Arnold Dugsby floored him. Six foot tall in his stocking feet, with knuckles the size of walnuts, Arnold knocked Bobby to the ground with one punch. He kept himself to himself after that.

Watching fights was a purely female activity; Dick never stirred from his chair. He had probably witnessed more fights than he cared to remember (a photograph from Dick's brickyard days includes one chap with a real shiner). This particular spectator sport was left to the women: Betsy in her starched white blouse with a neat brooch at her throat; Eva and Annie fingering their beads.

My grandma and Cora rarely left Wheeldon Mill until after ten o'clock. The last leg of their journey, as they neared Racecourse Road, was frequently illuminated by Old Man Burton peeing his way home from the local pub, but even that did not persuade Annie to set out earlier. No matter how often Betsy and Eva remonstrated and Dick insisted, 'Shouldn't that little duckie be home in bed?' Annie went her own sweet way.

There were cross words and remonstrations about another aspect of Annie's timekeeping: my grandma never put my mum to bed. Cora fell asleep on the sofa and was taken upstairs when Annie went to bed herself. Cora was not kept awake, but had no fixed bedtime and so always spent the first few hours of sleep downstairs. I wonder if Annie wanted the company (though she kept Cora with her whether Willie was there or not), or if she was trying to shield Cora from how she had felt as a very small child, put to bed in those dark workman's cottages; or, even as a slightly older girl, sandwiched between who-knew-what in the attic up the next flight of stairs, and her parents, fastened behind a door one storey below. Whatever the reason, Annie did as she liked;

once she made up her mind about anything, she would not budge. The same went for her thoughts about Willie.

Cora came into the living room one afternoon to find Annie swaddling the silver cake stand in pieces of cloth from the rag bag. She wrapped the silver sweet basket in its own cotton strips and laid these treasures side by side in the bottom of Cora's old pram. Next, the silver-and-cranberry-glass cones were tucked into a blanket and patted down. The sideboard was denuded of silver. 'I'm taking these to Mam's,' Annie said, with that look of hers that resisted questions.

The sideboard was buffed with a duster and a glass vase moved into prime position in the centre, but it was a while before the vase ceased to look like the impostor it was. Annie's silver was the first thing that struck you when you opened the living-room door, but Willie said nothing when he came in.

The constant grinding sensation in Willie's gut was best chased away with a beer or subdued with a pint of milk, but not that flyblown stuff that gathered dust unless Annie was in the house when it was delivered. Willie preferred bottled milk with a top that sealed which, though more expensive than milk ladled from a can, was at least not warmed in the porch half the day.

Fresh, bottled milk was only sold by one shop at the far end of Whittington Moor, so Willie's preference involved a long walk which, on bad days, was beyond him. One afternoon, he asked Cora to collect the milk instead and promised her sixpence in payment. Sixpence was a great deal of money for a child. This was typical of Willie: always generous, whether or not he could afford to be. (Friends of Cora's occasionally stopped Willie in the street: 'Give me a ha'penny, Mr Thompson.') A ha'penny was the usual tip an errand could command; if a child received a penny they were extremely grateful. Sixpence meant untold riches. But it was a hot afternoon and a long trail up to the top of Whittington Moor and back again, and Cora and neighbour Grace Blake were in the middle of a game and Jimmy Davis said he'd go instead. Jimmy had never had sixpence of his own. And, of course, Jimmy told Willie how very pleased he was, and, for the first time ever, Willie was extremely quiet with Cora.

Another emergency ambulance came to the door and there were the same dark-green disinfected corridors to wander down and get lost in, but this time it was worse because the severity of Willie's situation was hardening into irrefutable facts. After his ulcer burst the second time, Willie was warned he would not come through a third. 'But perhaps there won't be a third time,' the doctor said, suddenly becoming interested in his shoes.

A friend from the Caged Bird Society came to remove Willie's budgerigars and canaries. With bad days gaining on good ones, looking after them had become too much for him.

'Are you alright, then, lad? 'Well, let's be doing it.' Willie led him to the bottom of the garden. Before transferring the birds to their travelling cages, he took each one on to his forefinger, making his finger into a perch and tenderly stroking their tiny head. Willie spoke quietly to each bird, as if to ensure they knew how sorry he was to lose them. When, at last, he straightened up, Willie was holding the key to an empty aviary.

18

Chocolate Fudge for Alice Faye

LIKE EVERY YOUNG SOPHISTICATE, MY MUM HAD A HANDBAG
which fastened with a satisfying click. And her very own driving
licence, albeit in her father's name. Despite never owning a car,
Willie kept his licence up to date and passed the expired one to
Cora. Ever the cock-eyed optimist was Willie. Nestling at the
bottom of her bag was the toy handgun essential to any gangster,
and cigarettes, fine cylinders of white paper, lovingly rolled and
glued by Eva, and topped off with filter tips made from strips of
the sticking plaster sold in the corner shop. Cora was particularly
proud of these – no wonder – and kept them in a pink celluloid
case; a pearlised hand with impossibly slender fingers formed its
delicate clasp.

'Have one of mine.'

'Sure. Don't mind if I do.' Sometimes she was quite the
Hollywood young lady.

Not surprisingly, for someone who first glimpsed the screen as
a babe in arms, my mum was schooled in the cinema. By the time
she was seven or eight, the Lyceum vied with Woolworth's as her

place of worship and George Formby was losing out to more exotic fare. Deanna Durbin was a favourite; Cora saw all her films, but liked *Three Smart Girls* the best, especially the ending, when, thanks to the sisters' scheming, their warring parents are reunited. Cora, Grace Blake and Ada Porter adopted their roles and gave themselves new names – Babs, Betty, Billy – Cora naming herself 'Billy' after her Dad. There were mysterious alphabets and codes to unravel, whose magic letters **x** (**v_** * remain secret to this day; and Wild West adventures to create. If Cora wasn't a cowboy like Jesse James when she grew up, she'd be fast-talking, sassy and clever. In a few years' time, she'd want to be a newspaper reporter

---

FILM STAR WHO'S WHO

Twelve Hundred Biographies – Twelve Hundred Photographs

All About Your Favourite Film Stars –
Here's a book to add zest to every film you see!
80 photogravure pages; 1,200 biographies; 1,200 photos –
all for a nimble sixpence…All those facts you have wanted
to know about attractive stars – their age, their birthday,
their private lives and ambitions

LEG ULCERS AND SKIN DISEASES CURED

Why do you suffer so long?
…if you suffer from psoriasis, varicose veins and painful legs…

– Advertisements on facing pages, *Woman's Weekly*,
8 February 1936 (2d)

---

like Rosalind Russell in *His Girl Friday*, or a smart office-worker like Mopsy in the comic-strip cartoon. For now, she practised touch-typing on her own typewriter (rows of buttons stitched on to a cardboard box), and invented adventures for the film stars who occupied her doll's house.

My mum's doll's house, a fourth-birthday gift, though loved for several years thereafter, was bought from shopkeeper Mr Nield when his daughter Madge outgrew it. Built in the early '20s, this double-fronted house, with its sloping roof papered in imitation slate, and cotton-reel chimney stacks, was a symbol of suburbia, with four main rooms, an inviting hallway, a bathroom on the top landing, and two attics at the back.

Its only drawback (as with so many houses of the period) was the size and position of its kitchen, which had to be tucked behind the stairs. A kitchen had not figured in the thoughts of its designer, Mr Nield. (What 1920s' draper's daughter aspired to invent kitchen stories?) And so (as I discovered when the doll's house came to me), you had to overlook the tight squeeze for the kitchen cupboards, stove and sink. Other than that, it was perfect.

Despite its exterior decor and domestic drawbacks, this was no miniature Acacia Avenue, but a far more glamorous abode: home to Alice Faye, Tyrone Power, Jeanette MacDonald, Shirley Temple and Nelson Eddy. And, as its daily routine was moulded on stories gleaned from 1930s Hollywood, a Black Mammy stood behind the kitchen stove.

The doll's house sleeping arrangements would have satisfied even the strictest arbiters of the Hays Code, that period legisla-tion designed to keep sex out of the cinema. The women slept in one room, the men shared the other; Shirley Temple had a cot on the landing. At night, Alice Faye and Jeanette MacDonald smeared their faces with Vanishing Cream and ate chocolate fudge in bed, draped in the slinkiest of robes (remnants purloined from Annie's rag bag and tacked into cylinders, with slits snipped out for armholes). Empty pill boxes from the corner shop made perfect hat boxes (Beechams' pale pink drums were ideal); no film star travelled without one. While 'the girls' made plans, Tyrone Power and Nelson Eddy exchanged wisecracks in the next room.

For all Cora's fantasies of glamour, there were no sweeping chrome staircases or cocktail shakers: the stairs were carpeted in corduroy and fashioned with a banister made from a knitting needle; its knob made a satisfying newel post. The stars drank pretend-tea and their furniture came not from California, but a Sheffield toy shop. But there was a grand piano in the lounge where Jeanette MacDonald trilled up and down the scales and Alice Faye crooned in husky tones.

Thompson's Bakery was still producing 'Grade A' bread and, in keeping with the times, proclaiming the healthy goodness of its products. Annie's *Woman's Weekly* contained advertisements featuring photographs of ordinary little girls: 'Yes she's cute, but she's not Shirley Temple…' Cue Monica Poynting of Glasgow, transformed by a mass of Shirley Temple curls, courtesy of a 3d bottle of Amami shampoo. 'Are you like any of the stars? If so, please send us your photograph.' Amami paid successful candidates two guineas.

If Amami wanted photographs, why not Jim? What better endorsement than a healthy-looking child, and one of the family? For several nights, after she had collected Provident, cooked and cleared away tea, Annie set about making a miniature baker's outfit – white cotton trousers, tunic, baker's pinny, and a small baker's cap, everything down to the very last detail. The costume required considerable effort (and the demise of a linen sheet), but Annie wanted everything to be perfect. As soon as the outfit was ready, she and Cora gathered their props – a couple of Thompson's free-standing advertisements and the all-important Grade A loaf – and decamped to Arthur's Studio.

Cora was photographed against a plain dark backdrop, the darkest Arthur could provide, all the better to highlight her crisp white suit. Smiling, she pointed at her Uncle Jim's bread in its colourful waxy paper and the advertisement propped against the table: 'Grade "A" Bread. All OUR bread is impregnated with the Ultra-Violet rays of Health. Thompson's Sunshine Bread Sold Here.' The perfect thirties sales pitch: charming, healthy kiddy, healthy bread. The whole thing was irresistible. Yet, Jim resisted. My grandma's foray into advertising was over before it began.

*

'If a tiny stick is floating about in your tea you may expect a visitor'
– so said Eva's copy of *Household Management*, a compendium of
quaint old beliefs, fortune-telling and palm reading, along with
essential recipes (boil cauliflower and all greens for twenty minutes), instructions on engaging servants, and on buying or building
a house. Tiny sticks must have been constantly afloat in Eva's tea
– there was no let-up in the weekend mix of visitors.

Kitty and Margaret; George – with a bunch of flowers for Betsy
and a wish that he could present one to her eldest daughter; Ethel,
still giving as good as she got, and Auntie Liza still regaling the
family with tales of Staveley folk, and scenes witnessed and over-
heard while she sipped her glass of beer in the Foresters. No one
told Liza women did not drink alone; I suspect few people challenged Liza about anything. 'Our Liza's a cock bird,' Betsy
frequently remarked of her favourite sister, a strong endorsement
coming from her.

Cousin Charlie's wife still visited, and was as gentle as ever with
her tentative smile but, these days, sweet Edie came alone. After
nearly twenty years of bronchitic gasping, her precious Charlie
had gasped his last. With Europe limbering up for a Second World
War, the poor man finally died from the first one.

Liza's daughter, Emily, and her husband, Sidney, came via
motorbike and sidecar. Uncle Sidney was a whizz with electrics
and, on one occasion, strapped a wireless cabinet into the space
normally occupied by Emily, and rigged up the set for Dick and
Betsy. From then on, the wireless became a prominent feature:
Saturday evenings were 'In Town Tonight'.

Betsy's nephew Johnny provided a difference spectacle again.
A hefty miner, with permanent black patches on his face, the

typical marks of his calling, Johnny's vast chest strained against Betsy's damask tablecloth. His large fingers looked incongruous holding a slice of Eva's sponge cake, and even more so cradling a china tea cup. A special constable in his spare time, Johnny delighted in telling the assembled company how he and his fellow specials knocked seven bells out of the worst offenders the minute they had them cornered in the cells.

And, Sunday or not, there were the neighbours and weekend visitors to the shop. Every month or so, the Prentice sisters called with their young boys, rounding off a visit to relatives higher up the hill with a bag of boiled sweets for their return journey. The sisters were a curious combination: Sarah placid and well-made (as Betsy described her), Hannah as sharply spoken as she was angular. Sarah adored her young son, Ralph, who drove everyone else to distraction. 'Oh, Eva, there's the Prentice lad,' Betsy would say, if she spotted their arrival through the sweet window. Little Ralph Prentice had fingers into everything and would not stop talking. 'Mrs Nash, Mrs Nash, what's this for, Mrs Nash? What does it do?' ('It's a thing-a-purpose, Ralph. Now, put it down.') 'What's that on the wall?' On and on with constant questions, and all expressed with a clack-clack in his throat, thanks to the poor boy's infected tonsils. Betsy explained to Ralph that he needed to be quiet to let the adults talk. 'But Mrs Nash, I only wanted to know…' and off he went again, like a wind-up toy.

'Hush now, little man,' doting Sarah would say, smiling at Ralph who, until pulled up short by a warning glace from Eva, was advancing on the sweets with grubby hands. Sarah's sister, Hannah, was itching to clobber him but, as she could not hit her sister's lad, made up for it by clouting her own. Typically, this sisterly exchange of indulgence and abuse was Dick's signal to retreat to the wood.

Do not feel that you must have an elaborate display of cakes, or very rich ones. It is much more important to have excellent and very hot tea, and nicely cut bread and butter, scones, or small sandwiches. Besides these, a few *petit fours* or simple small cakes and a plate of cut cake will be ample. Jammy or stickily iced things are undesirable, however attractive they may look.

When a guest rises to leave, you will rise too, but you do not go to the door with her so long as other guests are present. (Don't forget to ring the bell warning the maid to be in the hall, will you?)

– 'Entertaining', *Home Management*, 1934

Some neighbours also needed side-stepping. 'Oh no,' Dick would groan, at the approach of Mrs Cartwright, lapdog tucked firmly under her arm. 'There's "just a minute" coming.' She never stayed for less than half an hour, and was still full of praise for Our Pearl. Or there was Mrs Jenkinson, another great talker. 'Our cat's got a long tail,' Dick would mutter, as she embarked on her umpteenth story.

Ten strides from the boundary fence, four trees from the path – Cora decided to bury some treasure in her grandad's wood: a string of beads, a diamanté brooch and a toy watch. Precious jewels, were it not that the beads were a washed-out shade of blue, the diamantés clashed with their bakelite setting and the watch strap was not quite as elasticated as it once was. Not the perfect treasure trove, then, but – who was to know? Betsy provided a casket (an old tin with a broken hinge and slanting lid). Cora dug a hole. **X** marked the spot on the map she folded into four and slipped into her pocket, in case she needed to retrieve her treasure later. The map lived with the lucky horses' teeth Cora discovered in the wood and carried everywhere – until Annie found them.

The wood was an ideal spot for playing by herself but, on most weekends, Cora played with the Mill kids. Games belonged to Friday evenings and Saturday afternoons. (Sundays did not usually figure as a day for communal play – though not because everyone else was at church.) The short terraces had their share of matriarchs and families whose kids you wouldn't cross – if you were planning to knock on a neighbour's door and run away, you wouldn't try that prank on the Lowthers – but, for the most part, everyone muddled along pretty well. The Mill kids looked after my mum. They asked Betsy if they could take her on their walks to the Meadows and beyond, and reminded Cora when they should head back: 'Your grandma will be worrying.' Though abrasive in speech and manner, these rough and tumble kids were kind. They weren't spiteful like some of the children my mum knew at school, nor did they put on airs – not that many had much worth boasting about – or speak against her grandparents or aunt, although it would have been the easiest thing for someone to repeat a story or disparaging remark about Betsy, Dick or Eva. As far as the Mill kids were concerned, my mum was Cora Nash: she belonged to the corner shop.

The lamp post in front of the shop served as starting point, winning post, marker, the lot, and was good for monkeying up, if you were feeling athletic. The rope suspended from the tree near the entrance to the swampy field by the canal could be clambered up at any time; rounders and other ball games were likewise played in all weathers. Any season was good for skipping too, although skipping required a huge rope, with often ten or more children waiting their turn, and up to half a dozen leaping beneath it. The thickness of the rope, the strength required to turn it (and the burn if it caught you), made this a game for older children. Occasionally, young adults joined in, sixteen- or seventeen-year-olds lifting their heavy boots or factory clogs clear of the rope, free of their adult selves for a moment.

Most games belonged to daylight, but 'leakey' was only ever played at dusk, the encroaching darkness adding an extra dimension to the search. Cold night air wrapped itself round bare legs, chilblained hands and chapped lips; it was hard to be sure whether your shivers were due to the cold or delicious fear. Apart from the 'looker' leaning against the street lamp, shielding his eyes and counting into the silence (Betsy could hear the countdown inside the shop) and the light from the shop itself, there was no other lighting close by. All other players dissolved into darkness. My mum and the other young girls hid with someone older (and were always caught quickly for this reason), but even the youngest boys hid alone. Backyards, doorways, privies, beside chicken coops and rabbit hutches, inside coal houses or the enclosed porch of the pub; behind canalside trees, and as far up as the stone cottages – all these were valid hiding places: anywhere you felt brave enough to crouch and could make yourself invisible. Excited whispers faded into silence. Then the shout: Coming, Ready or Not.

My mum saw how some children lived. One family at the Mill could not afford mats or lino: there was nothing to distinguish their kitchen floor from the cinder path beyond their back door.

She saw, too, the casual slaps and cuffs and clips around the ear some kids endured; the 'I'll knock your block off,' and much worse. (The discovery that children could be beaten was a revelation to Cora: the first time she understood this was aged six, watching Steerforth thrash David Copperfield in the film.) And so, when Annie sometimes told her, 'You were born under a lucky star,' she knew what her mam meant. She had no idea that Annie was thinking of something else altogether.

Despite the supposed drawbacks of the close community at Wheeldon Mill, the living in one another's pockets and everybody knowing everyone else's secrets – or perhaps for this reason – not one child (or irritable adult) confronted my mum with the fact of her adoption. It was the children on a slightly higher social rung, the mind-your-own-business (though don't think we don't know what that is) council-house dwellers of Racecourse Road. Not Annie's closest neighbour whom she took into her confidence when the family moved in and who never breathed a word to my mum. Someone else told.

'Your mam's not your real mam,' or words to that effect, Molly Stapleton flung at Cora one afternoon, a small projectile designed to wound, though Molly could have no idea how powerful her weapon was. They were playing in a neighbour's yard, my mum somewhat reluctantly. Molly was visiting her grandma who lived nearby and was aware that, though the adults thought it nice if all the children played together when she came to stay, Cora and the other local kids were less sure. Molly knew that she was merely tolerated (or worse: some of the others shouted 'Clear off' whenever she popped her head above the fence). She was younger than them too, and so enjoyed having this big stick to wave. It stopped my mum as surely as a real stick.

'Yes, she is.'

'She's not. My nan says.'

That extra stab of confirmation put my mum on guard. Puzzled and disbelieving, but wary now, she took the story home. 'What nonsense,' Annie reassured her. 'Of course you're my little girl.' But she was cross. She'd go straight round and speak to Mrs Stapleton about Molly's hurtful fib. She was in her coat before she reached the end of the sentence, and back home again almost as fast. Not another word on the subject was said by Annie or Molly. One sharp pinch and that was that. Until the next time.

It was a bigger girl, this time, in the year above my mum at school. Hers was a playground jibe, pitched out of nowhere. 'Oh, do you know you don't belong to your mam?'

Her question seemed quite casual, an afterthought almost, by the by – yet it must have been sucked on and savoured beforehand and judged for the right moment to lob. Once again, Annie put on her coat and went visiting. Then, silence. Like the last time. The whole thing was put down to schoolgirl spitefulness.

My mum had no reason to doubt this. Yet, there were times when she felt herself to be different from Annie and Betsy, situations in which their reactions were not necessarily the same as hers. She was too young to pinpoint exactly what these were, and perhaps it was merely a generational thing – but, for whatever reason, Cora sometimes felt different, despite the fact that everything around her – their love, affection and the attention she received – confirmed how much they loved her and that she was theirs. Why would she not be? Just as Annie and Eva were sisters, and her grandma's sisters visited, and Dick's nephews too. There was evidence of family all around her. As yet, Cora had no idea how complicated those connections were.

Chapter 19

Fast Cars and Darker Stories

JACK HARDY'S SCRAPYARD WAS A WELL-KNOWN GRAVEYARD for clapped-out cars, decrepit vans and broken gaskets. Any local vehicle that 'won't pap nor nowt' ended up here. The yard included an old railway carriage which Jack's father and younger brother had helped to convert into an office of sorts. The father said nothing and the brother not a lot. This taciturn pair remained in the office; amiable young Jack greeted all comers.

Like father, like daughter, my mum loved cars when she was young. Low-slung getaway vehicles with their engines ticking over on darkened streets – step on the gas and quick about it – or sleek purring limousines that steered Hollywood vamps to new horizons just before the credits rolled. For games like these, Jack Hardy's scrapyard was perfect. Cora asked Jack if she and two of her neighbours, Grace and Tommy Blake, could play with his cars. And, amazingly, he said yes. No other children were allowed near the yard – 'Clear off, you little buggers,' Jack shouted, if they so much as ventured near the gate. I suspect Jack knew and liked Willie.

Somewhere among the old carburettors, greasy axles and great hulks of rusting tin, there was usually a car that had not quite succumbed to dereliction, and still boasted seats and a steering wheel, even if it lacked one or two niceties like an engine or doors. The occasional cracked veneer dashboard was a considerable plus. The yard mostly fielded broken commercial vehicles, private cars still being treated with kid gloves. Relatively few of those landed here, but – oh, the ones that did. They had chrome knobs to twiddle and play with, starters to pull out or push; heavy pedals to depress, if you could reach them, and enormous steering wheels to get you where you wanted to go. For a child reared on the cinema

– and Willie's love of cars – afternoons at Jack Hardy's were bliss.

After a few fantasy miles and adventures, Jack gave Cora and Tommy some car seats of their own. Hers did service in the back garden: pushed up against the gate on the days when she and Grace had had enough of Tommy; or else providing seating for a card school. The kids at Wheeldon Mill taught my mum how to play pontoon; she passed on the favour to her neighbours. Cardboard coins stood in for currency; she wrote their monetary value on each one. The car seats also served as a useful buffer if the fastest girl on wheels achieved too high a speed roller-skating across the concrete strip by the back door.

My mum was about eight years old when Willie hurried into the house looking excited and extremely pleased with himself. He had borrowed a car, he told her and Annie, with a walnut dash and soft red seats that still smelled of leather. Its bodywork was absolutely gleaming. Could he take Cora for a drive?

Annie was peeling potatoes at the sink when Willie opened the back door and she barely considered his request before she squashed it. I can hear her knife scraping potatoes and feel the power behind that ordinary kitchen task and her refusal: knife, water, potato skin. I'm reminded of that game – scissors, paper, stone. Annie's domesticity trumped Willie's fanciful notion.

It was a school afternoon and she was preparing Cora's tea, but I wonder how long Annie paused before answering. Was she angry at being excluded from the invitation, nervous of his driving, or just plain infuriated by Willie? He left the house and did not return until the next day. It was not the only night Willie spent with the Kiplings.

*

On the days when he was feeling well, Willie walked up to Billy Kipling's garage mid-morning and spent several hours watching him at work and chatting on the forecourt. Usually, he wore baggy trousers held up with braces and an open-necked shirt; a flat cap had replaced his trilby. The natty dresser was gone but there was still an insouciance about Willie, even if, now, the figure he cut was more dustbowl than dandy.

Walking back from the garage one afternoon, Willie was chuffed to see a car draw up ahead and his doctor stop to offer him a lift. Riding home in Dr Sutcliffe's car, accepting one of his cigarettes and matching the man puff for puff, Willie could almost forget his predicament. He was still the kind of person his doctor was happy to ride with. No job, no prospects (no caged birds anymore), but he was still himself. Still Willie.

At Wheeldon Mill, someone had scrawled 'Jam Rag' across Mrs Sugsby's coalhouse door. The lettering was patchy, but the chalked words were clear enough. Noreen Carter explained to Cora that Nella Sugsby had a terrible disease which made her feet bleed and meant she had to wear special bandages.

When not gossiping, misleading one another or engaging in general misrule, there was time to sit on the causey edge and teach one another the latest songs. The Mill kids taught Cora 'Hometown' and other popular tunes, which they sang while walking along the canal path and when waiting to be picked at rounders. They showed Cora how to flick her wrist so the dice landed on the back of her hand in a game of snobs and took turns in swigging from one of Mrs Spencer's halfpenny bottles of nettle beer while 'pickin flies off folk' (noting adults' peculiarities): Mrs Taylor carrying her handbag as if her arm were in a sling; Mrs Rudge with her suspiciously black hair, or Violet Jakes taking the downhill slant of Station Road at full tilt: 'me 'ead's 'ere and me arse is comin''.

Most of Cora's friends at Wheeldon Mill were older than her; and some too old to ever be considered playmates. But whatever their age, they all underwent an immediate transformation on starting work. Boys who had dammed the riverbank and scudded stones across the water one day were wrenched from childhood the next. Equipped with a jacket and one of their father's old belts with new holes punched in it for this occasion, they instantly left their younger selves behind. From that day on, they formed part of the adult ranks, with rarely more than a cursory glance for those remaining on the other side. With girls, the change was even more startling: they seemed to burst from their childhood chrysalis into women, and, in the case of young women, could be just as easily crushed.

There was a new vitality about Amy Foster as soon as she started work. With a home perm and a smart dress – not one her mam had made over – she seemed to blossom into herself. Amy and her siblings had always had a sullen appearance; everything in their lives was scarce or begrudged, but, for a few short months, that changed. Amy splashed out on a studio photograph to record her brand-new self, but, in no time at all, she'd a ring on her finger and, all too soon, a baby, her new-found freedom erased as easily as the lipstick she no longer had much call to wear.

Or there was Sarah Cooper, with her broad, slow smile, too smiling always, too ready to placate. Running to catch up in every sense, she was included in childhood games as much through sympathy as friendship. As she grew older, Sarah found new ways of making friends; she became very pally with one boy in particular. They were often seen together on the grassy bank, insufficiently screened by the trees. 'I see Sarah's down the canal again,' someone would say to Betsy, who'd draw in her breath and shake her head. What prospects for a big slow girl – hardly a young woman – with a too ready grin and an eagerness to please that made you fearful on her behalf? Most neighbours felt sorry for the girl and turned a blind eye, though some objected: it's not nice, this canoodling; a disgrace. Then, the inevitable happened: she became pregnant. That was the last my great-grandma saw of Sarah Cooper.

There was much to discuss in the corner shop as the thirties drew to a close, and little of it optimistic. In October 1938, an accident at the Markham Colliery, some two miles away, brought death to the neighbourhood in the worst mining disaster Derbyshire had witnessed to date. At 5.30 a.m. on 10 May, 171 men were near-ing the end of the night shift when an explosion blasted the Blackshale Seam; seventy-nine were killed and forty injured. One of the deceased, Alfred Furness, had lived at Wheeldon Mill. Annie and Eva took Cora to the graves so they could pay their respects. Those who lived within the shadow of a colliery never forgot what coal could do.

The last gypsies to arrive at the Mill before the Second World War were very different from Bud and his family. There was no scope for romantic illusions about gypsy idylls this time round. The Darbys camped in more or less the same spot as the previous family, but they lived in a trailer with tiny windows, the two oldest boys sleeping in a small tent pitched beside it. There were no graz-ing horses this time either: the Darbys' trailer was towed by a beat-up old car.

As with other visiting Romanies, Betsy and Eva supplemented Mrs Darby's meagre purchasing with anything they could spare from the shop, but her permanently weary expression showed how difficult it was to bring up five children by herself. When the family first pitched camp, some said her husband was in jail; on the few occasions he did appear, he stayed only a few days, looking almost as grey as his suit.

The most significant difference between the two gypsy families, as far as the Mill kids were concerned, was that most of the Darbys were old enough to join their games. There was nearly always one of them looking to play and generally two: Harry and Marky.

Harry was the oldest of the children; he shared his mother's dark colouring and features, whereas Marky had blue eyes and auburn hair. Though they did not look alike, the brothers were close in age and of a similar height and build, and so, initially, were assumed to be twins. They dressed alike too, which reinforced this impression. Their clothing also distinguished them from the Mill kids. At a time when most boys their age dressed in grey shorts, nondescript shirts and pullovers, Harry and Marky wore long black trousers and ginger shirts. More significant still, the brothers were inseparable and, even on the occasions when their behaviour was perfectly innocent (although, admittedly, there were fewer of those), looked as if they were up to mischief.

Marky introduced himself and his siblings to Cora. She could hardly believe the grandeur of his full name – Marcus Cornelious Darby – yet knew he was telling the truth. Most of the time, however, Marcus was plain Marky and, sometimes, 'that damn Marky' was nearer to it.

The brothers were unlikely to sit quietly in a classroom, but they could certainly write and spell four-letter words. If any adult reprimanded them, their lavatory door bore the brunt of it the following day. Knowing who was responsible was one thing, catching them red-handed quite another. No one ever saw them at their chalking and each was capable of denying anything with the straightest face. Harry and Marky's vocabulary further set them apart: the Mill kids' swore, but their repertoire was less extensive. And, as for my mum, Betsy made it very clear: 'They swear. You don't.'

The two boys joined in with all the Mill games, were fast runners and eager playmates, but adults regarded them differently. Several neighbours complained to Betsy and Eva about those two young scoundrels. There was no prank Harry and Marky would not contemplate; no devilment was beyond them. They behaved themselves in the shop, however, thanks to Betsy's usual tactics: 'Now then, Marky, what is it you're after?' the friendly but firm greeting conveying, 'And don't think I haven't got my eye on you.' She adopted the same tack when talking to Punka Stokes, especially after he passed Cora a counterfeit pound note (which she, having never held such a large sum of money, immediately gave to her grandma). Betsy liked Punka but was nobody's fool; she was also a match for Harry and Marky.

One of the houses opposite the gypsy field was occupied by Mrs Lane, a middle-aged woman who looked much older because of her scrunched-up face: she was constantly angry about something. One day, inevitably, her anger was directed at Harry and Marky. Though they could swear, and excelled at it as far as the local children were concerned, they did not have Mrs Lane's years of practice. No one was more proficient at hurling abuse. She raged at them across her garden fence and when the boys ignored her, chased them towards the corner shop, shouting and waving her arms.

The following morning, two brown steaming parcels appeared on Mrs Lane's doorstep. It was not difficult to guess who had deposited them (two piles being something of a clue) but, as with the over-night chalking, there was no proof. Everyone expressed their disgust and disapproval, but there were one or two private smiles at the thought of cantankerous Mrs Lane being the recipient of Harry and Marky's summary justice.

One weekend, however, the Darby boys went too far. Cora arrived at Wheeldon Mill to be told that, this time, they were in real trouble: Mrs Jenkinson had received a lewd note and marched straight round to Mrs Darby's trailer. Mrs Jenkinson played merry hell and did not care who heard her. If those lads did not sort themselves out, she was going to the police. The family left the Mill shortly afterwards.

A few months later, Cora was standing outside the Lyceum waiting for Annie when Harry came out of the chip shop. 'Marky wants to give you a kiss,' he said, smiling, and they chatted until Annie joined Cora for the film. That was the last she saw of the Darbys, who disappeared again as quickly as they'd reappeared.

Their story has a terrible coda. During the 1950s, my mum saw an article in Annie's *Daily Express*. A young woman had been strangled on her first date and Marcus Cornelious Darby arrested for her murder. For all his misdemeanours, Cora could not believe this of Marky; the picture did not fit with the boy who'd joined in with the Mill kids' songs. Week after week, she scoured the paper, looking for a further report. Eventually, Cora found one: 'Gypsies Weep for Killer.' Marcus Cornelious Darby was hanged at Strangeways Prison.

20

Wartime Snow and Ice

FOR TWO OR THREE YEARS BEFORE THE WAR, THE WOMEN OF Brimington and Wheeldon Mill enjoyed a late summer mystery tour. Annie and Eva booked places for themselves and Cora. The price of a charabanc ticket bought a drive through Derbyshire, the sightseeing an excuse for a port and lemon in a country pub and a singsong on the way home, following a rare afternoon free of responsibilities. Ashover, Bakewell, the plague village of Eyam, Monsal Dale, the stone circle at Arbor Low. Meandering through millstone grit and limestone, past acres of rolling green before rising on to bleak moorland, the White Peak succumbing to the Dark. No matter how many times you saw it, Surprise View was always as exhilarating as its name, and there was the bubbling softness of Burbage Brook and the elegant stature of Chatsworth House, sitting low but commandingly within ancient parkland, the tip of its hunting lodge peering through the treetops.

The trip reaffirmed a sense of belonging, of being stitched into the landscape, that tug of knowing those Derbyshire miles were home. Mistress of ceremonies, Mrs Clark paraded the aisle issuing

Floss stood at one window of the cab, and I stood at the other. Now we were going to see the wonderful sights of London...

What did we see? Long rows of tall, dark houses, with hard, stony roads between them. Crowds of people were walking along the sides, and all sorts of carts and horses were clattering down the middle.

'If you see the King, Floss, you must tell me,' I said. 'If I see him... I will call you...'

Mother smiled. 'I am afraid you will have to look a very long time before you see the King.'

'O Mother,' I said, 'when the Pussy Cat went to London *she* saw the Queen... If a *cat* can see the Queen why cannot Floss and I see the King?'

Mother smiled again. 'Well, perhaps, some day, if you are very good, I will take you to see him.'

Floss and I looked out again, but we did not see anything wonderful. There was not a tree or a bit of grass to be seen. Only the dull, dark houses, the carts and the people.

The Hard Words in this chapter: crowds; won-der-ful; sights; rows; ston-y; walk-ing; mid-dle; smiled; puss-y; Queen; per-haps

– From *Up to London to See the King*, read by Cora at the Edmund Street Infant School

jokes and the introductory lines of songs which she proceeded to conduct with the tip of her feather boa; chatting to neighbours, Maud Cartwright, Kathleen Driver and Ellen Taylor, leading them in holiday revelry, until, with a growing piquancy, in 1939, the post-pub singsong swelled into 'Jerusalem', as the clock counted down through that last hot summer.

Annie took Cora to London in August 1939. She wanted her to see the capital city before who knew what destruction befell it. It was my mum's first sight of London, or so she thought, and Annie did not contradict her. As far as Cora was aware, her mam was also seeing London for the very first time. They saluted the Changing of the Guard and stood where Charles I had stood in Westminster Hall; they gazed at the Houses of Parliament, attempted to count all the windows in Buckingham Palace, and even made their way to Dirty Dick's pub, but the highlight of their day, as far as Annie was concerned, was 145 Piccadilly, home to the King and Queen when they were Duke and Duchess of York. There, Annie and Cora saw the childhood bedroom of the Princesses Elizabeth and Margaret Rose, its sky-blue ceiling pricked out with yellow stars.

Theirs was a whistle-stop tour, something to remember if the worst came to the worst, a phrase often repeated, though never fully explained to Cora. On the way home, just when it seemed all treats had been exhausted, they discovered *The Adventures of Robin Hood* on a St Pancras bookstall. Glorious technicolour pictures of Olivia de Havilland, Basil Rathbone and Errol Flynn. Cora spent the return journey in silent rapture.

My mum was sitting with Annie and Willie when Mrs Blake knocked, but came into the house without pausing. Britain was at war. She had just heard the news on the wireless. Almost as memorable as the announcement was the look of horror on her face.

Official advice recommended that, regardless of whether or not they were going to be evacuated, a child's name and address should be written on a luggage label or envelope and pinned to a piece of clothing where it could not be removed. Annie and Willie thought that idea shoddy and inadequate, and ordered a silver expanding bracelet with a silver identity disc for my mum. Cora was also taught to memorise her identity number: RBGO219/3, the /3 indicating her position in the family. But what do the letters stand for, she wanted to know. 'It means you're a rum bugger, good for nothing,' Willie said and winked. All three of them laughed; Annie, grateful for once, for Willie's insistence on seeing the joke.

January 1940 was the coldest month Derbyshire experienced for a century; temperatures remained below freezing for weeks. The whole country was muffled by snow, besieged by ice and frozen pipes as much as wartime. And, just as it had during a similarly significant point in my mum's life, the River Thames froze over.

At Racecourse Road, an elderly neighbour died and on the day of his funeral, as was the custom then, Cora joined her parents and other neighbours in standing at their gates to watch the coffin leave for the church. The hearse passed by and, as they were turning away, Willie said, 'I shall be next.' A moment's silence followed this announcement before Mrs Blake managed to quip about her own aching bones, to which Willie joked that, when her time came, the wash-tub and peggy-legs would have to be buried with her.

The January day that Willie died was bitterly cold; the roadside snow was thick and deep. It was 23 January, his forty-seventh birthday. It was also a Tuesday, Annie's washday. The kitchen and living room were a fug of blazing fire and steaming clothes, their heat all the more pronounced because of the desperate chill outside and the icy rooms upstairs.

Cora had a cold and was kept from school that afternoon. (She must have been unwell because Annie was a tyrant about illness. If you could stand up, you went off to do your duty.) Willie was in bed, where he remained all day, which was unusual. Upstairs, there was silence; downstairs, the afternoon passed in a blur of washday steam and shifting coals.

Darkness descended. The electric light was on, and my mum was sitting at the table, painting in a colouring book. In the way that memory fixes details, she remembers she was wearing a red Scotch kilt. Annie was preparing stew and dumplings, and when she went upstairs to see Willie, he said, 'Leave Cora and look after me.' Another rare occurrence – he rarely asked Annie for attention. My mum knew that if her dad asked, he must need Annie's help.

Late evening came on quickly, the heat and the stuffiness of the laundry combining with the stuffiness inside Cora's head. She had fallen asleep on the sofa (still downstairs, still not put to bed) but woke to the sound of Willie moaning. The sitting room was full of people. Eva was there; and Jim and Edith, both standing with their coats on, Jim's hands shoved into his pockets; Bernard and Ida were also present, every one of them summoned to the house by neighbours.

The hall door opened; Willie's doctor appeared and, shortly after that, an ambulance. Willie was carried downstairs on a stretcher, waving his arms and shouting, 'They've taken my arms.

Give me my arms.' That was the last time my mum saw him alive. He died shortly before midnight.

Heavy snow continued falling throughout that week; roads were piled high and crusted with it; temperatures remained exceedingly low. On the day of the funeral Cora came downstairs to be greeted by a strong, pleasant smell. Ahead of her, at the far side of the room and leaning against the wall, was the lid of Willie's coffin. It was a bitterly cold day but, of course, there was no heat in the room. The unusual heady scent issued from the coffin wood.

My mum has written an account of her father's death, and so the words that follow are hers: 'I saw the coffin near the front window, and there inside was my darling Daddy. His body was covered in a gorgeous white satin shroud covered with beads or pearls. He looked so beautiful. I remember being struck by seeing him in something so regal.

'My Auntie (Eva) was there and she said something, very gently, like, "Isn't he lovely. Look at his lovely hair," and she put her fingers into the dark golden curls and carefully curled them round and

they just fell back on to his forehead. She said, "Give him a kiss. He would want you to give him a kiss." I don't know if I was lifted up to kiss him but I kissed him on his lips – more than icy cold and I can still feel it. I have always been thankful that I saw him and that I kissed him. I knew his ending, and I knew then that he did not mean to leave me.'

Annie was getting dressed upstairs; by the early afternoon they were on their way to church. Jim and Edith were Mayor and Mayoress that year and so Annie and Cora travelled in the mayoral car, a Rolls-Royce, complete with uniformed chauffeur wearing a peak cap and gaiters. Willie would have been delighted. As the hearse passed through Whittington Moor, all the men on the street stood straighter and removed their hats.

Christ Church stands some distance from the road and its churchyard was deep in snow. The mayoral chauffeur carried my mum all the way down the sloping path and into the church. The coffin bearers were friends of Willie's: members of the Caged Bird Society and local shopkeepers, including the owner of 'Herrings' chip shop and confectioner, Mr Wardle. It seems ironic that a man whose health was so poor was laid to rest by some of those who'd sold him fish and chips and fags, but that's how it was.

Two jet-black clips bit into the lapels of Annie's mourning jacket as she welcomed friends and family back to the house; Mrs Blake had stoked the fire while they were at the service. 'I'll pay for this,' Jim said, gesturing towards the funeral tea, 'and all the rest of it,' and my grandma was grateful, of course Annie was, though she wished Jim had waited until the two of them were alone before speaking.

The smell of the coffin wood permeated the house for several days; my mum's grief lasted years. After her father's death, it seemed that even the electric light in the living room grew dimmer, although Annie insisted she had not changed the bulb. For Cora, nothing blazed fully without Willie.

21

Shoot Straight, Lady

'Mayor's Brother Dies,' the newspaper said. Once again, Willie's fate made local news, and, again, on a sorry occasion. After his death, many things remained the same, except that nothing was ever the same afterwards. It was impossible for Cora not to see how much easier life was for Annie, but she had lost her Daddy and her Pal.

There were immediate practicalities to consider; their most pressing need was money. Annie's widow's pension was ten shillings a week, with an additional five allocated for Cora. (In two years' time, when my mum started senior school, half of those five shillings would be swallowed by the cost of school dinners.) Annie was not sorry to lose her Saturday-morning humiliation at the dole office, but the money had to be made up somehow: Providenting would not be enough.

The tailoring course Annie had taken during the last war now came into its own. She decided to set up as a home dressmaker; it was an advantage to be able to tell customers she was properly trained. At the time, Annie had cursed her pricked fingers and

the evenings she was required to stay behind to unpick a waver-
ing seam. Now, she was grateful for such rigorous teaching.

Next, Annie bought a wireless, a purchase she'd resisted while
Willie was alive, insisting they would always be fighting over
the programme, him wanting to switch on for music and her the
story, though Annie was as keen on the old songs as he was, and
Willie liked a tale of derring-do. From now on, the house was
rarely silent. Breakfast was accompanied by Dr Hill on our good
friend the prune; evenings hummed with orchestral sounds and
cliff-hanging serials. The handle of Annie's Singer kept time with

Yours is a full-time job, but not a spectacular one. You wear no
uniform, much of your work is taken for granted and goes un-
heralded and unsung, yet on you depends so much. Not only
must you bring up your children to be healthy and strong, look
after your husband or other war-workers so they may be fit and
alert, but you must contrive to do so with less help, less money,
and less ingredients than ever before. In the way you tend your
family, especially, your skill – and your good citizenship – are
tested. Thoughtlessness, waste, a minor extravagance on your
part may mean lives lost at sea, or a cargo of vitally needed
bombers sacrificed for one of food that should have been unnecessary... We leave it to you, the Good Housekeepers of Britain,
with complete confidence.

– Advice to the housewife from *Good Housekeeping*,
August 1941

the different theme tunes. Detective stories provided the best accompaniment: the more involved the narrative, the faster her needle sped across the seams.

Rationing complicated life for everyone, and especially for the corner shop: so many rules and regulations and so much paper-work. Quite apart from the palaver of neighbours registering with the shop and presenting their ration books, was the need to cut out coupons and return them to the Food Office. Until the system changed, and ration books were stamped, one night a week became coupon night for Eva.

Gaps started appearing on the shelves – soap and soap powders, tea and pepper; what was not rationed was scarce. As before, butter and sugar were immediate casualties; cheese and preserves soon followed. There was universal umbrage at the prospect of dried eggs. Dick's hens laid sufficient for the family, plus some for the shop, but too few to supply the whole neighbourhood. Colour began to be stripped from labels and packaging; tins looked naked without their wrappers. The newly drab shelves gave the shop its own peculiar camouflage. Things looked even drearier with the blackout blind pulled down.

Anyone wanting groceries wrapped had to supply their own paper; Charles Parks brought the Sheffield *Star* to wrap his polony; waxy sweet cones were now a thing of the past. Some hardships meant less than others: the shortage of lavatory paper was not much remarked upon, newspaper having done that job for years; an initial meat ration of 1 s 10d a week seemed generous to women who had trouble affording 1 s 6d.

If rationing complicated trading, the blackout regularised shop hours: everything had to be achieved before darkness descended.

..*Shoot straight, Lady*

You've got a fighting job on hand, too. These are significant days and anyone — man, woman, or child — who is less than fighting fit is a pull back on the total war effort.

FOOD is your munition of war. The Government sees that you get the right stuff and it's vital that you should know how to use it to full advantage . . .

These days, the only neighbours calling in the evenings were those considered friends, but that did not stop the occasional bit of business. Zoe knocked on the back door, asking for butter, just the tiniest amount, the merest smidgen – 'I can't do without my bit of butter, Mrs Nash.' Zoe was a rare recipient of under-the-counter goods. Aside from the difficulty of seeming to favour one customer over another, Betsy was risking her licence.

Eva joined the ARP and was issued with a regulation tin hat and whistle and a rattle with which to alert neighbours in the event of a gas attack. The first-aid classes she attended were enormous fun. She and her fellow wardens – middle-aged men, mostly – took turns to bandage one another and practise shepherding imaginary crowds. Eva tested Cora on the Bones of the Body and added making splints, plus a hazy knowledge of how to stem arterial blood, to her legendary successes with pulling teeth. But she hoped someone else would be called upon to operate the telephone in a real emergency – unused to speaking on the phone, Eva regarded it as an alien instrument.

Night after night, the streets she patrolled were silent, bar muffled jocularity and curses come chucking-out time. She learned to read the outline of Brimington by moonlight, and came to know which pavements dipped or plunged without warning and were likely to pitch her into the gutter, but it was a tiring end to a day spent handling ration books, and shaking a bit on and then a bit off the weighing scales and parrying requests for just that little bit extra of whatever was currently in stock.

The only time she blew her whistle was during practice sessions in the church hall. 'You go on home,' Eva's fellow wardens told her after several uneventful weeks. 'We'll do your shift. It's not right for a woman to be walking about alone after dark.'

She accomplished one heroic deed, however. Coming along the canal path one afternoon in her usual breezy style, Eva saw Nora Parks some yards up ahead, flailing in the water. Unused since the 1900s, the canal was a murky broth: you'd sooner spit in it than swim there. But old Mrs Parks was not swimming: she had slipped on the grass and tumbled in. Her saturated clothes were already spreading like a black water lily, filling with water and beginning to drag her down. Eva leapt in and saved her. My great-aunt's first-aid training came in useful after all.

Annie had too few pots and pans to donate to the war effort, but the railings along Racecourse Road soon disappeared, leaving an uneven iron stubble. No more satisfying rattle of sticks for Robin Hood during sword fights; Zorro would have to do without acoustics from now on.

Zorro is the flavour of the moment. Annie makes a cloak (two arm holes and a neck cut out of blackout cloth) and Cora swishes her way to school with garden canes complete with cardboard guards, one for herself and two for the conquistadores she'll do battle with at playtime. Walking there one morning, she passes the Infants' School to find the playground crammed with men. Some are sleeping, side by side, overshooting their canvas beds, their heavy boots obscuring scribbled hopscotch markings and the white lines painted on the ground for drill. One or two perch, knees to chin, on minuscule infant chairs.

There is something unsettling about this huddle of grown men. It is not just the sight of so many unknown adult faces, and in the wrong place, but their cumulative expressions conveying strain, exhaustion, relief. One man hands Cora two small coins: French, he tells her. Survivors from Dunkirk washed up in the most unlikely places.

Sewing could be done at any hour. Housework, shopping (queuing, mostly), collecting Provident: these had to be accomplished before blackout and so completed by 3.30 on winter afternoons. There was little time for sewing during daylight. My mum fell asleep to the sound of Annie's Singer, with Tommy Handley murmuring in the background.

The living room became a one-woman workshop of cutting, letting out and taking in. Mrs Sew-and-Sew had nothing on Annie. The women she sewed for were already well versed in Make Do and Mend, and needed no government ministry to advise them. Few neighbours presented Annie with fabric they wanted making up; more often, they arrived with a dress now required to do service as a blouse and skirt; a blanket to transform into a coat; or a man's jacket to make over for his son. My grandma lost count of the number of contrasting or complementary panels she stitched into frocks to enlarge them. People were forever knocking on the door. In time, she became well known: 'Take it to Mrs Thompson. She'll do it.'

There was a new addition to the household too: Annie's tailor's dummy. Though pigeon-chested Nellie was a relic of an earlier style, she was an essential dressmaker's tool. Clothes hung from every hook and inch of picture rail; those awaiting attention were piled on the piano, finished garments occupied the back of the sofa. 'Oh, Mam,' became Cora's frequent greeting, coming in from school. No surface was without its pile of mending, cotton reels or pins. (Girl guides appealed for discarded bobbins: empty reels made useful holders for signalling wires.)

Sewing at all hours was how Annie came to be summoned for showing a light. Bundling her Bluebird Toffee tin of cottons on

to the window sill in a sleepy fashion one night, she disturbed the blackout blind. 'Put that bloody light out,' an invisible voice shouted, as if on cue. Mr Woodruff, the warden, lived in the row of houses behind my grandma's. As they were near neighbours and this was her first (and last) offence, he could have issued Annie with a warning, but Mr Woodruff was a most punctilious warden. He reported her.

My grandma was charged that on 28 July 1940, at 11.30 p.m., she allowed a light to be displayed. The summons was signed by the Justice of the Peace, J.W. Thompson: Annie was called to appear before her brother-in-law. My mum accompanied her and waited in the corridor for the verdict. Jim issued the summons, fined Annie five shillings and promptly paid it.

Cora drew a succession of khaki soldiers. 'Bless 'Em All'. Tall, short, thin: all stood to attention in her notebook. Hilda stepped out in her siren suit, clutching her gas mask and handbag. Toni, Pamela and Rosemary sported fashionable arrowed toques. Even Yvonne and Mary tackled the housework in water-coloured beads and neat frocks. Cora painted heart-shaped pockets, trim clutch bags and sharp-edged gauntlets. The war did not dim fashion sense.

The biggest excitement for the young women of Wheeldon Mill was munitions work, a repetition of their mothers' roles, though this time with stocking seams painted on with gravy browning, hair coiled tight in Victory rolls, overcoats with 'Air Force' pleating, and two dabs of Max Factor pan stick (if they could find it in the shops).

Some linked up with servicemen stationed in the area. Pearl brought a paratrooper to meet Betsy and Eva, one of the young men stationed at Hardwick Hall, now commandeered as a parachute training centre, its once ornate corridors scuffed by army boots. He came to the corner shop on several occasions, Pearl's blushes growing with each visit, and offered to lift jars and boxes from the highest shelves to save Eva getting out the steps.

Before he left for active service, Pearl brought her soldier to say goodbye. Slightly tearful but full of smiles, she told Betsy how, on his next leave, they planned to become engaged. The paratrooper was standing behind her. Pearl did not see him frown and shake his head. Odd – cruel too – that he wanted Betsy to know something he did not tell Pearl. Betsy would not be the one waiting for letters that did not arrive.

One Saturday morning, young Winnie Driver appeared in the shop. 'I'm off then, Mrs Nash.' She'd been talking of it for days: her week in Blackpool with some Clark Gable lookalike in naval blue.

'Have a nice time, then, Winnie,' said Betsy, who knew what was required of her even when she did not approve. 'But where's your suitcase?'

'It's alright, Mrs Nash.' Winnie produced her brightest smile. 'I've a clean pair a' knickers in me handbag.'

Every Chesterfield company engaged in the production of iron and steel turned its capabilities to the war effort. Bomb and shell cases, landmines and gun barrels manufactured locally were said to be on every British fighting ship; the BBC reported on the town's inaugural production of high-explosive cylinders. The area within a few miles of my great-grandma's shop contained some key sites: Sheepbridge produced components for Rolls-Royce aircraft engines, while the Staveley Works manufactured anti-tank guns and the man-made fog that would help camouflage troops on D-Day. Far more sobering was Robinson and Son's production of

more than seven million dressings, 25 million bandages, 75,000 yards of bandage cloth and 450 tons of cotton wool. The Peak District played its own distinguished part: Ladybower Reservoir became the vital practice ground for the bouncing bombs used in low-level raids over Germany.

Ethel's son joined the RAF. She was pleased as punch, or so she insisted. And, of course, she was proud, her smart young man a pilot, the most glamorous job of all, but she was frightened too, and with good reason. Young Rolly was killed during the Battle of Britain. Her only child, shot down in a burst of flame, somersaulting into the endless blue.

The car seats from Jack Hardy's scrapyard were put to new use as makeshift beds in the Anderson shelter kindly neighbours erected for Annie and Cora. It was cold and damp in the shelter, with only night lights and candles for company and who knows how many spiders. But they had a piece of old carpet for the floor, pillows and plenty of blankets, food, a thermos and, if they were lucky, a square of chocolate left over from the sweet ration.

Annie buys Cora an exercise book and suggests she record their experiences. For the first few weeks, Our Adventures are described each night until Cora is too tired to write; most episodes have to be completed the following day. She is soon bored with the project, however, finding nothing new to say about sitting in the dark every evening. Unlike one of the heroines in her *Girls' Crystal Annual*, Cora never chances to encounter and challenge a Nazi spy.

It is often dawn before the All Clear sounds. Giddy with tiredness, they stagger back to the house clutching their pillows and blankets. No matter how many times they emerge from the shelter, Annie is always amazed. Rubbing shoulders with the Sheepbridge plant and a railway line, let alone their proximity to Sheffield, she feels they are living beneath an arrow on the map.

My grandma was wrong, however. The family's only wartime casualty was Betsy's youngest brother, Jack, who died, probably as a result of shock, a few weeks after being flung to the ground when a bomb exploded in nearby Duckmanton. The closest anyone else came to a bombing raid was Annie and Cora's experience of the Sheffield Blitz.

Home to Vickers' steel works, which produced crankshafts for the Spitfires that won the Battle of Britain, Sheffield was said to contain a half-square-mile that was more essential to the production of munitions than anywhere else in the country. From the moment industry was targeted by German bombers, the city anticipated aerial attacks.

The evening of 12 December 1940 was crisp and clear; people were hurrying across the city, returning home after a day's work

MR CHURCHILL

Mr Churchill is a man,
A man of great renown,
To whom at last, in deadly fear,
Tyrants must bow down.

Mussolini and Hitler,
These gangsters cruel and sly,
Must answer to our worthy –
(John Bull) by and by.

He is the Premier of England,
A loyal and noble man,
And our job in this war today,
Is to help him all we can.

The British people are proud,
Very proud indeed,
Of this 'fine old English gentleman',
Who helped them in their hour of need.

And when the war is over,
And the roaring guns are still,
How we will cheer this great leader,
Mr Winston Churchill.

– Cora Thompson, age 10

or a little shopping, concentrating on how to make this, the first real Christmas of the war, feel as festive as any other year. Shortly before 7 p.m., an unmistakeable sound filled the sky. The first planes were heading for Sheffield, guided by a near perfect moon.

Over the next nine hours, three hundred planes bombarded the city. At this stage in the war, there were too few fire-watchers on duty to safeguard its buildings. Shops and offices blazed through the night; the city centre was almost obliterated. A direct hit on the Marples Hotel reduced this seven-storey complex to rubble. Offices, a concert hall, hotel rooms and all their furniture crashed into the cellars on top of sheltering guests. Seventy people died there; the search for survivors lasted twelve days.

Throughout that long unquiet night, Annie and Cora heard the planes overhead. Like everyone else, they had quickly learned to distinguish between Allied and enemy aircraft. They heard the bomb blasts too and hoped they were not next in line. The following morning, the whole neighbourhood was agog with tales of how Sheffield 'got it' the night before; some neighbours had left their shelters to watch the inferno. Annie and Cora had no time to stop and compare notes, however: my mum was due in Sheffield for a ballet exam.

In true Blitz spirit, she and Annie caught the bus. They had no telephone, no means of verifying how bad the bombing really was and, anyway, exams were exams. Everyone knew what was required: Courage, Cheerfulness and Resolution.

Nothing prepared Annie and Cora for what greeted them as they walked into the city centre. Dust coated their throats; smoke rose from crumpled heaps of masonry. The doll's-house furniture shop (usually their first port of call) was still intact, but Walsh's department store was now rubble.

On a recent visit to Sheffield, Cora had admired an enormous panda in Walsh's window, his giant paws raised on strings, as if walking; his ears, soft caps of fur; his enormous head nodding up and down as his great, gentle strides took him nowhere. Confronted with this new and shocking sight, the first thing my mum considered, aged ten years old, was that big cuddly body, blasted to coiled wires and matted fur.

The Royal Academy of Dancing examinations took place on the outskirts of Sheffield. There was an unfamiliar bus to catch, which took them on a different kind of mystery tour altogether: past the gaping wounds of eviscerated buildings with cables dangling over plumes of smoke and uniformed men clambering over their remains. Street after street was cordoned off. They were driven past broken roads where roofs dangled perilously over collapsed houses and incongruous strips of wallpaper exposed the innards of people's homes, past zigzag markings delineating stairways where stairways no longer existed. A peculiar silence wrapped itself about them.

The RAD examiner lived in London and knew that bombers come back. Far better take her chances in the bombed-out capital than in the alien North of England. She was keen to take the students through their paces as quickly as was decently possible. While Annie and the other mothers attempted small talk in the changing room, Cora and her fellow examinees strove for perfect pirouettes. Outside, the city smoked.

The ballet examiner was correct. Three nights later, the bombers returned. Thousands of incendiaries raised fires across the city; factories and railway lines were bombed. More than 750 people were killed or listed as missing and around 500 seriously injured, while damage to property left 6,000 civilians homeless and thousands unemployed. But a few days after the bombardment, the Sheffield *Star* went to press with a cartoon on its front cover and a one-word caption: 'Defiant'.

By the time my mum was ten, dancing permeated everything. There were books to read, routines to devour on film, dances to create in the back garden. Council-house concrete made a perfect surface for tap dancing; lino provided a reasonable grip for ballet shoes. Judy Garland and Mickey Rooney were not the only ones who sang and danced as they walked along the street.

When war was declared, Cora's dancing certificates were put into the music case my grandma packed for emergencies. The case

held no mementoes, just certificates and vital documents, she told my mum, 'insurance papers and things like that'. Whenever there was an air raid, one of them grabbed it en route to the shelter.

Alone in the house one afternoon (Annie was out Provident-ing, I expect), my mum decided to look at her dancing certificates. I can see her now, sitting on the bottom stair in the little vestibule with barely sufficient space for bags and coats; it was a good job they never used the front door (except for Willie's last journey). Cora started sifting through the documents, but, as she withdrew them, something unexpected caught her eye: a blue-grey file that begged to be opened.

This imposing file contains official-looking documents, typed questions and answers and, among the carefully printed lines, the word, ADOPTION. There is a girl's name too and a city: London. Cora feels hot and cold and absolutely nothing and everything at once but, this time, she is certain. This time, she knows she is the girl in this file.

The words bounce back at her. Their details are impossible to absorb; it is like trying to grasp something fastened under glass. She is herself and someone else as well, the girl she would have been had she not become Annie's daughter. On top of this shock, and just as intense, is the knowledge she is trespassing among Annie's private papers. She has no sense that these documents are also hers. Instead, my mum feels guilty. The papers belong to Annie and Annie does not want her to see them.

Cora loves her mam and knows Annie's love for her needs no formal documentation. She folds the right board back to the centre and the left board on top of that, and taking one final look at the stiff blue-grey cover, restores the file to the music case. Annie does not want her to know she is adopted and so Cora decides to pretend that she does not: 'Annie wanted me to belong entirely to her. I wanted to belong to Annie. I felt very secure and happy with Annie, although I still very much missed Willie. But Annie was my mother and she was also my friend. The present was my life and I'd get on with it. I also knew that unless Annie told me all she knew, there was no way of finding out.'

22

Silver Shoes

IN THE EARLY 1940S MY MUM WAS ALLOWED TO WALK unaccompanied from Racecourse Road to Wheeldon Mill. She had seen The Wizard of Oz and, during summer months, often walked to her grandma's in the gingham 'Dorothy' dress Annie made for her. The yellow-brick road Cora followed held its own perils in the form of two major junctions. The easiest place to cross Sheffield Road was by the council-cut patch of grass which afforded the clearest view. Then began the long walk up the Coal Road, past the allotments spiked with raspberry canes and pea sticks, and taking especial care at the busy spot where her grandad came to grief in the accident that partially crippled him.

The jam factory announced its presence with its usual cloying sweetness before Cora ducked under the railway bridge, the first of three, shouting loud enough to startle the echo before it could surprise her. Out once more into the air again, past the stubby row of houses near the little shop whose exterior wall shone with a sheet of dark blue tin advertising Five Boys' chocolate; trailing her palm along the dusty hawthorn bushes that lined this part of the route, pausing to say hello to Eva's friend Mrs Healey, if she happened to be in her front garden. The houses on the left side of the street petered out here. This was the scrag end of town, with more scrubland than houses, but that did not worry Cora. She had no ruby slippers to protect her, but Betsy and Toto were waiting up ahead.

The ground beyond the second railway bridge was sharp with pottery breakages. This was one of the grey tips (shord rucks) where Pearson's Pottery dumped its apologies and failures. There was often an adult scavenging for something: a pie dish in one piece, ideally, one not so cracked as you'd notice once it was filled with stew, or whose clay protuberances would disappear beneath a pie crust. There were clay moulds, too, bulky ornaments kids presented to their mothers who thanked them for these offerings and eventually shoved them in the bin. For a child, 'pickin on't tip' offered contemplative pleasures, an urban equivalent of shell seeking. There were never any glorious discoveries, however. Pearson's Pottery manufactured functional stoneware in brown, khaki, beige. Still, its lumps of clay were good for chalking on walls and pavements, as some at the Mill knew to their cost.

Just past Pottery Lane was the house built by George Harding, no longer a terrifying figure in a battered hat, but a friendly milk-man, who nearly always had a cheery message for Betsy and Eva. Just beyond the third and final railway bridge, near some damp, spare ground, a young woman had set up camp in a gypsy wagon. Though she used the corner shop occasionally, she was not one of the gypsies Cora knew. She thought her brave, living alone on this waste ground, an odd place for a woman by herself. On the opposite side of the road, the low baby wall, so-called because toddlers liked to run along it holding an adult's hand, revealed how easily you could reach the River Rother. Too easily: this was where one of my mum's Wheeldon Mill playmates drowned.

She is not far from the corner shop. Were it not for the rising gradient and the trees, its doorway would be visible already. Over the little railway bridge and, finally, the bridge across the canal. Betsy is looking through the sweet window. She knows to expect Cora, and waves.

George wrote to Annie. He was now a Major passing through Chesterfield. Could he call and see her?

Annie had had to pinch herself the last time she saw George. It was shortly before the war, and she and Cora and Eva were at the Lyceum, when the programme switched to the news, and there he was. Up on the screen, a participant in the unfolding drama: the will we/won't we question that hung over everyone in the late 1930s. While a plummy voice spoke in modulated tones of on-going efforts, the grave political situation, and so on, there was George, in a pinstriped suit and bowler, being handed papers by another pinstriped suit, and preparing to leave for France

'Well I never,' Annie said, when she finally found her voice. 'I wondered where that fellow had got to.' The Twentieth Century Fox searchlight raked the screen and the theme music announced the main feature, but Annie remained transfixed by the thought of George and his mysterious hush-hush role. Not everything he did could be predicted.

George said nothing of his pinstriped moment when he reached Racecourse Road, and the war meant Annie could not enquire. And, anyway, there was plenty to distract them. This was his first visit to the house. George could not call while Willie was alive. I wonder what he and Annie thought when she opened the back door to greet him? But theirs was not an evening *à deux*. Cora and Eva accompanied them to the cinema.

There was nothing like walking out with a Major. Their progress was continually interrupted by sharp salutes. This was no trip to the local Lyceum, with commissionaire Bobby Teasle issuing commands on where they all should sit, but a bus ride into town and the Chesterfield Regal. There was no munching on a wartime carrot either (ice creams being unattainable), but an extremely rare treat, also courtesy of George – a large box of Black Magic chocolates, with a scarlet tassel dangling from its lid.

They saw *Dark Victory* and watched Bette Davies smoulder and suffer. 'There's been no one but you,' she said, a sentiment surely not lost on George. But this was one evening only and a curfewed evening, at that. No sooner had he escorted them all back to Race-course Road (more salutes on the return journey), than it was time for their farewells. George said goodnight at the gate. Brass buttons, officer's khaki, shiny leather; Annie watched him retrace his steps.

George's story did not conclude with him striding into the sunset, followed by crisp salutes. Many years later, after his wife's death, that honourable man wrote to my grandma. But they were both in their eighties and the prospect of meeting too daunting for Annie. It was all too late. My grandma never saw George again.

Once my mum was at senior school, Annie was slightly less concerned about leaving her alone for an hour while she finished Providenting. The key was slipped beneath the push-pull mower in the lavatory; a sharp twist of the knob opened the back door, and into the kitchen with its invariably dripping tap. There was always a fire – Annie returned mid-afternoon to stoke it, all it needed was a little encouragement from the poker – but even a fire could not cheer the empty house. There were no songs, no laughter, no teasing questions about Cora's day. There was no whistling, either. When Cora was alone, the house was a small tight capsule of grief and silence.

It broke, of course, the minute Annie came bustling through the door, carrying the night air with her; 'Put the kettle on, while I start tea. Guess who I've just seen?'; fishing for her apron in the kitchen drawer while Cora laid the table. They were companions as well as mother and daughter.

Much would have been different had my mum not been an only child. When she was small, Cora longed for a sister and used to tell new friends she'd once had a sister who died. However, unlike most only children, she was not often by herself. When at Racecourse Road, she was usually with the Blakes, and even bathed there. Mrs Blake's brother was a miner and assisted her with coal, some of which she passed on to Annie. But it took a lot of coal to heat water for a bath and so sometimes Cora bathed next door, despite Mrs Blake having her own large family; their neighbour constantly helped Annie and Cora. Their kitchen windows faced each other. Each night, just before the curtains were closed, the children of each household stood in pyjamas and waved to one another, like characters in a storybook.

Cora had now progressed to the Iliffe School of Dancing. (Miss Mason had married and taken her last curtain call.) My mum's first classes with her new teacher took place on the sprung maple floor of the Odeon ballroom. She felt she was dancing on Broadway.

Marjorie Iliffe could not have been more different from Joan

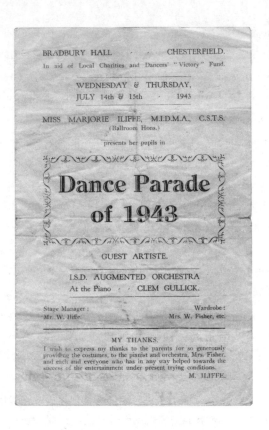

Mason. Her clothes were plain, verging on drab; there was nothing fashionable about her appearance. To see Miss Iliffe in the street, you would think her anything but a dancer, but she had a string of letters after her name and her abilities as a teacher more than made up for any lack of flamboyance. Hers was a larger, more disciplined school; Miss Iliffe's girls wore uniform, sleeveless tabards (more cutting out of blackout cloth and sewing for Annie). Marjorie Iliffe inspired tremendous loyalty.

All dancing schools put on shows, but the demand was even greater during wartime. Willing mothers ran up stage clothes out of yards of American cloth for troupes rehearsed as rigorously as soldiers on manoeuvres, and begged and borrowed props wherever they could (in Joan Mason's days, the corner shop pitched in with clay pipes and marshmallow 'ice cream' cornets).

Dancing on stage was a tremendous thrill, but my mum also organised her own shows, each one a little more ambitious than the last. Annie's kitchen provided rehearsal space, Grace Blake and Janey Davis perching on the mangle while Janey's sister Mabel practised her solo. Local children paid a ha'penny to watch the result. Concerts performed with friends from the dancing school enjoyed a little more finesse and commanded a higher ticket price. For a penny, neighbours saw Cora and Daphne Edwards dance in Marlene Hill's backyard, dressed in the outfits they'd worn on stage.

'I want 'er,' one hulking lad shouted from the audience, point-ing at Cora, 'Er in t'middle, 'er in t' pink,' and started clambering over the other kids to reach her. The dancers paused mid-step but Reg was evidently in earnest. Daphne and Cora flung their clothes into their suitcase and ran, with Reg and a group of younger boys in pursuit. They were saved by hopping on to the Whittington Moor bus.

The girls were given the opportunity to perform at a bigger venue the next time round, and raised ten shillings for Mrs Churchill's fund by dancing in the backyard of the Railway Inn. Clementine Churchill wrote to thank Cora and her friends for assisting 'the Brave Russians in their terrible struggle' (a steno-graphed letter, but a signed letter nonetheless). There were larger, formal fund-raisers too, via the Iliffe School of Dancing. The war enabled Miss Iliffe's pupils to dance on every stage in Chesterfield – the Regal, the Odeon, the Victoria, the Corporation Theatre, Hippodrome, Lyceum and Market Hall – the last under the auspices of white-haired 'Auntie Minnie' who organised shows for the servicemen stationed nearby. After the dancers had taken their bows, hundreds of male voices raised the rafters and the hairs on the back of the neck with 'Let the Great Big World Keep Turning'.

The best shows, though, were the ones at the Regal which ran for several nights, replacing the B-movie and preceding the main feature: a hour or so of ballet, high kicks and acrobatic poses, and then *Lassie Come Home*. Some rehearsals began after the cinema closed for the evening. It was nearing midnight by the time the dancers reached their homes; another long walk for Annie and Cora through Chesterfield's empty streets. Almost everyone else was a-bed, but all around them blazed the bright, bright light of double summertime.

Nightly shows, greasepaint; stage lights, sequins and taffeta: it was just like being a real dancer, especially when Warner Brothers sent the Regal a congratulatory telegram – 'Chesterfield should be proud of its amateur talent' – when Miss Iliffe's school staged its own performance of *Hollywood Canteen*. But the best write-up belonged to a different show altogether and came courtesy of the *Derbyshire Times*:

'Visitors to Chesterfield on Saturday afternoon would view with some amazement the monster queues outside the Regal Cinema. That for the better-class seats stretched from the entrance, down Cavendish Street, round the corner into Saltergate, and up as far as Elder Way. The queue for the cheaper seats was as long. They waited from 3 p.m. to 6 p.m., not to see Clark Gable, Garbo, *Gone with the Wind* or *Mrs. Miniver*, but the purely local talent appearing in the *Salute the Soldier* stage show.'

They were waiting to see my mum – and all the other dancers who performed that night in 1944. Annie and Eva were among them, settling into their gold plush seats with a cone of caramels

between them. Dick and Betsy were too elderly to attend, but would hear all about it later, back at the shop. And here comes Cora now, tap dancing across the stage in a whirl of pendulum wings and triple-time-steps, arms outstretched and smiling, cuffing the boards with her silver shoes.

23

Endings and Beginnings

ON THE AFTERNOON OF 21 AUGUST 1944, A DOODLEBUG HIT Tower Cressy. Glass shattered in the windows of its capacious nurseries; flames shimmied up the metal fretwork of the NCAA's sun balconies. Those extravagant towers were reduced to desiccated dust. A second blast underlined the dereliction one week later. On 27 August, shortly after 7 a.m., smoke rose once again from Tower Cressy.

The hostel was unoccupied at the time. The NCAA's Sloane Square offices remained open throughout the war, but the Association moved to Wokingham for the duration and was without a children's hostel for some years (its Sydenham branch being commandeered by the fire department).

I think of how easily paper catches fire, and see flames lick the edges of pages containing irreplaceable details: the stories of all those women who gave up their babies for adoption, my mum's birth mother included. But this may be pure fantasy. My mother was told that the NCAA hostel was bombed during the war, the implication being that papers were destroyed along with it, but this

Monday 21st August 1944

Today we nearly caught a Doodle Bug! It fell on the imitation Tudor Castle on Campden Hill. This afternoon at 3pm I was busy sorting things for the Fair when a Doodle got nearer and nearer. The office was full of people and no one bothered. Having dived under desks so often and the Thing has been far away that I took no notice. Then I turned to run, but it dropped, and did the house shake and did we hear falling glass...

We ran in all directions to find out where it was. We mounted to the roof and just saw the smoke blowing away. Martin, Miss M's nephew, set off and brought back news it was Aubrey Road and Walk at the corner – Cressy House. Auntie Nell rang up at once as she realised it was near me. We also rang around. It gave us quite a turn. So I made some tea to settle us down. Miss Ashton and I set forth on an expedition of enquiry. Most of the shops round Holland Park tube station had lost their windows. We found the shell of the house. It used to have four towers. All that pretty property is blasted. Mrs Bennett, one of our voluntary workers, was in the baker's, and the owner dragged her to the back as the windows cracked right down. I returned to my flat only to find I could not get in at the front door. The blast had blown off the lock. Two windows also gone. But my room was intact...the bomb had blown the curtains right across.

– From *Few Eggs and No Oranges*, the wartime diary of Vere Hodgson, who worked near the NCAA hostel, Tower Cressy

was probably an assumption on someone's part, many years after the event. You do not plan to evacuate a building and leave all paperwork behind. Whatever the facts of the matter, details of my mum's brief sojourn with the NCAA no longer exist.

Did fire obliterate my grandma's blue-grey file too? I can't think how else she destroyed it; my mum never saw it again. Thankfully, she saved the Tower Cressy brochure. My mum came upon it shortly before Annie's death, and felt it should come into her keeping. I don't know if Annie had intended to pass it on, but she was proud of 'the posh adoption' home my mum came from. Even when Cora was small – and knew nothing of her adoption – Annie entertained her by singing, 'I Dreamt that I Dwelt in Marble Halls,' and hinted of her mysterious beginnings. (Back to those heady thoughts of Princess Alice.) 'I think you were born in marble halls,' Annie used to tell her, though my mum took this to be one of the tall stories of childhood. My grandma kept Cora's Adoption Order, but that blue-grey file was different, I suspect, because it represented my mum's life prior to Annie and Willie. In destroying those papers, however, my grandma was merely doing what adoptive parents were actively encouraged to do in those days hemmed in by secrecy and taboo – completely eradicate the past.

My mum was sixteen when Annie finally told her she was adopted. A friend (having no idea that two little girls had already spilled the beans), advised her to do so before someone else did. Annie said relatively little, spoke of the adoption home, 'the grandma' who was present in court, and of 'the girl' – a nameless 'girl' – it was made clear that my mum's birth mother was some mere chit of a lass. My grandma clearly did not want Cora to have much information. And, for an extremely long time, that is how things remained.

*

As the 1940s continued, there was more greasepaint and further dancing exams for Cora, and she even contemplated life on stage – if Ruby Keeler could tap dance her way out of the chorus line in *42nd Street*, then why not Cora too? *Rhapsody in Blue*, *Dancing Highlights*, *Night and Day*… the list of local shows continued. One year, she was a pearly queen. (Picture all the mother-of-pearl buttons passed on to me when that particular dance dress expired.)

Annie continued to encourage her, but she wanted Cora to have skills to fall back on and to delay her decision for twelve months, and so Cora exchanged her button-box typewriter for the real thing and got to grips with technical college and shorthand. A year later, she was introduced to and fell in love with office life. She had also learned, via a dancing friend, that the bright lights involved dingy digs and a rumbling stomach. She continued dancing, however, and, generously, was allowed days off for exams, but regular hours claimed Cora: from office girl to junior typist, to assistant secretary to a boss who, though not quite as legendary a figure as Charles Paxton Markham, had a reputation for hard talking nonetheless.

On her very first day in the secretarial department (£72 a year), Cora typed a letter to her granddad. Though frail by then, Dick still wanted to hear all about his 'little duckie' and the details of her job. Collecting and delivering post, running errands; Gestetnering, typing and dictation; making tea and distributing the weekly office cakes (dry trifle-sponge-fingers seemed manna from heaven with post-war austerity hitting hard) – initially, Cora's tasks were none too demanding. Her supervisor enjoyed poetry and promoted knitting and sing-songs; when work was slack, the typists took up their needles: Knit one, purl one. Life Is Just a Bowl of Cherries.

In 1951, at the age of eighty-nine, Dick died. He had sold his precious wood a year earlier, thinking it time a younger man had grass to keep down and hazel to twist into fencing. The Wheeldon Mill Plantation was bought by Albert Mowbray who ran the greyhound track established in the area in the late 1930s. Mowbray lived in Thompson Street, the street named after Jim (and full of his houses). In provincial towns, connections are endless.

Dick took to his bed a few days before his death. Usually, when Dick suspected he was developing a touch of the tickatalaroo – my great-grandfather's name for any kind of 'flu or fever – he'd send Eva to the Great Central Hotel for a bottle of whisky and disappear upstairs. By the time he reappeared, the bottle would be empty and his fever fled. But, this time, it was different. Dick felt unwell, developed pneumonia and was dead within three days.

'Mam won't last without him,' Annie said. Eva and Cora were disbelieving, but Annie's assessment was correct. After Dick's death, Betsy took to sitting in his chair, something she'd never done before and, though strong, and in good health for someone in her late eighties, seemed to diminish by the week. She died three months later. (A relative insisted she had known there'd be a death: that morning, her tulips had drooped.)

My grandma and great-aunt asked two near neighbours they'd known for many years if they would prepare Betsy's body for burial; this was not a task they could face (or would have expected to perform) themselves. They would be glad to help, the women said.

When Annie and Eva came back upstairs, they saw their mother's body washed and laid out neatly on the bed, but her wedding ring was missing. It had gone. They guessed straightaway who had removed it, but the last thing they wanted at this grief-stricken time was a confrontation with a neighbour. They visited one of the women and explained the situation, asking if she'd call on the other and say the ring was lost, and would she please help them find it. Then the four of them went back upstairs and made a great to-do of shaking out the sheets and – would you credit it? – a rose-gold band rolled down the middle of the bed.

A difficult situation neatly resolved and without accusations, or with anyone losing face: it was the kind of negotiation Annie and Eva had learned from Betsy. How sad that they now had to practise it on her behalf. I'm shocked to think of a close neighbour stealing from my great-grandma, and especially in these circumstances. But I suspect my shock was greater than Annie's and Eva's. They knew what their neighbour's life was. Life had taught her harsh practicalities: the living need money, the dead do not. What seems a dreadful disrespect was as much a mark of desperation. Either way, it provides a coarser tale, as well as a finale to my great-grandma's story and life at the corner shop.

My mum was married by the time my great-grandparents died. She met my dad at a New Year's dance in the late 1940s. Didn't most couples meet at dances then? The 1950s were no kinder to married women than previous decades. No sooner was Mum married than she had to circumvent the constant banter of the (married) male office wags, asking when the little ones would be coming. 'Oh, don't you worry,' Cora said. 'I'll catch up with you soon enough.' Like many women of her generation, she gave up paid work to start a family. My brother came first, and then me. My brother is named for our great-grandfather; me, after noirish film star, Lynn Bari: Hollywood habits die hard. Until I started school, Cora's dancing fell by the wayside. By the time she took up classes again – Latin American, for her own fun and fitness – she was also tying my ballet shoes, just as Annie had helped tie hers.

After Dick and Betsy died, the lease on the shop was surrendered and Eva went to live with Annie. That's where I came to know them, in the house at Racecourse Road. The cupboard that once housed my mum's books and toys – and which Annie had opened to show the mystery lady – was mine now, as were the books and toys. At bathtime, Eva blew my brother the same pendulous soapy rainbows she'd blown for my mum, and (some years later), thanks to Annie, he was the only boy we knew with his own Dennis the Menace jumper. I can see him now, lying on their rag rug before a blazing fire, drawing cartoon John, Paul, George and Ringos, sporting his own Beatle cut.

My grandma and great-aunt were invariably together, though Annie was still Providenting, and, for several years, Eva worked at a grocer's shop, swapping the family counter for another, less pleasing one where she was, at least, visited by women she'd known at the Mill, who kept her up to date with its goings on. Annie and Eva (Mama and Auntie to me) were nearly always mentioned as a pair, a kind of double act, although their personalities were very different. They eventually performed a final, heartbreaking double act of sorts, by dying within ten days of each other. In the absence of a maternal grandfather (Willie being long dead), they were my maternal grandparents: my relationship with Eva was much closer than the title 'great-aunt' usually suggests.

When I was small, Annie had more time than she'd had during Cora's childhood. As well as dressing me and my dolls, my grandma had other impressive talents. By some means, whose method

baffles me still, she crocheted a doll's cradle, some six inches high, which, when stiffened with sugar water, stood proud on its silk rockers. Annie reupholstered the three-piece suite from my mum's doll's house, complete with antimacassars: individual lace florets. Such loving care and artistry on my behalf; the hours she must have spent cutting out and gluing velvet on to that miniature furniture. Now, I notice that a patch of glue escaped from one of the seams; then, all I saw were plump red seats fashioned with love.

Mealtimes at Racecourse Road were always a treat, whether eating Annie's meat pies, served in jam-tart-sized pastry cases; Eva's fat chips (as good any gastro-pub offering and dashed into hot fat with characteristic abandon), or a kind of children's meze they invented, offering several diminutive dishes tempting to a child. Sometimes, during Eva's stint at that other grocery store, we ate mystery teas. With the tin opener at the ready and the bread and butter waiting, we discovered whether tea would be tinned salmon or peaches. Tins that had slipped their labels were no good to sell, but made for some entertaining mealtimes. Annie and Eva were always willing to enter into a child-eye's view of the world. If dinner was too hot, my brother and I were instructed to take our plates for a walk down the garden. Willie's aviary had long since disappeared, but Ginny the cat would be toasting her back against the boundary wall, conjuring phantom birds.

My mum used to hear Annie and Eva telling their stories and wonder how she could match their vivid tales. Yet this book could not exist without her memories of the childhood places and people she knew. There were many other people too; still are. They are not omitted accidentally. My mother's later story is her own.

The possibility that my great-grandfather was Romany was one of the tales my mum wove for my brother and me during childhood, and was part of his enchantment for us. Stories about Dick invariably involved 'Grandad's wood'. He was an almost mythical figure and the wood itself a magical spot. Long after my great-grandfather died, Eva walked me along Pottery Lane and up to Wheeldon Mill to see the wood and the bullock grazing there. En route, there were more stories: of Eva dodging in and out of the trees with Teddy the dog, and of my mum burying treasure. The wood's there still, but the steps Dick created from living tree roots are gone.

There were other walks with Eva, walks going nowhere in partic-ular, but always with an element of surprise or adventure, whether through 'the jungle', an area of overgrown shrubs and trees, or along unknown meandering lanes where Eva introduced me to 'bread and cheese', the hawthorn she'd nibbled during similar walks in her own childhood.

My mum knew nothing of Dick's and Eva's beginnings until after Dick and Betsy died, when she was told by Annie and Eva. I knew of my great-grandfather's history from a very early age, but was about fifteen before I learned of Eva's orphanage years, and eight-een when knowledge of my mum's adoption added another layer and further dimension to the mix. Having unrelated relatives has always intrigued me, but it's taken me much longer to explore almost (but not quite) the full story.

Questions of naming and identity are central to any adoption. Naming has a complex place in this family's story too, and I've added to it by changing some of the names in this book. All three adopted children acquired new names, Eva and Cora gained forenames as well as fresh surnames. My great-aunt spent a consid-erable part of her childhood as 'Annie' before becoming 'Eva', an extreme change to contemplate, although probably less disturbing than those she'd already encountered before she came to Wheeldon Mill.

My great-grandfather's 'adoption' document gave him a second name, which looks like 'Darnce' or 'Durnce' but which Dick understood to be Dorance: he was Richard Dorance Walker and became Richard Dorance Nash. Despite the evidence of the actual document, however, Dick understood Dorance to be his original surname, and attempted to pass this on to his daughters, and so maintain a link with his original family line. Unfortunately, his attempts were fogged by poor learning and spelling 'by ear': the name appears differently in almost every instance – 'Doran', for example, and even, on one occasion, 'Durham' – each recording clerk interpreting it in their own way. Poor learning led to another complication too – ironically, for Annie, the one child who was always sure where she came from – my grandma's birth is not registered under her full name.

Official documents have a way of revealing only part of the narrative and of foxing those of us who look into the past. Despite never marrying, Eva had three surnames during her life: her birth was registered under her father's name, she became Ball and, finally, Nash, with a wealth of stories between each alteration. And, although the name was not used within the home, my great-aunt was also called Doris to create an echo with 'Dorance' and so bring her more into the family.

There is a further aspect to my great-aunt's history, though Eva knew nothing of this, and it belongs to her father, that ordinary man doing what he had to do to get by. By 1908, he had a new life, a new 'wife' (I've found no evidence of their marriage) and, soon afterwards, a new family.

And he who gives a child a treat

Makes joy-bells in Heaven's Street

And he who gives a child a home

Builds palaces in Kingdom Come

– From 'The Everlasting Mercy' by John Masefield. Published in 1911, the poem became widely known and was copied into an old Provident register by Annie, together with other quotations. Masefield's mother died in childbirth when he was six.

By making representation to the Poor Law Guardians, he had the power to release his three girls from the orphanage once his circumstances changed, and provided they were judged 'satisfactory'. Yet again, he had to make a choice between his old life and his new one; it is unlikely he could afford to combine the two. His new 'wife' may have known nothing about this aspect of his past, or else had been told about the girls and refused to take on any children other than her own – old and new family combined would have brought them all closer to calamity. The decision may not have been calculating irresponsibility, but yet more harsh reality.

Eva remained in touch with Kitty and Margaret throughout her life. Despite the best efforts of the Industrial School, all three seem to have avoided domestic service. Ironically, their oldest sister did not. By 1911, Nellie, who disappeared from this story at their mother's death, was a junior maid. Until I looked into the family history, I had no idea she existed.

*

The abandoned or orphaned children of Victorian and Edwardian literature frequently had well-to-do guardians or benefactors (cruel as well as kind), but working-class families also took in children, as Dick's and Eva's beginnings show, and these children were expected to work. The view that children should be useful was by no means confined to the workhouse or Industrial School, but was fundamental to an ethos of service and duty that extended beyond the First World War – hence Dick holding the candle for Joe Nash, and Eva being kept at home – and the idea of a child being schooled in the family trade or business ran well into the twentieth century, irrespective of social class.

One of the anxieties surrounding adoption in its early years was the fear of children being taken into families to act as unpaid servants. I think, with immense dismay, of one parallel between the life the Industrial School envisaged for my great-aunt, and the life she actually led, and that's the common view that servants should have 'no followers' (no suitors). But, for all my discomfort at that similarity, Eva's life was not that of a servant. My mum, who knew nothing of Eva's beginnings during her own childhood, had no sense of her aunt being anything less than a vital – and vibrant – part of the family, on the same terms as everyone one else. The idea of Eva being the-daughter-at-home brings into sharper focus that complex equation between family and service, whereby wives (and, in some instances, daughters), perform for free the duties servants are paid for.

Clara Andrew of the NCAA spoke of adopters wishing to take girls because, in later years, they would be companions for their adoptive parents. Contemplating this subject in 1920, the Home Secretary of the day remarked that 'a good many people looked upon children as a legitimate investment for their old age'.

Daughters have long been expected to fulfil the role of comforter.

Though her role as daughter-at-home took away freedoms most of us take for granted, Eva knew she was loved. Had she married, her life would have been very different, though it may have been even less free: in those days, marriage to a blue-collar worker, plus two or three children (possibly more), would not have allowed Eva much time for herself. It would nonetheless have given her experiences she never had the chance to have – most obviously, sexual love and, probably, her own children. Instead, she had my mum and, later, my brother and me.

Dick's life and Eva's were as thoroughly constrained by attitudes to childhood (and young women) during the nineteenth and early twentieth centuries as by adoption. My mum grew up in a different era, albeit one with bogeys of its own: she was the one child who had no idea where she came from, and whose origins were actively hidden, the greater focus on the family unit at that time paradoxically encouraging concealment. I can stand back a little (though admittedly not that far) when considering Dick and Eva, but that is hardly possible when it comes to Cora. Hers is obviously the story closest to me.

24

Beginnings and Endings

FOR A LONG TIME, I WAS NOT PARTICULARLY CURIOUS ABOUT
Jessie Mee. This was partly life going on, but it also seemed that
knowing more about her would be disloyal to Annie. My mum
and I still speak of what Annie would have wanted; neither of us
wished to hurt her. But an even greater imperative existed, and that
was my desire to see if I could help Cora find out what she could
about her birth mother.

When I started researching this book, there was still much to
uncover and much I wanted to find irrespective of this memoir.
I wept on reading Emily Ball's death certificate – dead aged
twenty-seven and reduced to a housekeeper by the man whose
children she bore, and died for – though it took me a moment
or two to register the document's full implications. And thinking of how Emily's young life was swept away on paper and in
fact, and of how impossibly hard it must have been, she seemed
to stand for all the other young women before and after her who
never stood a chance. I was also crying, I suppose, for another
young woman; someone of whom, at that point, I knew little,

beyond her name. But then (on paper, at least) I found her.

My mum started trying to trace her birth mother after the change of law in 1975 that enabled adopted children (following counselling) to have access to their original birth certificates and thus the possibility of tracing their birth mothers. Knowledge of a name, an address and, in this instance, an occupation is an extraordinary thing to acquire when you have waited nearly forty years to discover it, but unless that name is unusual, it does not get you very far in identifying a person; you also need some idea of their age and place of birth. A name alone produced multiple candidates of childbearing age in different parts of the country. The helpful (and logical) advice that you pursue marriage certificates next shows how many people assume a geographical stability domestic servants and many working-class families did not have. The documents that would also have helped – the censuses of 1921 and, especially, 1931 – were, of course, inaccessible (1931 will remain so, having been destroyed by fire).

The most obvious route is via the actual adoption, but the court records pertaining to my mum's adoption were apparently non-existent and the NCAA is now a defunct organisation, its records taken over by Westminster City Council. It is extremely difficult to trace adoption records that pre-date the Second World War: No. Nothing. No. I'm Very Sorry. Lost. Gone. Each letter or call, however sympathetically expressed, a rebuff so strong its kickback dammed up further enquiries. Months passed; months and years.

A chance repeat enquiry turned up some archival tidying in an office initially contacted years before, and, this time, produced court records. I'm sure my mum was not the only adoptee of her generation to discover how scant these details are in files dating back to the twenties and thirties. Those with some knowledge of adoption today would be aghast at the flimsy documentation. All those 'satisfactory' arrangements barely recorded; birth mothers' stories forgotten and not passed on. Even into the 1960s, it was customary to advise adoptive parents to conceal the child's origins and tell children their biological parents had died – and sometimes violently at that: in a car crash. A sure way to end probing questions, but what a brutal legacy to hang round a child's neck.

In my mum's case, however, there was one lead. Together with the details on her birth certificate, an index card existed in the files of the NCAA (which was almost but not totally defunct when my mum began her search: the Association existed until 1978, when local authorities took over the responsibility for adoptions). This index card included a further name, F. M. Wood: Jessie was not alone when she took my mum to Tower Cressy. My brother discovered this when he made some preliminary enquiries. Thank goodness the index card was found when it was. Some time later, that stray documentation also vanished, and, with it, all evidence of Cora's connection with the NCAA. For many years, there were three mysteries in my mum's adoption story: the 'mystery lady' who visited Racecourse Road; F. M. Wood, and the most significant mystery of all, the woman I've called Jessie Mee.

The 'mystery lady' has haunted my mum's story for years. For a long time, we imagined she was Mrs Sedgwick, Jessie Mee's employer and, possibly, the wife (or mother) of the man who made her pregnant, who wanted to ensure the child was safe (chauffeur-driven cars being more likely to belong to leafy north London and to a past I cannot fully recreate). But the 'mystery' visit to my grandma came several years and accumulated paperwork after an adoption bound and stitched together in secrecy, though, back in the 1930s it may just have been possible for Mrs Sedgwick to unlock those doors. Annie would certainly have wanted to impress upon someone of her standing how well she was looking after my mum. After all, my grandma told Cora that their visitor was 'a very nice lady,' and 'very well off'. Yet why did Mrs Sedgwick wait so long before making an appearance? This is where the theory stumbled.

More recently, my greater knowledge of the National Children Adoption Association suggested an alternative, if imperfect, scenario. Ladies with chauffeur-driven cars were exactly those the Association cultivated and attracted: women with means who could attend their fund-raising dinners and had a use for those evening gowns and mah-jong sets. However, Clara Andrew wanted adopted children to make fresh starts, so it seems strange that the NCAA would risk the awkward questions that could so easily have stemmed from the mystery lady's visit. Its literature makes no reference to occasional inspections or follow-ups of any kind (though some of those involved with children – the NSPCC, for example – would have been happier if these had taken place), so there seems to have been no apparatus for a visit like this one. Unless news of Willie's ill health and receipt of the dreaded Means Test had percolated down from Relieving Officer to Health Visitor, though, in that case, the visitor would have been a gabardine-clad woman arriving on foot, not in a chauffeur-driven car; and that version of events would also suggest a far more rigorous approach to adoption than I believe existed then. (Clara Andrew is on record as saying she thought that adopted children, like all others, should, to some extent, take their chances.) So, the 'lady' continued to be a mystery.

And a further aspect of her visit puzzled me: if she was acting on the NCAA's behalf, why did she allow my grandma to head off to my mum's school in that fizz of anxiety? Perhaps her polite protestations went unheeded and Annie set off before she could be stopped; or else, while Annie was away, the mystery lady realised the complications that would ensue from meeting Cora, and that she'd overstepped the mark. Both would account for her hasty withdrawal. Yet, my grandma's behaviour on that afternoon does not sound a bit like Annie, who was always composed, no matter how anxious she was feeling. Unless she felt wrong-footed by this apparition in marocain silk, thought she was being questioned about her ability to care for my mum. She had the same rights in law as a birth parent, but, like any parent, if questioned, would have felt intensely distressed. If she felt the need to prove that care, and thought her love in jeopardy, Annie would have done anything.

For a while, F. M. Wood, the person named on the index card, seemed much less significant, though, in fact, she was the key to unlocking my mum's story. I'd assumed her to be a middle-class woman, someone else well-connected who assisted Jessie (at one with the mystery lady and Mrs Sedgwick). And Annie always hinted that my mother's father was 'posh'. Of course she did. Why wouldn't she? And perhaps he was. The different threads appeared to fit.

F. M. Wood lived in London, N1. Fastening on the postcode, I pictured Georgian houses and nicely turned pavements and squares. I forgot how easily, in London, smart bleeds into down-at-heel. So I was surprised when her address turned out to be Hoxton, unlovely in those days. The house is not there anymore, slum clearance managing what Hitler did not get round to.

She revealed her identity quite quickly, although I've given her another one here. Frances Wood was the married name of Jessie's elder sister. At last I was on the right track, except it was not quite as straightforward as that. Try as I might, I could not make the pieces fit. Large contingents of people with the same surname in far-flung parts of the country provided the usual baskets of red herrings. Though it looked as if Frances would be easy to trace, and, through her, Jessie, the trail very quickly went cold. My researches continued: court records, hospital archives, electoral registers, census details; birth, death and marriage certificates, trade directories, on and on... trying to piece together a narrative from the poor threads available. Though England had seemed full of possibilities, these led nowhere; Ireland was where I needed to look.

I still know the strange calm I felt when, sat at my computer, I knew, without doubt, I'd found Jessie. I know the date and the hour she came to light. She was waiting to be discovered all along. I can see myself picking up the phone to give my mum the news she'd thought she would never hear. I'd always imagined catching a train to reveal that news in person, but some information will not wait.

Jessie Mee was in her early twenties when she gave birth to Cora. In some ways, she was barely more than the 'girl' Annie described. She was one of eleven surviving children, the eldest already married before Jessie started school. Her beginnings do not surprise me. Her mother's was the same old story: in and out of pregnancy from a very young age, the latest baby barely weaned before the next one stirred inside her.

Jessie's father was a builder; her eldest brother followed him into the trade, but things were more difficult for girls. As in England, domestic service was their best option. Once they reached their mid-teens, it was time they put their feet under someone else's table. At least two of Jessie's siblings were in service at some point, including Frances, before, and possibly after, she came to London.

Women left Ireland in greater numbers than men in the early years of the twentieth century and provided a significant proportion of London's domestic staff. London-born girls were said to look down their noses at the work and were disliked by prospective employers for that reason, being thought too independent and too knowing. Expanding opportunities in factories, offices and shops beckoned them. Provincial young women and migrants, like Jessie, took their places. The high proportion of Irish-born women living in Kensington, Hampstead, Westminster and St Marylebone at the start of the 1930s was almost entirely due to the demand for domestic servants, despite anti-Irish feeling among some employers.

How Jessie's life must have changed from the days when she raced her brothers and sisters along Main Street, past the draper's, the boot shop and the Temperance Hall, to when she became Mrs Sedgwick's cook. Days serving breakfast, luncheon and high tea; evenings off at the cinema. But, of course, there was more than this to Jessie's story: in 1929, she was pregnant with my mum.

Inter-war London could be every bit as overwhelming as the city can seem today, albeit on a smaller scale. And just as capable of swallowing up the desperate, the poor and the lonely – young and vulnerable servants among them. But Jessie Mee was not alone: she had her sister Frances, and another sibling was also in London around this time.

Frances was a married woman with small children when her younger sister became pregnant. Like many working-class families in London between the wars, she and her husband rented rooms in shared houses, and then upped sticks to another shared house nearby. Life seemed to catch at their coat tails. Addresses previously occupied by two couples housed three when the Woods pitched up, making for even more of a squeeze.

Even if she wanted to, Jessie could not make a permanent home with Frances and her pregnancy may have been a source of some tension between them, older sisters being supposed to look out for younger ones. Nor would Jessie have wished to return to Ireland pregnant. A certain carelessness surrounded illegitimate births. In 1930, one in four illegitimate babies born in Ireland did not survive their first year. Also, in 1930, a Custom House official, a doctor, uncovered an extremely high rate of infant mortality in a Cork home for unmarried mothers: more than 100 of 180 babies born in the previous year died. The matron (a nun) and the Home's medical officers were entirely complacent about covering up an infection that had the babies in their care dropping like flies. No, Ireland was not her best option. Jessie may have sought spiritual advice from a Catholic priest, but I doubt she sought practical help because, for the time being at least, she remained at Hazelmere Avenue.

Whatever the circumstances surrounding my mum's birth, Jessie took pride in her child: she named her after herself. The name by which my mum is known was chosen by Annie and Willie. She also held on to her for as long as she could – the NCAA took babies far younger than Cora.

Women who placed children for adoption between the wars did not intend to be traced years later, nor did the authorities wish them uncovered. Better by far that they dissolve into the background, their stories swept under the carpet; the slate wiped clean. Funny how such phrases describe domestic acts. How Jessie must have wished it were that simple.

I don't know what happened to her in the weeks after she gave up my mum. I try not to think of Jessie's empty arms, her damp blouse. If she did squeeze in with her sister, she only did so for a very short time – by the autumn of 1930, the Woods had moved again and Jessie was not with them. Within a year or so, she was back in Ireland and, although I don't know the full story of her life, I do know how it ended.

I was right to cry on reading Emily Ball's death certificate. She was not alone in her ghastly fate. Jessie Mee also died in childbirth, another young woman who gave up her life too soon, and left behind young children. This was a discovery I had not wanted or expected to make.

She is lying in a small graveyard now, with some members of her family beside her. Two sides of the cemetery are bounded by trees; hills and further trees shape the horizon. Those green hills that hold centuries of secrets hold Jessie's secrets too. Though not unkempt, the graveyard is gently overgrown and lacks distinct paths between gravestones. Dotted among the long grass on the day that I was there, were clusters of the deepest purple clover I have ever seen, groups of slender 'chimney sweeps' and richly yellow vetches. When I stood before the grave with my brother and my mum, I heard the distinctive notes of birdsong. It is quiet there, peaceful. Finding Jessie is about leaving her be.

Except that it is hard for me to do exactly that. I think of all the difficulties Jessie must have faced, and how closely she was required to guard the story of her time in London. And, knowing a little more about Jessie now, my thoughts return to Mrs Sedgwick, who may not have been the chance employer I'd always assumed her to be. Mrs Sedgwick was herself Irish, and shortly before she and her husband settled in London, occupied a sturdy villa in one of the better parts of Belfast, with a gabled window and room for a servant girl. Did one of the Mee sisters work there? Young women from small towns and villages made their way to Belfast and Dublin, as well as London, and sometimes tested the shorter distance before embarking on the longer, saltier journey. Who knows? Perhaps one of the Mee girls knelt beneath that gabled roof to say her prayers. Perhaps, perhaps. It is a tempting and not wholly implausible thought, especially considering what came later. A prior connection provides a more solid foundation for Mrs Sedgwick's understanding than the story of a pregnant-young-servant-who-confessed-to-her-employer (although there were plenty of those).

And, thinking again of Mrs Sedgwick, I am drawn back to the mystery lady who came to Racecourse Road – for surely it *was* she who appeared all those years later? Until now, I've not felt able to make sufficient sense of the gap. What brought her to Chesterfield when my mum was six, if not a letter from Jessie? Jessie had other children by that stage, each one a reminder of the child who was not with her, each birthday cake (if the family ran to birthday cakes) a reminder of the date she could not acknowledge. Blow out the candles. Make a wish.

I write Mrs Sedgwick's reply – imagine her describing all the colourful books on my mum's bookshelves; her Minnie Mouse bag, doll's house and motorcycle man, and all the photographs of her which Annie proudly displayed on the piano, and dusted every week. I think of Jessie receiving this letter. I want that for her, and of course I want it for Cora.

My grandma will always be Annie, and my great-grandparents and great-aunt Betsy, Dick and Eva. If I could choose my relatives, I'd choose them, but discovering the identity of the woman I've called Jessie Mee closes the circle, and makes me consider all over again what complex layers of loving, losing, wanting – and leaving – children underpin my family story.

My mum is the last link with this vanished world, but, in my mind's eye, all these stories continue. Cora and I will always be talking of Dick sitting in his wood with a small dog at his heels, and Betsy standing behind her counter. Annie will be forever seated at the table in the back room, fashioning a new dress with her pinking shears, and young Eva will be beside her, peeling an apple in one long straggling piece to see which letter forms when she flings the peel over her left shoulder.

IN DERRY VALE, BESIDE THE SINGING RIVER

In Derry Vale, beside the singing river,
so oft I strayed, ah, many years ago,
and culled at morn the golden daffodillies,
that came with spring to set the world aglow.
Oh, Derry Vale, my thoughts are ever turning
to your broad stream and fairycircled lea,
for your green isles my exiled heart is yearning,
so far away across the sea.

In Derry Vale, amid the Foyle's dark waters,
the salmon leap above the surging weir,
the seabirds call – I still can hear them calling
in night's long dreams of those so dear.
Oh, tarrying years, fly faster, ever faster,
I long to see the vale belov'd so well,
I long to know that I am not forgotten,
and there at home in peace to dwell.

– Lyrics written by W. G. Rothery to the tune of 'Londonderry
Air', and sung by Cora at the Cavendish Junior School

Sources

p.12   'We found Derbyshire…': *The Diaries of Mrs Philip Lybbe Powys, of Hardwick House, Oxon*, edited by Emily J. Climenson, Longmans, Green & Co., 1899, pp.24–5.

p.22   'NURSE CHILD WANTED, OR TO ADOPT: James Greenwood, *The Seven Curses of London*, Basil Blackwell, 1869, p.24, quoted by Dorothy L. Haller, 'Bastardy and Baby Farming in Victorian England', http://www.loyno.edu/~history/journal/1989-0/haller.htm; 'ADOPTION… a good home', an advertisement placed by Sarah Ellis, Brixton baby farmer, in *Lloyd's Weekly Paper*, 5 June 1870; Lionel Rose, *The Massacre of the Innocents: Infanticide in Britain 1800–1939*, Routledge & Kegan Paul, 1986, p.98.

p.28   'Besides the fumes and the gases…': Florence Bell, *At the Works: A Study of a Manufacturing Town*, Thomas Nelson & Sons, 1911 (2nd edition), pp.58–9.

p.43   'It must be remembered…': Maud Pember Reeves, *Round About a Pound a Week*, G. Bell & Sons Limited, 1913; Virago edition, 1979, pp.143–4.

p.46   December 7, 1910…: Example of Mrs E's household budget, from Maud Pember Reeves, *Round About a Pound a Week*, pp.135–6.

p.52   'Families too large…': Elizabeth Dean, interviewed aged 101: Angela Holdsworth, *Out of the Doll's House: The Story of Women in the Twentieth Century*, BBC Books, 1988, p.184.

p.64   'My mother died…': Elizabeth Dean, in Angela Holdsworth, *Out of the Doll's House*, p.184.

p.66 'The New Industrial Schools of the Chesterfield Union', *Derbyshire Times*, 26 March 1881.

p.67–77 Information relating to the Chesterfield Children's Homes during the 1900s: D522/C/W/5/1, Children's Homes Committee Minute Book, Derbyshire Record Office, Matlock.

p.98 'Q. What illustrious lady…': *Simple Catechism of the History of England, from the Invasion of the Romans to the Present Time, Adapted to the Capacities of Young Children*, from 'Mrs Gibbon's Simple Catechisms of', Relfe Brothers, School Booksellers & General School Stationers, Charter-House Buildings, Aldersgate, 1890.

p.116 'In the early twentieth century, stillborn babies…': based on an interview with Rose Ashton; Angela Holdsworth, *Out of the Doll's House*, p.112. See also 'Out of the Doll's House', 80DH/02/, The Women's Library, London Metropolitan University.

p.118 'It is more dangerous…': Slogan for the UK's first National Baby Week, 1917: Jenny Keating, *A Child for Keeps: The History of Adoption in England, 1918–45*, Palgrave Macmillan, 2008, p.22.

p.124 'Xmas Day and such a sad one…': Extracts from Maria Gyte's Diary: Gerald Phizackerley (ed.), *The Diaries of Maria Gyte of Sheldon, Derbyshire, 1913–1920*, Scarthin Books, Cromford, 1999, pp.156–7.

p.160 'Big strong men cried…': Veteran Collier, Coalville, Leicestershire: Gerard Noel, *The Great Lock-Out of 1926*, Constable, 1976, p.206.

p.174 'Lately in the press…': Beatrice Harraden, Foreword, *The National Children Adoption Association Report 1927–28* (with '1928–29' handwritten on the cover), author's own.

p.176 'They enter our offices…': Clara Andrew, founder of the National Children Adoption Association, NCAA booklet *c.*1919, p.10; quoted by Jenny Keating, *A Child for Keeps*, p.50.

p.178, 180 'Until the 1926 Act was passed…': taped interview by Brian Harrison, 8SUF/B/099, 2 July 1976, Hodgson, Mrs Mary, The Women's Library, London Metropolitan University; 'The underlying idea was experimental…': Ethel Smyth, *Female Pipings in Eden*, Peter Davies Ltd, 1933, pp.237–8. For further information, see David Mitchell, *Queen Christabel: A Biography of Christabel Pankhurst*, Macdonald & Jane's, 1977, and June Purvis, *Emmeline Pankhurst: A Biography*, Routledge, 2002.

p.179 'including the professional classes…': Clara Andrew, evidence to the Hopkinson Committee, 5 October 1920, in Jenny Keating, 'Struggle for Identity: Issues Underlying the Enactment of the 1926 Adoption of Children Act', *University of Sussex Journal of Contemporary History*, 3 (2001), p.5.

p.181 'insist on the strictest medical examination…': typed copy of undated article for *Good Housekeeping* by Susan Musson, head of the National Council for the Unmarried Mother and Child; 50PF/04/01, c.1927, Adoption Act 1926, The Women's Library, London Metropolitan University.

p.181 'destitute or orphaned or friendless or neglected children': 50PF/04/01/1, Voluntary Social Services Handbook, 27 September 1929, The Women's Library, London Metropolitan University.

p.185 'a menial, a nobody': Winifred Foley, general maid, quoted in John Burnett (ed.), *Useful Toil: Autobiographies of Working People from the 1820s to the 1920s*, Allen Lane, 1974, Penguin Books, 1984, p.227.

p.185 'Do not speak unless necessary…': Mrs C. C. Peel, *Waiting at Table: A Practical Guide*, Frederick Warne and Co. Ltd, 1929, p.23.

p.186 'You must remember…': 'Nursery Routine: The Threshold of Motherhood', *Home Management*, Daily Express Publications, 1934, p.499.

p.189 'huge private house…': 'Finding Homes for Babies!' *Woman's Own*, 25 April 1936.

p.218 'Mrs D of Derby is 35 years old …': Household budget quoted in Margery Spring Rice, *Working-Class Wives: Their Health and Conditions*, Penguin, 1939; Virago edition 1981, pp.176–7.

p.230 'In the modern house…': 'House Decoration: The Kitchen', *Home Management*, p.433.

p.264 'Does Detective Fiction Lower our Ethical Standards?': Helena Normanton, *Good Housekeeping*, July 1931: 7HLN/C/03, Articles from 'Good Housekeeping' by Helena Normanton, 1924–1939, The Women's Library, London Metropolitan University.

p.288 'Do not feel that you must have an elaborate display of cakes…': 'Entertaining (With information on Weddings and Christenings)', *Home Management*, p.587.

p.304 'Floss stood at one window…', *Up to London to See the King*, *A Story for Six-Year-Olds*, Nelson's Supplementary Infant Readers I, Thomas Nelson and Sons, 1904, pp.40–41.

p.312 'Yours is a full time job…': *Good Housekeeping*, August 1941, quoted by Juliet Gardiner, *Wartime: Britain 1939–1945*, Headline, 2004, p.182.

p.322 'Mr Churchill': author's own.

p.340 'Today we nearly caught a Doodle Bug…': Vere Hodgson, *Few Eggs and No Oranges, a Diary showing how Unimportant People in London and Birmingham Lived through the War Years, 1939–1945*, Dobson Books Ltd, 1976; reprinted by Persephone Books, 1999.

Select Bibliography

I've drawn on numerous family sources to write this memoir – documents, newspapers cuttings, photographs and notebooks, even a partial stocklist from the corner shop, as well as my own recollections of childhood stories and many, many conversations with my mum. The public sources I've found most useful include the following:

ARCHIVES, LIBRARIES AND MUSEUMS

The British Library; The British Newspaper Library at Colindale; Chesterfield Library, Local Studies; Chesterfield Museum; Derbyshire Record Office; The Foundling Museum; Kensington Central Library, Local Studies; The London Library; London Metropolitan Archives; The Museum of Brands, Packaging and Advertising; Library Archives, London School of Economics; The National Fairground Archive, Sheffield University; Royal Free Hospital Archives Centre; The Women's Library, London Metropolitan University.

DIRECTORIES, NEWSPAPERS AND MAGAZINES

Debryshire Courier; *Derbyshire Times*; *Directory of Sheffield*; *The Era*; *Good Housekeeping*; *History and Gazeteer of Derbyshire*; *Home Chat*; *Kelly's Directory of Derbyshire*; *Modern Home*; *Punch*; *Reflections*; *The Times*; *T. P. Wood's Almanac*; *Woman's Weekly*; *Yorkshire Telegraph & Star*.

BOOKS ON CHESTERFIELD & DERBYSHIRE

Boden, F. C., *Miner*, J. M. Dent & Sons, 1932.

Brelsford, Vernon, *A History of Brimington from the Doomsday Survey to 1937*; with new illustrations and an update by Mandy Hicken, Brimington Parish Council, 1989.

Cousins, Philip J., *Brimington: The Changing Face of a Derbyshire Village*, Brimington Parish Council, 1994.

Dimbleby, David, *A Picture of Britain*, Tate Publishing, 2007.

Jenkins, David E., *Sheepbridge: A History of the Sheepbridge Coal & Iron Co. Ltd*, Bannister, 1995.

Markham, Violet, *Return Passage: The Autobiography of Violet Markham*, Oxford University Press, 1953.

Pendleton, John and Jacques, William, *Modern Chesterfield: Its History, Legends and Progress*, The Derbyshire Courier Co. Ltd, 1903.

Phizackerley, Gerald (ed.), *The Diaries of Maria Gyte of Sheldon, Derbyshire, 1913–1920*, Scarthin Books, Cromford, 1999.

Priestley, J. B., *English Journey*, 1934; Folio Society, 1997.

'Tatler' [Pendleton, John], *Old and New Chesterfield: Its People and Steeple*, J. Toplis, Derbyshire Courier Office, 1882.

Williams, J. E., *The Derbyshire Miners*, George Allen & Unwin, 1962.

ON ADOPTION, BABY FARMING, ILLEGITIMACY, INFANT MORTALITY

Behlmer, George K., *Friends of the Family: The English Home and its Guardians, 1850–1940*, Stanford University Press, 1998.

Brookes, Barbara, 'Women and Reproduction 1860–1919', in Lewis, Jane (ed.), *Labour and Love, Women's Experience of Home and Family 1850–1940*, Basil Blackwell, 1986.

Davies, Hunter, *Relative Strangers: A History of Adoption and a Tale of Triplets*, Time Warner Books, 2003.

Llewelyn Davies, Margaret (ed.), *Maternity: Letters from Working Women*, G. Bell & Sons Ltd, 1915; Virago Ltd, 1978.

Greenwood, James, *The Seven Curses of London*, Basil Blackwell, 1869.

Keating, Jenny, 'Struggle for Identity: Issues Underlying the Enactment of the 1926 Adoption of Children Act', *University of Sussex Journal of Contemporary History*, 3 (2001).

Keating, Jenny, *A Child for Keeps: The History of Adoption in England, 1918–45*, Palgrave Macmillan, 2008.

Moore, George, *Esther Waters*, 1894; J. M. Dent, Everyman's Library edition, 1977.

Rose, Lionel, *The Massacre of the Innocents: Infanticide in Britain 1800–1939*, Routledge & Kegan Paul, 1986.

Smyth, Ethel, *Female Pipings in Eden*, Peter Davies Ltd, 1933.

Swift, Rebecca (ed.), *Letters from Margaret: Correspondence between Bernard Shaw and Margaret Wheeler, 1944–1950*, Chatto & Windus Ltd, 1992.

ON DOMESTIC SERVICE

Light, Alison, *Mrs Woolf and the Servants*, Fig Tree, Penguin, 2007.

Peel, Mrs C. S., *Waiting at Table: A Practical Guide*, Frederick Warne & Co. Ltd, 1929.

Powell, Margaret, *Below Stairs*, Peter Davies, 1968.

Taylor, Pam, 'Daughters and mothers – maids and mistresses: domestic service between the wars', from J. Clarke et al. (eds), *Working-Class Culture: Studies in History and Theory*, Hutchinson, 1979.

Woolf, Virginia, *A Moment's Liberty: The Shorter Diary*, abridged and edited by Anne Olivier Bell, Hogarth Press, 1990.

AUTOBIOGRAPHY, MEMOIRS, DIARIES

Arthur, Max, *Lost Voices of the Edwardians*, Harper Press, 2006.

Broad, Richard and Fleming, Suzie (eds.), *Nella Last's War: The Second World War Diaries of Housewife, 49*, Profile Books Limited, 2006.

Burnett, John (ed.), *Useful Toil: Autobiographies of Working People from the 1820s to the 1920s*, Allen Lane, 1974; *Destiny Obscure: Autobiographies of Childhood, Education and Family from the 1820s to the 1920s*, Allen Lane, 1982.

Cookson, Catherine, *Our Kate: An Autobiography*, Macdonald & Co. Ltd, 1969.

Davies, Margaret Llewelyn (ed.), *Life As We Have Known It* by Co-Operative Working Women, Hogarth Press, 1931; Virago Ltd, 1977.

Foley, Winifred, *A Child in the Forest*, Futura, 1977.

Forster, Margaret, *Hidden Lives: A Family Memoir*, Viking, 1995.

Hodgson, Vere, *Few Eggs, No Oranges, a Diary showing how Unimportant People in London and Birmingham Lived through the War Years, 1940–1945*, Dobson Books Ltd, 1976; reprinted by Persephone Books, 1999.

Mitchison, Naomi, *All Change Here*, The Bodley Head Ltd, 1975; *You May Well Ask: A Memoir 1920–1940*, Victor Gollancz Ltd, 1979.

Thompson, Flora, *Lark Rise to Candleford*, Oxford University Press, 1939.

Uttley, Alison, *Country World: Memories of Childhood*; selected by Lucy Meredith, Faber & Faber, 1984.

Woodward, Kathleen, *Jipping Street*, Longmans, Green and Company, 1928.

FURTHER SOURCES

Alexander, Sally, *Becoming a Woman and Other Essays in 19th- and 20th-Century Feminist History*, Virago Press, 1994.

Bell, Florence, *At the Works: A Study of a Manufacturing Town*, Thomas Nelson & Sons, 1911 (2nd edition).

Bott, Alan and Clephane, Irene, *Our Mothers: A Cavalcade in Pictures, Quotation and Description of Late Victorian Women 1870–1900*, Victor Gollancz Ltd., 1932.

Crawford, Elizabeth, *The Women's Suffrage Movement in Britain and Ireland: A Regional Survey*, Routledge, 2005.

Dallas, Duncan, *The Travelling People*, Macmillan, 1971.

Davidoff, Leonore, *et al.*, *Family Story: Blood, Contract and Intimacy, 1830–1960*, Longman, 1991.

Flanders, Judith, *The Victorian House: Domestic Life from Childbirth to Deathbed*, HarperCollins, 2003; *Consuming Passions: Leisure and Pleasure in Victorian Britain*, Harper Press, 2006.

Floate, Sharon Sillers, *My Ancestors Were Gypsies*, Society of Genealogists Enterprises Ltd, 2005.

Gardiner, Juliet, *Wartime Britain 1939–45*, Headline, 2004.

Gittins, Diana, *Fair Sex: Family Size and Structure, 1900–39*, Hutchinson, 1932.

Hartley, Jenny, *Charles Dickens and the House of Fallen Women*, Methuen, 2008.

Holdsworth, Angela, *Out of the Doll's House: The Story of Women in the Twentieth Century*, BBC Books, 1988.

Hughes, Kathryn, *The Short Life and Long Times of Mrs Beeton*, Fourth Estate, 2005.

Loveridge, Pat, *A Calendar of Fairs and Markets Held in the Nineteenth Century*, Romany and Traveller Family History Society, 2003.

Marwick, Arthur, *Women at War, 1914–18*, Croom Helm, 1977.

Mitchell, David, *Queen Christabel: A Biography of Christabel Pankhurst*, Macdonald & Jane's, 1977.

Nicholson, Juliet, *The Perfect Summer: Dancing into Shadow in 1911*, John Murray, 2006.

Nicholson, Virginia, *Singled Out: How Two Million Women Survived Without Men After the First World War*, Viking, 2007.

Noel, Gerard, *The Great Lock-Out of 1926*, Constable, 1976.

Owen, William, *Owen's New Book of Fairs*, J. Cornish, 1859.

Cullen Owens, Rosemary, *A Social History of Women in Ireland: 1870–1970*, Gill & Macmillan Ltd, 2004.

Paxman, Jeremy, *The Victorians: Britain Through Paintings of the Age*, BBC Books, an imprint of Ebury Publishing, 2009.

Purvis, June, *Emmeline Pankhurst: A Biography*, Routledge, 2002.

Reeves, Maud Pember, *Round About a Pound a Week*, G. Bell & Sons Ltd, 1913; Virago Ltd, 1979.

Roberts, Robert, *The Classic Slum: Salford Life in the First Quarter of the Century*, Manchester University Press, 1971.

Spring Rice, Margery, *Working-Class Wives: Their Health and Conditions*, Penguin, 1939; Virago Ltd, 1981.

Thompson, Paul and Harkell, Gina, *The Edwardians in Photographs*, B. T. Batsford, 1979.

Walkley, Christina, *Dressed to Impress, 1840–1914*, B. T. Batsford Ltd, 1989.

White, Jerry, *London in the Twentieth Century: A City and Its People*, Viking, 2001.

Acknowledgements

A large posthumous thank you is due to Kate Jones without whom this book would not even have got started. I am immensely grateful to my agent Clare Alexander for her faith in the book and for her unfailing wisdom and calm counsel; to everyone at Atlantic Books for the care they have taken in producing and publishing this memoir, most especially Karen Duffy for commissioning the book and Sarah Norman who has shepherded it with patience and enthusiasm. Thanks too to Victoria Millar for her attentive copy edit, to Elizabeth Minogue for her drawing of Wheeldon Mill, and to Lindsay Nash for going the extra mile with the 'text boxes'. Enormous thanks are due to Kate Kellaway for her invaluable comments on the manuscript; my thanks also to Melanie Silgardo for her sensitive reading and to Gordon Willis for his keen editorial eye.

An Authors' Foundation Grant from the Society of Authors helped me financially and was a very welcome boost in the early stages. A Carlyle Membership from the London Library was also much appreciated and assisted my researches throughout. I am also grateful to Sue Peach and her colleagues in the Local Studies Department of Chesterfield Library; to the Derbyshire Record Office, Matlock; the National Fairground Archive, Sheffield University; and the Women's Library, London Metropolitan

University. Thanks also to Hilary Youde of Chesterfield Borough Council for supplying the deeds of my great-grandfather's wood.

Various individuals have helped with information and advice of one kind or another. My thanks to John Auton, Nick Barrett, Dr Lynette Challands; Margaret Hewetson-Brown; Victoria Rea; Philip Riden of the Chesterfield Victoria County History Group, and Stephen Wakelam.

The final, but largest thank you of all goes to my mum without whom this book could not have been written. Annie and Willie, and Betsy, Dick and Eva passed their generous spirit on to her.

Lines from Elizabeth Bowen's short story 'The Tommy Crans' are reproduced with permission of the Curtis Brown Group Ltd., London on behalf of the Estate of Elizabeth Bowen. Copyright © Elizabeth Bowen 1934.

Thanks are due for the following illustrations: to Derbyshire Libraries for supplying the Spoof Race Card, Chesterfield Races, November 1863, and the images from 'Chesterfield at Swallows: a shopping carnival souvenir of Autumn goods' issued by J. K. Swallow & Sons, September 1923; to Robert Opie of the Museum of Brands, Packaging and Advertising for permission to reproduce the advertisement for 'Dolly Blue, Dolly Tints, Dolly Fast Dyes'; the photograph of the Chesterfield Industrial School is courtesy of the *Derby Telegraph* via www.picturethepast.org.uk; the list of Christmas presents received by the Chesterfield Children's Homes, 29 December 1903, D522/C/W/5/1, is reproduced with permission of Derbyshire County Council, Derbyshire Record Office; the advertisement for Sunlight Soap, 1916, is reproduced with kind permission of Unilever; the line drawing of Tower Cressy, Aubrey

Road, by Frank Emanuel, is reproduced with permission of the Royal Borough of Kensington & Chelsea, Family & Children's Services; the classified advertisements for domestic servants, 7 July 1927, are reproduced with permission of *The Lady*. 'Come out of the kitchen!', advertisement for the Parkinson New Suburbia Gas Cooker, is from Brian Braithwaite and Noëlle Walsh, *Things My Mother Should Have Told Me: The Best of Good Housekeeping 1922–1940*, Ebury Press, an imprint of the Random Century Group, 1991, p.88; 'Shoot Straight, Lady', Ministry of Food Advice, is from Raynes Minns, *Bombers & Mash: The Domestic Front 1939–45*, Virago 1980, p.115. Copyright unknown for 'When You're in the Money...' and 'Oh Flo, ...'